What Others Are Saying  About

*Reading and doing the work in **Conquer Crisis with Health-Esteem** was an extraordinary experience for me. I was awakened into the possible underlying causes that have led me to where I am today — diagnosis with Multiple Sclerosis. The book asks all the right questions that enabled me to take a close look at my life and then showed me, with detailed suggestions, what to do with that information. I am sure that anyone who takes the time to become familiar with this book will not only be more knowledgeable about themselves, but will also become highly enlightened. It's as if the book was written directly for each reader.*

Sandra Burman
Burman Industries, Inc.

__Health-Esteem__ is not just another self-help book. It is a very positive message which makes you think and work through your problems in a very logical way. It makes you appreciate the best within yourself and gives you the tools to explore your own value and the means to change. Modern medicine can only do so much with pills. Supplementing modern, traditional medicine by helping yourself is something surely needed to assure a healthy existence.

Leslie Paris Dornfeld, M.D.
Founder, Protective Medicine, Inc.
Publisher, "Health-A-Bits"©

*Descartes philosophized 300 years ago that our thinking makes us know we're alive. Through **Conquer Crisis with Health-Esteem**, we enter the millennium with a qualitative way of thinking that keeps us alive.*

Loreen Arbus
TV Producer and former Head of
Programming, Cable Health
Network/ Lifetime and Showtime

The examples and memories shared in this workbook feel like they're coming through me, except with a very clear view of the picture. Each chapter helps me heal my deepest pain and keeps me from repeating the same patterns in my life. The book is a great tool to use with friends and family.

Diana Sinay
Wife, mother, teacher

This special book provides a practical road map to your own personal awakening. A must read for anyone wishing to heal and grow!

Lisa Kaz
President, ANSAP Productions

CONQUER CRISIS WITH HEALTH-ESTEEM™

A Workbook For Women and Men

by Judith Parker Harris

Published by:

SAYRITE Publications
Post Office Box 3755
Beverly Hills, CA 90212

copyright © 1998 by Judith Parker Harris
Printed in the United States of America

Publisher's Cataloging-in-Publication
(Provided by Quality Books, Inc.)

Harris, Judith Parker, 1950–
    Conquer crisis with health-esteem : a workbook for women
and men / by Judith Parker Harris ; illustrated by Cheri
Mann. -- 1st ed.
        p. cm.
        Includes bibliographical references.
        ISBN: 0-9662826-0-4

        1. Mind and body. 2. Mental healing. 3. Emotions.
    I. Title.

RZ400.H37 1998   615.8'51
                                  QB198-251

Conquer Crisis with
HEALTH-ESTEEM™

A Workbook For Women and Men

by Judith Parker Harris

with illustrations by Cheri Mann

SAYRITE Publications
Beverly Hills, CA

Disclaimers

The author of this book does not dispense medical advice nor prescribe the use of any technique as a form of treatment for mental, emotional, physical or medical problems without the advice of a trained therapist or physician, either directly or indirectly. The intent of the author is only to offer information of a general nature to help you in your quest for mental, emotional, and physical fitness and good health. The purpose of this workbook is to educate, motivate and entertain. The author and Sayrite Publications shall have neither liability nor responsibility to any person or entity with respect to any loss or damage caused, or alleged to be caused, directly or indirectly by the information contained in this book.

It is the purpose of this workbook to complement, amplify and supplement other texts. You are urged to read all the available material, learn as much as possible about alternative health and tailor the information to your individual needs. For more information, see the many references in the Appendix.

If you do not wish to be bound by the above, you may return this book to the publisher for a full refund.

Acknowledgments

I wish to thank my dear husband, Jack H. Harris, who first suggested that I write a book and has lovingly and patiently guided, consoled and encouraged me every step of the way. It is he who took the photographs on the front and back covers of this book. His words "Don't get angry, write a book," got me started. And, his philosophy — "You must wake up every day with joy in your heart for what the day can bring" motivated me to rise and write!

You will meet my healing team and many others who helped make my new healthy life and this workbook possible in Chapter 4. I'd like to give special thanks, however, to my three largest workbook contributors; Tobes Reisel, Elizabeth Harlow and Nancy LaPidus for their wisdom, their brainstorming and their attention to the healing details of this book. I went to each as a patient/client and as my health-esteem evolved, I became a partner in a process so exciting I had to document it for others. Our relationships evolved into a dynamic force with a story to tell and a program to follow that could awaken the healing answer center within those who use this workbook.

My mother who has always done the best job she could, even though she felt ill-prepared to deal with life's challenges, also deserves my gratitude and understanding. I am most proud that my mom had the courage to grow, change and become her own woman when my father passed away. It's never too late, and my mother is proof of that! Her common sense has helped a lot, too.

Book design by John Bellanca

Cover by Jack H. Harris and John Bellanca

Copy editing by Susan Moss

Editorial Assistance by Colette Caggiano

Process drawings by Tobes Reisel

Cartoon and diagrams by Cheryl L. Albrecht

Preface

Throughout most of my life, I made my existence much tougher than it needed to be. Some of the pain in my life was unavoidable, but some was magnified by my inability to connect to the healing wisdom within both myself and the world around me. I kept making the same mistakes in relationships, kept coming down with the same number of horrible colds and spells of bronchitis each year, kept sacrificing diversity of life to workaholism, and kept burying one life event after another out of sight if it didn't fit into my act of perfectionism.

Then crisis hit in 1985 and I was forced to start looking both inside myself and outside of myself if I was going to heal the numbness and partial blindness that came with my diagnosis of multiple sclerosis.

I did it! I've been symptom free since 1990. Nothing about my life today is the same as it was in the year of my diagnosis. I did the work which was sometimes frightening, always enlightening and definitely worth it! The completion of this workbook represents the most fulfilling work of my lifetime to date. It includes years of my research and direct experience as well as guidance and advice from alternative health experts to help you through whatever crisis you may face.

The difference in this book from others you may have read is that I'm seeking to be the friend in whom each of you can confide. I'm opening myself to you just like I had to open myself to me by saying, "I've got no more secrets locked inside to make me sick. Here's the truth about me. Now, let's look at your truth."

There's elation that comes with conquering crisis, and in that elation I had an immediate question. "How can I share this knowledge with others? How can I make it easier for people to start and maintain the healing process in their own lives?" As I interviewed people across the country and began lecturing to groups about crisis recovery, I was asked over and over again for a workbook. Men and women wanted to look at and work with the same procedures I had used so successfully. Like me, they wanted to facilitate their own healing process and bring their awareness to a higher level.

Then I had a brainstorm. I would take my healing team, Tobes Reisel, Nancy LaPidus and Elizabeth Harlow on a retreat and have them focus with me on creating just such a book; one that would accompany the reader like a guide and friend out of life's crisis situations and into successful outcomes.

To do that, each one of us had to go back and recreate the turning point in our lives in which we decided to heal. Then we had to look at the step by step process that evolved from that decision. We rediscovered how unique the process is for each of us. We didn't talk or write from books and degrees. We talked and wrote from experience and from our hearts. We realized we were putting a blueprint together that everyone could use to come to their own unique conclusions. We stuck to one filter, however. Every process and procedure had to be one that I used in the years of my research and journey to wellness. I became the every-one-of-you that says, "Yeah, sure, but how can I do this?" The answer is, "Like me, one question and one connection at a time."

As we worked together over the months that it took to write this workbook, we all experienced increased insight while endeavoring to create insight for others. What that means is, that the healing process is never-ending for each of us.

I am happy to present a workbook full of energy designed to spark readers into growth, change and healing.

I do not claim that what is contained in this book is the ultimate "truth" about life. This is the process I used to find my truth which will vary for everyone. Of course, the knowledge presented in this book should not be used in the place of any professional therapeutic or medical assistance that you might need to resolve your health challenges. If you have problems with your health, mentally or physically, it is important to consult a qualified physician or health professional.

I simply invite you to take the first step in creating your own health-esteem team by inviting the friend that is this workbook into your life.

Contents

Appendix

Why Did You Buy This Book?

Something in your life is making you feel uncomfortable enough to take action: So you did, by buying this book. That's an important first step. If you're like me, however, the next steps may be making you feel a little *more* uncomfortable. Perhaps your bookcase is already bulging with self-help and motivational books. Or, perhaps this is your first one. Either way, the nature of this type of book requires that you do something. And that's where true panic can set in, causing a mental tirade like this one:

"Do something! I don't have a spare moment in my day. I've already shaved my sleeping hours. I rush through my meals. Work pressure is unbelievable. I barely have time for conversation in my various relationships, let alone intimacy. The piles of magazines, books, newspapers, phone messages, junk mail, e-mail and faxes are running me out of my office and my home. Experts are coming out of the ozone telling me how to eat, exercise and care for my physical and mental health, and I've just got one thing to say in my defense, 'I'm too busy!' I'm peering over the edge of my out of balance life and it's not a pretty sight! I've got one day to get through and that's today. Nobody told me it was going to be like this!"

I've got one answer for the above. "Boy, do you need this book!" I identify with every sentence of the above paragraph. My associated behavior threw me out of control in my workaholic, business life and into a disease, multiple sclerosis. Following the advice contained in these pages took me from being numb from the waist down and partially blind, to being healthy, successful in new business ventures, fulfilled with new community involvement and completely in love with my soul mate to whom I've been married since 1987.

"Sounds too good to be true," you say.

You're right! Yet, it is true! I'm not a doctor or a psychologist. I am an accomplished business woman whose walls were covered with my over-achievements, but whose life was strangely empty. (My bio's included in the workbook for those who need credentials.) I do have a Ph.D. in EXPERIENCE, however: The experience of plunging into holistic medicine to find my way to health. And that was not an easy dive. I was last on my list for care and nurturing and the first to question all the New Age mumbo jumbo enlightenment philosophies. Who knew??? Meditation and Ayurveda from India — Acupuncture and Tai Chi Chuan from China, Jin Shin Jyutsu and Reiki from Japan, herbs and teas — Please! I was raised to get married and have children like Cindy McDonald down the street and to survive a childhood with an alcoholic dad, a helpless mom and a dramatic financial downfall.

Well, I did all of that, and a big crisis still hit! My crisis was of the health variety. Yours may be of another type, but one thing is certain; to come out feeling better than you do now, you need the enlightenment I found by doing everything on the following pages. Yes, I did it all, while struggling to save my business and find a personal life. Very few people have the luxury of putting their lives on hold while trying to find solutions. The most important additional time you can find in your day, however, is the time for you, because without that nothing else matters.

O.K., what else do we have in common? I'm a baby boomer, born in 1950. One of the 77 million who turns 50 every 7.6 seconds. I'll do that in the year 2000, and yes, that makes me a little anxious.

What about younger readers? I had a woman come up to me after a recent speech and clasp both my hands in hers as tears poured from her eyes. I thought she was going to share a similar story with me, but instead she thanked me for saving her. Like me, she was being pressurized in the advertising business. My vanity had not allowed me to see that she was 20 years my junior. I tend to look at all women and think we are the same age. She said, "I saw so clearly what I could become in 20 years if I don't change my ways. Thanks for keeping me from turning into you." That's the least I can do, I thought — shocked, but oddly flattered.

Now, what was I keeping her from becoming? Sleep deprived, anxious, stressed — perhaps even ill? Do any of these problems strike home for you? Were they motivators in buying this book?

How about relationship difficulties? Have you had any of those? I had one divorce and more broken hearts than I care to detail before discovering that I didn't have a clue about love.

Have you recently experienced the death or loss of a loved one? Do you feel like you're missing out on too many parts of life? Is your energy all going in one or two directions, leaving your total life picture completely out of balance? Speaking of energy, do you have enough to go around, or does it seem to fizzle out just when you're ready to relax or have some fun? Are the questions "Who am I?" and "What am I doing with my life?" creeping back into your thoughts after you thought you'd answered them years ago? Are you having to change career direction and feeling frightened at venturing into uncharted, new territory? Do the rules of life seem to keep changing just when you had mastered the old score card? Are the major occasions in your life — birthdays, anniversaries, holidays — leaving you even more stressed out?

Are you waking up feeling frightened and anxious instead of joyful and eager to see what another day brings? The good news is, you're not alone. The bad news is, that is not a healthy way to live. I lived in the shadow of all of the above questions — which all denote a crisis of some type. I believe one or more of them must apply to you, too. It was finding my Health-Esteem that helped me to climb out of each dilemma.

When my biggest crisis to date hit, I felt like I was damaged goods. I was broken, not unlike a 24-year-old cancer patient that Dr. Rachel Remen discusses in a wonderful healing story found in the book **Feminine Healing**, by Jason Elias and Katherine Ketcham. The patient's leg had been surgically removed at the hip, and his recovery was slow and painful. In one therapy session he drew a picture of a vase with a jagged crack running through it and insisted that his body, like the vase, was broken and therefore useless. As time passed he emerged from his solution and self-pity and announced that the picture of the cracked vase was not finished. Pointing to the black line running through the vase, he explained that the crack in the vase was where the light was able to shine through. This workbook is about finding the cracks and broken places we all have sustained — to stop hiding them — to allow the light to find them so we can find the healing power that lives inside us all.

Now, back to you and a question you might be asking. How do I find the motivation to conquer my particular crisis? You started by taking this book into your hands. By reading a section each day you will be taking your own journey to Health-Esteem. One of the key members on my healing team and a contributor to this book wanted it to have this subtitle: *An Introduction and Guide to Recognizing When You're Not Well and Directions You Can Take To Get On The Road To Wellness*. A subtitle? Maybe not. Valuable and truthful benefits to making this workbook your best friend? Absolutely! When you finish, you will know the key part Health-Esteem plays in helping you through most any crisis.

Like you, a crisis took me to a bookstore and to lectures in search of answers. Unlike you, I've already done everything included in these pages. I can honestly tell you, it works! I'm a person, just like you who wants to let you know, if I can do it, you can do it, too! I did it, and now I'd like you to fill in the rest of this sentence:

I _ _ _ _ _ _ _   TOO!*

*Answer: I Can Do It, Too!

Chapter 2

What Is Health-Esteem?

I often define Health-Esteem with a declaration, "I am worth being healthy!" To act upon that declaration, you may have to actually change much of the mind set you have adopted, inherited or been taught throughout most of your life. You must discover respect for yourself and knowledge that you are what you think. Every experience you have had in life has left you with both a physical and emotional memory. Good or bad, whether you can recall the events or whether you have buried them out of sight and mind, they are imprinted in your cellular memory. That means they are rooted in the essence of what makes you uniquely you.

Embracing Health-Esteem means making a commitment to the one part of healing we can take charge of — our thoughts and emotions. Critical lessons come from the lives we live. Everything we need to know to initiate healing is available by accessing the data banks of our lives. Illness or crisis is inseparable from the fact that we are everything that has happened to us.

Health-Esteem is a process of discarding sick-making lessons in our lives and replacing them with

I Am Worth Being Healthy!

healthy thoughts and actions. For instance, spending two decades as a frenzied workaholic was a sick-making pattern for me. I learned to push everything that I didn't have time for and couldn't deal with out of sight and out of my mind. Unfortunately, all those things hid out in my body waiting to be dealt with, or if ignored long enough, waiting to deal with me. I'm talking about disappointing love affairs, failed friendships, confused spirituality, lack of community involvement, sadness, fear, anger, frustration, and other emotions I simply had no time for. I was torn between who I wanted to be and who society expected me to be. I completely mixed up my identity with my work. The result was that I got sick. To get well, I had to *un*learn my obsession with work, separate myself from what I did for a living and literally birth a self that was willing to participate in all the other parts of life.

Sounds like a big job doesn't it? I'd be guilty of false advertising if I said you can do it overnight. Gaining the power of Health-Esteem requires time devoted to discovery and self-awareness and a desire to connect with the environment and the people with whom we share this life on earth. One of my favorite definitions of health, hangs on the wall of a father/daughter chiropractic team's office and reads, "A state of optimum physical, mental and social well-being, not merely the absence of disease or infirmity."

At this point, I would like to clarify the difference between healing and a cure. By healing, I am not speaking about a cure, but rather an evolution into consciousness. When it comes to disease, whatever the label, AIDS, MS, cancer — the experience differs as much as each individual's personality. Every person's healing process is

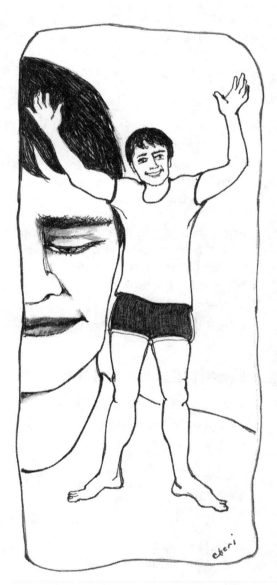

I Am Worth Being Healthy!

unique. We don't necessarily get over a disease. What we do is become conscious of the disease process and what underlies it. Then we set out to change as much as possible about cultural conditioning and mechanical thinking. As one of my healing partners in this workbook, Elizabeth says, "We either heal into living or heal into dying. Nobody's in charge of that — it's a soul process."

I've chosen to heal into staying in remission from MS for as long as possible, hopefully for my lifetime. The process of doing that is no mystery — it takes work, concentration and dedication — all of which I hope to motivate within you. Each chapter of this book is devoted to an aspect of achieving Health-Esteem. Health-Esteem engenders a rebirthing of yourself, independent from other's perceptions and completely tuned-in to your own wisdom: Wisdom that connects your mind and your body, your heart and your brain, your energy with that of the healing universe.

I cannot give you a time table. It's different for everybody. I can tell you how to start, however. Start by saying out loud, "I am worth being healthy." Look in the mirror and say, "I am worth being healthy." Repeat, "I am worth being healthy," five times before you meditate. Say it to yourself while you're walking, jogging or doing your morning exercise. When someone hurts your feelings, or cuts you off in traffic say, "I am worth being healthy," before you reply to the offending party. Repeat it, and before long you'll mean it, and at that point the phrase will be your guide to using this workbook and finding your Health-Esteem.

Test how far along you are on that road by taking the Health-Esteem quiz that follows:

Health-Esteem Questionnaire

1) Do you feel illness is a natural part of life? Just something that happens with age?

2) Do you feel like you're being punished when you get sick?

3) Do you find it hard to place value in your health?

4) Do you resent spending time and money to stay well?

5) Do you think it's more important to look good than to feel good?

6) Do you feel like you should be doing something more important when you are exercising?

7) Is it fun or "comforting" for you to eat foods that are bad for you?

8) In your childhood, was your family unable to teach you health-esteem?

9) Does illness make you feel helpless?

10) Does illness fill you with self-doubt?

11) Does illness make you feel sorry for yourself?

12) Do you spend more time being critical or appreciative of your body?

13) Do you feel like you must change your body in order to be loved?

14) Are you afraid to look at someone who is handicapped or who is in a wheelchair?

15) Are there negative parts of your personality that you work very hard to keep hidden — even from yourself?

16) Is your own care and maintenance often the last thing you get around to?

17) Do you feel that your health care practitioner, alone, is responsible for your health?

Every "Yes" to one of the previous questions is a sign post indicating an area where work needs to be done to improve your Health-Esteem. Look at each question as a point of departure to research your own feelings on the subject. There is not one right answer. We have provided a few thoughts to prompt your thinking on each question. In the space following each question, immediately jot down the feelings these thoughts provoke in you. Please don't hesitate — just write whatever comes to mind — positive and negative. For instance, after #1 some disgruntled feelings might be: *Are you nuts? Everybody gets something. You've just got to wait and see what life has in store for you!*

1) Do you feel illness is a natural part of life? Just something that happens with age?

While death is inevitable, death from any one of the illnesses of our times is not a law of the universe. Age and illness do not equate. Illness is not one of the words used to define age. It is possible to be healthy until the day we die and simply wear out and pass gently in our sleep. Isn't that the optimum situation and something worth our aspirations? Illness isn't natural. It is a body's way of getting it's occupant to pay attention to something that is out of balance. Symptoms relate to physiology out of balance. The body is designed to work and function perfectly and it will do so if there is no interference.

FEELINGS: _____

_____

_____

_____

_____

2) *Do you feel like you're being punished when you get sick?*

I did because I believed in a lot of false assumptions such as bad things don't happen to good people. If illnesses or accidents were punishments — who's doing the punishing ? And why did that outside authority to whom you are giving this power select you? No — don't give your power to that authority. Instead, I ask you to rest assured that somewhere in your body there is an answer for whatever has befallen you. The answer may be a cure, it may be a way to use and learn from your situation, it may be a sign to change the direction of your life, it may be a way to find peace, to let go of something harmful, to help others... Whatever the answer is — it is found on the inside, and finding that answer will bring Health-Esteem.

FEELINGS: _____

_____

_____

_____

_____

Questions 3 and 4 actually go together. If, as question 3 asks, you do find it hard to place value in your health, then as question 4 posits, do you resent spending time and money to stay well?

I don't know about you, but health was never a topic of conversation in my family until someone got sick. Then it was a problem to be dealt with that made us feel quite helpless. Big illnesses — like polio, leukemia, cancer — were all something to be feared. The vicissitudes of life left us powerless and totally dependent on our doctor/deity to save us. There was certainly no mention of emotional health and feelings being in any way connected to physical dis-ease.

I submit all of the above lessons learned from my childhood household as faulty programming in desperate need of being rewritten and re-learned. Health takes work, not dependence, and it affects every decision we make in life. Learning to be conscious of our every thought and action, as well as their consequences must become as natural as breathing. We have the power to create our own wellness. We are born with that power. Unfortunately, we are seldom taught to use it and we are often taught to give it away.

FEELINGS: _____

_____

_____

_____

_____

Question 5 — Do you think it's more important to look good than to feel good?

I certainly did. With the right hair, make-up and clothing I could hide almost everything I didn't like about my body or life. The feelings I was racking up, pushing aside, and shoving down were falling through the cracks in my brain, down into my body to hide out and show up later in aches and pains, crises and illness.

Buried feelings don't go away, they gang up on you. Imagine looking at another person and tuning into their feelings instead of their hair style or wardrobe choice. Imagine that instead of snapping angrily at your husband, "You're not going to wear that awful shirt are you?" you confessed that you were really hurt last night at the dinner party when he got up and left the table while you were telling a story.

FEELINGS: _____

_____

_____

_____

_____

Question 6 — Do you feel like you should be doing something more important when you are exercising?

You know that little gnawing feeling that creeps in when you look at the clock and panic about all you have to do and you say, "OK, I'll just do 20 minutes of aerobics not 40, I've got to get to work." Or, you constantly apologize for cutting meditation out of your life because you were just too busy! Too busy for health? — The thing that's ultimately going to either prolong or curtail every other activity you had planned for your life? When I was interviewing a wealthy, powerful entertainment executive with MS and told him about my daily exercise routine, he counted up the minutes and said in shock, "That's over 2 hours you spend on yourself — everyday?"

How can you do that? I say, "How can't I?" when it improves the quality of every thought and action I take throughout the day.

FEELINGS: _____

_____

_____

_____

_____

_____

Question 7 — Is it fun or "comforting" for you to eat foods that are bad for you?

You may ask "Is that a rhetorical question or what?" I know, I'm human. Hot fudge sundaes are my downfall and when I eat the one I allow myself every three months — it's almost as much fun as great sex and as comfortable as a down quilt on a freezing, snowy night. This is kind of a trick question, however. Food is fun, comforting, nourishing and wonderful. Where I got in trouble was using it as a substitute for feeling my emotions. For instance, in my workaholic frenzy, I'd go home and often feel sorry for myself and my lonely existence. "I'll just eat junk food," I'd say to myself. (Translation: It's not worth cooking a nourishing meal just for me.) Like a robot, I then ate my chips and dip, followed by ice cream — followed by a pack of cigarettes — all while I looked mindlessly at the TV. (Translation: Keep your hands, mouth, and eyes busy — swallow the loneliness and pain with every bite so you don't have to feel it.) I had to learn to be mindful of my eating and to find other ways to express my feelings. Suggestions follow in the Nutrition section.

FEELINGS: _____

_____

_____

_____

_____

_____

Question 8 — Was health low on the list of values taught to you by your family?

It wasn't even on the list in my childhood, unless we talked about sickness. In my house, health was one of those things you either were or were not born with — you just didn't think about it too much until it disappeared, until you were sick. Then you did what the doctor told you and waited to get well again. Health was passive not active. Imagine being taught from the very beginning of our thinking that our every thought and action is interconnected to our health. How empowering to know that with every breath, we are making ourselves into what we will be. There's so much more to teach in school about health than hygiene.

FEELINGS: _____

_____

_____

_____

_____

_____

Questions 9,10 and 11 can really be grouped: Does illness make you feel helpless, filled with self-doubt, sorry for yourself?

The answers here and throughout most of the questionnaire depend on what you were taught, or what you absorbed from your childhood home. My answers were yes to all of the above. Sickness was a cause for alarm. If I got a cold, the flu was inevitable. My bruises were surely a sign of leukemia. How would I ever catch up in school if I was too sick to study? I was, indeed, helpless. Sickness made me a victim and, therefore, I could be sorry for myself. What a different attitude I might have had if I had learned to look at why I got sick — no rest, unhappy at home, pushing myself too hard — and then to look at what I could do to get well: Get rest, talk to someone about my feelings, lighten up and realize there was more to life than people pleasing. "Come on," you might say, "all of those things connected to a cold? Maybe you just caught it."

My answer — the immune system cannot ward off illness when it's in a weakened state, and sick-making feelings sap its strength.

FEELINGS: _____

_____

_____

_____

_____

_____

Question 12 — *Do you spend more time being critical or appreciative of your body?*

If you spend more time being appreciative — Hooray! And I mean that because it has taken me 46 years to like my body. So my answer to...

Question 13 — *Do you feel like you must change your body in order to be loved?*

has always been a resounding, "Yes!" All my life, I've been covering up my body with cute and or pretty and or sexy clothes. I was really using those clothes to cover up a lot of feelings, however. My mom had indicated that the body was somehow shameful — clothes to the rescue! TV had indicated that my body didn't measure up — I felt inadequate. Clothes could fix that! My work environment had indicated that my body could draw the "wrong" kind of attention. Ah, dress to succeed and simultaneously ward off sexual harassment. Defense is the best offense. Eventually I just stopped thinking about my body — it became a hanger for my clothes which created my image which was what was real.

I was shocked when I finally realized that I had allowed outside forces to define who I was and how I felt about myself all of my life. Exercises on ways to command your own self-definition are included in Chapter 17.

FEELINGS: _____

_____

_____

_____

_____

_____

Question 14 — Are you afraid to look at someone who is handicapped or who is in a wheelchair?

It's the old "There but for the grace of God go I" syndrome; also known as the "If I get too close, I might catch it" obsession. Why ignore the experience of a person by being totally wound up in your own fears? It's not about you — it's about that person. As my friend Ethel, who has been in a wheelchair for almost 20 years says, "Blowing out my candle doesn't make your candle brighter." That saying helps her realize that she has power and that it resides <u>not</u> in her wheelchair and not in her body, but inside of her.

What are you afraid of? There is an answer, but it may not be in the package you expect. Look inside, sideways and all around yourself because it's there.

FEELINGS: _____

_____

_____

_____

_____

_____

Question 15 — Are there negative parts of your personality that you work very hard to keep hidden — even from yourself?

Now we're getting to the nitty-gritty. The shadow side — the little monster in us all. That's where anger, jealously, envy, greed, hate, lust, resentment, worry, bitterness, fear and all those big nasties hang out. And believe me, if we feel the flip side, all those happy feelings we aim for, then we feel the shadow side, too. The problem comes when we try to hide those feelings even from ourselves. For instance, if we feel envy, it's important to acknowledge the feeling and trace it back to where it might have begun. Take a moment to trace a bad feeling you are familiar with all the way back to its roots.

FEELINGS: _____

_____

_____

_____

_____

_____

Question 16 — Is your own care and maintenance often the last thing you get around to?

Mine was, because my priorities were outside driven — relationship, career, money, friends, achievement. *There must be a way to get to ourselves before we almost destroy ourselves. Do we all have to make the same mistakes and wind up in a crisis before we meet ourselves coming to our own rescue?*

FEELINGS: _____

_____

_____

_____

_____

_____

Question 17 — Do you feel that your health care practitioner is responsible for your health?

This is the big mind-block standing in the way of health-esteem. Most of us were taught that doctors had the power. The truth is — they are scientists and they have research, knowledge, and skill that can be helpful. But, the power — the real power lies within ourselves. The secret is for patients to work with their health care practitioners in the pursuit of health. It's a partnership. You must become a co-creator of your health. There is no one answer. There are more answers everyday. You must be willing to ask questions and to look for answers inside as well as outside.

Chapter

3

Head Over Healing In Love — The Book

Do we all have to make the same mistakes and wind up in a crisis before we meet ourselves coming to our own rescue? That question and a very bad TV movie depicting all multiple sclerosis sufferers as complete victims sent me to my computer to write a book. I figured there were a lot of people out there like me; people out of touch with life, due to a single-minded obsession with work, love, money, accomplishment or some other force that was sending them straight into an appointment with a brick wall if they didn't wake up to the rest of life and signals coming from their own bodies.

The last thing I wanted to listen to in 1985 was signals from my body. So my body got mad as hell and sent two very scary messengers, numbness from my waist to my toes and partial blindness. I had just celebrated my 35th birthday, survived the near loss of my multi-million dollar advertising agency and limped through the sad ending to yet another relationship that I had hoped would be "the one." Suddenly I was forced to turn in workaholism for another disease, multiple sclerosis.

In 1985, the medical community had little to offer me. I stumbled through two years of denial on my own before discovering I had to find my own answers. Part One of **Head Over Healing In Love** takes you right into my out of control life at the moment the first frightening and bewildering symptoms occur. An automobile accident caused by a large black hole in my vision shocks me out of denial and into a search for healing partners. Soon I begin to discover the frozen, locked-in physical and emotional condition I was in that had been created in the social context of women's liberation, the sex, drugs and rock 'n roll revolution, political and heroic angst and the emergence of workaholic yuppies plagued by their overlooked shadow sides. I realize that I am only one example of how society's struggles are reflected in the illnesses and crises of a generation.

In Part Two of my book I become detective-like, chronologically tracking down lessons learned from my childhood, family and relationships that had turned into unhealthy patterns and behaviors. I recognize the scars received in an alcoholic, emotionally abusive home and how they set me up for an illness such as MS, which means "multiple scars." I document many others in my generation facing different crisis crossroads and offer prescriptions for various physical symptoms in the form of behavioral changes.

Part Three of the book offers the Health-Esteem program as a path of ongoing healing, no matter what the illness or trauma. Readers learn methods to apply to their own emotional health tracking and see what one experiences and feels in the process of getting well. Conversations with other wellness seekers with other ailments and crises besides MS provide inspiring stories and insights.

The title of my book refers to the many levels of love. To begin healing I had to open my heart to the possibility. I had to discover my health-esteem and that meant discovering that I was worth being healthy, in other words, I had to be able to love myself and to devote time, money and devotion to my own self-nurturing. Once my heart was open, further healing came by embracing family, friends and the environment and world around me. When I was finally connecting to the many feelings life has to offer, I was ready for the love that had eluded me my entire life to find me. Three years into my healing when I was completely content with my life as a single, fulfilled, active, productive and involved woman, my soul mate whom I would have been unable to recognize before, swept me off my feet as we both fell head over heels in love.

Convinced that I had learned to be vulnerable to the disease of MS by absorbing the pain, disappointments and hurtful thoughts and actions of others, I wrote the book to help others track down sick-making lessons from life that could put them in the path of illness or crisis. My health care policy is simple; to understand the one part of healing we can take charge of — our thoughts and emotions. Some say my MS symptoms are merely in remission. I emphasize the importance of what one does during the remissions. I am always mindful that in 1985 I was diagnosed with multiple sclerosis. I'm aware that I've had to change every pattern in my life to remain symptom free, and I quickly catch those slips that I might make into old, bad habits. I hope and believe this behavior will make my remission permanent.

I am combining a positive attitude with positive behavior and positive change. Through the example of an ordinary woman, like myself, and examples of other ordinary people who have all done something extraordinary — survive a life-changing crossroads and emerge better people — I help readers:

- Meet the other half of their personalities.
- Reclaim trust, nurturing, intimacy and love in their lives.
- Embrace their own sexuality.
- Document their personal "emotional" histories.
- Overcome crisis crossroads with proven methods.
- Separate from negative lessons learned from others.
- Own and live their own life lessons.

Why I Wrote the Health-Esteem Workbook

When the book was finished and began working its way through the laborious process of publication, my healing process continued, and the concept of Health-Esteem grew into a business. I began speaking to groups nationwide, and by request I began recording tapes to furnish my audiences with a health-esteem program they could take into their lives immediately. Still, I got requests for more detail. So, I took down my audiences questions and thought about how I could answer their questions in a way that would motivate them into action.

They would ask: How did you start? How do you learn how to listen to your body? How do I match a symptom or a signal with the right action to get better? Is it possible to mix allopathic and homeopathic medicine? Who was on your healing team? How do I put together a healing team of my own? What questions do I ask various practitioners to know if I've found qualified ones? How do I sort through all the claims, news, suggestions and warnings bombarding me daily? What if I'm not as strong-willed as you are? What does spirituality have to do with all of this? What if I don't get better, have I failed — does that mean I'm a bad person? Why do I have to spend so much time digging into my past for answers? How much time will this take? When is it too late to try? How do I use this if I'm facing a divorce, a job loss, death of a loved one, terminal illness, everyday stress... What if I don't want to feel all of my emotions? What if I don't have time for all of this? How do you meditate? What about exercise? What's most important? Do I have to change a lot? How do I get over the fear? I've got so much to worry about, why can't I just hire someone else, like a doctor to take care of all of this for me? I don't have years, I want to feel better tomorrow — can you help me do that? I just want to feel better, I don't have to understand everything — do I?

My answers to these questions and more took form as this workbook. I then approached three key members of my healing team, my chiropractor, my development consultant and my body therapist and asked if they would help me break down the healing process that I and others had been through in a form readers could use for their own experimentation. We brainstormed tests, questionnaires, experiments, exercises, diaries, interactive thought processes and more to get the mind and body working together. They are all in the following pages. Everything in these pages was helpful to me and others.

I am an idealist. It is my most fervent wish that my readers can avoid some of what I suffered by opening their hearts to the possibilities of life much earlier than I did. It took me years to discover what is in these pages. May this workbook save you some of that time and add to the quality of every day you live with Health-Esteem. Quite honestly, that is why I wrote this workbook.

The Health-Esteem Workbook Team

If credentials and backgrounds mean little to you, this chapter may be skipped, allowing you to dive into the next section. Otherwise, please accept this as my introduction to you of the Health-Esteem team. They are my healing guides, my dearest of friends, and now my partners in bringing this workbook to you.

First, I present my own profile. You already know that for the first 35 years of my life I worked myself into a well-honed example of a workaholic: achievement thirsty, accomplishment-driven, relationship-deprived, empire building female entrepreneur. I was completely successful in shutting off my personal needs for the good of my business. I looked in my mirror and saw not a woman, but the president of my solely-owned advertising agency. Here is my profile before I was diagnosed with MS.

Judith Parker Harris received her B.A. (phi beta kappa) with a double major in Dramatic Arts and Rhetoric from the University of California, Davis in 1972. Fifteen trophies for being a champion accordion player and 30 speech awards including California State Champion in humorous and dramatic interpretation preceded her college honors.

In the '70s, Judith produced and directed over 3,000 television commercials and served as on-camera spokesperson for a national retail chain. Throughout that decade she wrote almost everything she produced including magazines, newsletters for trade publications, travel documentaries, industrial videos and investigative journalism for public broadcasting. Many ad awards including Sacramento's Advertising Woman of the Year came her way.

In 1980, a long-distance love affair prompted Judith's move to Los Angeles. The relationship soon fizzled and she was left to start her career anew in the city of angels. Within one year, she turned a sales position with a new production company into a partnership which spun off into an advertising agency. One year after that, the advertising agency had over one million dollars in billings, clients nationwide, and a reputation as the pioneer of brand marketing for healthcare products such as plastic surgery and chemical dependency. Less than a year into the agency's success, Judith's partner wanted out of the risky, advertising business and she became the agency's sole-owner.

What was not included in the above narrative was the dysfunctional lifestyle of the over-achiever. I spent every waking moment of my life devoted to work. The ups and downs of the business often found me without a paycheck or food on the table while I struggled to save my business and the jobs of my staff members. I was numbed by the battering of my life and blind to anything that would side track me from my course. Then, MS came along and changed everything about my life as I had known it up to that point. Rather than allow my mind to triumph over my body, I united the two in a search for my health. Emotional pain was found and followed back to it's root, where I could choose to accept, forgive, discard or change it. Negative life patterns were isolated, understood and altered as needed. I met and married my soul mate, changed my career direction, became involved with the world around me, reached out to others, and accepted love into my life. Three years into these efforts, my last symptom of MS disappeared. I have now been not only symptom-free since 1990, but also healthier than I've ever been in my life. The rest of my profile reads like this:

Judith Parker Harris has turned the philosophy and research expressed in **Head Over Healing In Love** into a new career as she becomes well known on the speaking circuit for her talks, cassette tapes and motivational courses. She is also partnered with her producer husband, Jack H. Harris, as Vice President of Worldwide Entertainment Corporation. Judith oversees all new feature film development and has teamed with her husband to produce several projects.

On the Board of Directors of Women In Film, Judith has been instrumental in uniting the entertainment community in their donation of labor, materials and services to produce pro bono public service announcements for local and national organizations serving women and children. For this effort she was invited to the White House and personally congratulated by First Lady Hillary Rodham Clinton. Judith is also on the Board of Para Los Niños, serving homeless Skid Row children and their families, and is very active with MS Groups seeking to improve the self-image of MS sufferers as well as the opportunities they envision for themselves in both living and healing.

She currently lives in Beverly Hills, California with her husband Jack. Judith has become a step-grandmother to seven wonderful kids and she and her husband are the proud parents to a gigantically adorable 12-pound Maltese pup, Jessie.

What is written between the lines in Part Two of my profile is that I overcame the isolation of workaholism and disease diagnosis to create a new, exciting, fulfilled, connected life filled with love of self, my husband, family, friends and the world around me. (Translation: I'm now living a life of health-esteem.) I want to help you do the same and so do my partners.

My first wellness partner, Tobes Reisel, came to me through recommendation. After that, Tobes made further suggestions as the needs arose. As I became well enough to follow her advice and listen to the needs of my own body, one recommendation led to another and to another when the time was right for what each wellness guide had to offer. As I studied and opened myself up to healing, the people I needed to learn from, to be guided by and to be helped by came naturally into my life. I had to be willing to listen, to talk to others, to notice what was working for people I admired, to be aware of the many options surrounding me in life.

Tobes Reisel

Tobes, art therapist / consultant / elder wise woman and teacher, enticed every bit of healing wisdom out of a surprising source — myself. Just as she deftly guided my healing course, she gently guides the direction of this workbook to help you discover your own internal healing wisdom. Tobes is of my mother's generation, but she broke through her own traditional conditioning to find wisdom to share with and help heal all wounded daughters. Feeling she never fit into a family of older parents, three half brothers and lots of male cousins, Tobes turned to art to get her through a lonely childhood. Marriage at age 22 veered her away from a career in graphic art long enough to raise four daughters and live the accepted female image of the time — that of the perfect cook, the best mother and the wonderful wife.

Thirsting for brain food, Tobes continually audited psychology classes on the campus where her husband, a clinical psychologist, taught. Again, art manifested as Tobes began drawing from her unconscious. As a guide in her Jungian psychotherapy process, she got interested in using imagery as another language. Professors at the university in the behavioral sciences department began using her process drawings in class until finally, pioneering Tobes realized that in her search for a language to express herself, she had found a way to teach in what would now be termed "art therapy." Tobes experienced what she helps all women who come to her to discover — that usual accepted verbal language doesn't always speak for us; we have to find our own way of communicating — our own way of being.

Tobes was pushed into her own self-awareness through the physical manifestation of her own emotional frustrations — bronchial asthma. In her mid-30's, she suffered from bronchial infections. She recalls suppressing more and more of herself to fit the image of what she was supposed to be. Her congestion limited her breathing all of the time. She was unable to speak without coughing. Tobes dealt with her illness for a long time by becoming completely dependent on antibiotics and antihistamines. "That's what we did in the '50s and '60s," she relates, "we took a lot of pills." It took a full-blown bronchial asthma attack to make her realize that, "Something is happening here that is more than just physical."

Along her path to wellness, Tobes became a registered art therapist, which she combined effectively with her own individual development and psychology training. As Tobes furthered her own awareness and expertise in art therapy, she grew apart from what her marriage represented in the traditional sense. Tobes journey through the difficult passages of personal and professional development became the basis for her way of guiding countless women and men through their own complex roads to effective, creative lives.

She constantly reminds others that wellness is a continuing process, and this workbook is positive proof. She explains, "Working with Judith, Nancy and Elizabeth on this workbook brought me a sense of appreciation that enhances and continues to help me develop my own personal consciousness, creativity and effectiveness."

Elizabeth Harlow

Elizabeth is a body therapist and a healer, so gifted, she could literally read my body inside and out through touch, breath, circulation and profound intuition. Her hands were able to touch my body and receive communication from deep within me at a cellular level. She reads a body's energy and knows where she must go to work. Not only does she help endocrine, respiratory, circulatory and nervous systems to run smoothly, she also helps emotions, memories and a lifetime of stories surface; then they can be dealt with on the physical plane, where they can help heal illness-making patterns.

Elizabeth is uniquely qualified to help her clients discover the truth in their lives. She healed into living her own life after it began so traumatically that she had to bury the feelings of her early experiences or die remembering them. She understands what needs to be done when her clients come upon emotionally-laden memories and encourages them to experience the intensity of the emotions, as she explains that another step closer to the truth of one's soul has been taken.

Elizabeth survived life in an orphanage only to be brought home and raped by her alcoholic stepfather. Repeated molestation resulted in a pregnancy at age 14. She delivered a baby girl who was immediately given into private adoption. Thinking she was protecting her mother and younger children in the family, Elizabeth endured threats, beatings and overall abuse. Finally, facing death from a vicious knife attack from her stepfather, Elizabeth left home at 16 and began life on her own.

Upon graduating from high school with honors, Elizabeth, like so many women in the late '60s began a career, married and went to college simultaneously. Her marriage soon ended, and her straight A study path in psychology, plus voice and piano lessons and volunteerism in numerous care giving organizations still couldn't lift her feeling of being a failure.

Years later, a second marriage also ran into difficulty. In the early '70s, Elizabeth joined a women's consciousness-raising group. Seven women met weekly and shared the difficulty of breaking away from the expectations of their mother's generation, of making it in a man's world, of expressing feelings verbally or in writing, and of fighting the many revolutions of being a woman, including those waged for sexuality and equality. Six of those women have gone into the healing profession; Elizabeth is one of them.

The journey that would deliver her to the point of healing others would take her eight years. Eventually her high pressure work in the arena of community development and planning plus a move to the west coast would take their toll. In 1979, Elizabeth underwent a major healing crisis which altered the course of her life. The right side of her body began to shrivel. To understand why her body was betraying her, she had to get to the feelings and pain she had buried in self-defense. She began exploring a new territory in Eastern healing strategies often referred to as transformational studies with Dr. Richard Moss, M.D. Elizabeth recalls, "The high energy currents of living in a working community and practicing in the Mojave Desert began pressing up against buried feelings and physical pain from the traumatic beginning of my life. They were surfacing like an avalanche in my body and psyche. I knew the experience of cellular memory release before the phrase was coined."

To develop the knowledge she was gaining and continue her own healing, Elizabeth received her massage therapy certification from the Institute of Psycho-Structural Balancing in Santa Monica in 1982 and began a body therapies practice. With a lot of healing waters under her bridge, Elizabeth met her daughter, Linda (then 22), in 1985.

In 1984 Elizabeth started her body therapy practice with no advertising and no trouble because as she has said, "People were guided to come to me." In that same year, she was introduced to Dr. Carl Simonton and became the Senior body therapist working on his staff at the Simonton Cancer Center in Pacific Palisades, California.

Elizabeth's thirst for understanding continues to bring her into study and work with people on the leading edge of the healing arts. Her expertise ranges from the in-depth study and practice of ancient healing systems of Reiki, Jin Shin Jyutsu, hatha yoga, Tai Chi Chuan and Tai Chi Sword, to co-facilitating transformational wilderness explorations.

Elizabeth teaches what she has lived: "We are each, ultimately, our own healers and intimately connected to the whole of this existence." Elizabeth calls the healing process, "a coming together and listening. It's like picking up a telephone, only I'm dialing straight to inner communication." She tells her clients, "It's not what I know, as much as it is what your system wants to have me communicate to you."

Nancy LaPidus, D.C.

Nancy is my second wonderfully gifted chiropractor. Before I tell you about her, I'd like to say a few words about Natalie Miller, my first chiropractor, who died tragically at the age of 37 when a virulent, fast-growing form of cancer choked off her productive life. Natalie worked with me to successfully eliminate every one of my MS symptoms before she died. She introduced me to myself at various ages as she found pain locked inside my body, where I had stored secrets even from myself. Unfortunately, it may be that Natalie could not face many of her own emotional truths in order to help herself with the same zealous determination she gave her patients. Ironically, she lost herself in her practice, just as I *almost* lost myself in my advertising agency. Natalie's spirit lives on in the health of others she championed and is represented with love in these pages.

Nancy, unlike Natalie, has learned to follow her own advice and wisdom. She works with me to keep my body tuned, balanced and on the wellness track. A licensed chiropractor since January, 1986, Nancy specializes in nutrition-related illnesses and loves what she does. She had to try on a few other professions and find out they didn't fit, however, before she found the perfect match for her life's work. Born in 1954 and raised in Providence, Rhode Island, Nancy doesn't have many memories of her childhood. When she was nine years old her parents divorced, and she and her brother lived with her mom. Nancy's dad moved out of the area, but would come to visit one or two weekends a month when his work travel schedule allowed time. He stayed in touch with her and her brother through phone calls and letters.

Nancy describes herself as being a depressed kid. The changes in her family left her feeling very sad and lonely. As a way to shut out the pain and loss she felt, Nancy turned inward and spent huge amounts of time reading and listening to music. Nancy went to private school and on to Boston University, but dropped out to pursue a paralegal program at Georgetown University. Upon graduation, she moved to California and worked as a paralegal for four months — enough time to realize she hated her chosen field.

It was time to move on, so she went from Santa Barbara to Los Angeles and a Women's Employment Options Conference at the Career Planning Center. Nancy was so impressed with the Conference that she went to work for the Career Planning Center. She did career counseling and development, but felt uncomfortable with the sales end of the job. She describes herself at that time in her life as a naïve young woman, shy and lacking in self confidence. She says, "I had an underlying feeling that I was an intruder here — an uninvited guest at the party of life. I could do it now. I have such a different way of being in the world today."

One day Nancy looked around at all the people who were telling her what to do and how to do it and she thought, "I'm at least as smart, as talented, as capable as they are, so how come they're telling me what to do?" Thinking that what she lacked was a college degree, Nancy quit her job and went back to school at Santa Monica College. She enrolled in a nutrition class and bells went off in her head. "It was extraordinary. I thought physiology was the most fascinating thing I'd ever studied." The rest is history. Two years of pre-med. prerequisites and three and a half years of chiropractic college followed. Nancy excelled and blossomed into an individual with a mission: to help others obtain wellness, and to teach patients how wonderful it is to feel "healthy" as opposed to simply "not feeling sick."

Nancy's turning point to her own wellness came with the end to an intimate relationship and the onset of Epstein Barr Syndrome. She had to look at confidence, Health-Esteem, forgotten memory and spirituality issues to regain the energy she learned to treasure for her life and her practice. (See Chapter 30.)

Besides her busy patient schedule, Nancy always finds time to teach classes in nutrition. She loves her calling, and her patients love her. Several of them are quoted throughout this workbook. Without preaching, Nancy gently reminds her patients that they must also do their part to bring the balance into their lives that healthy bodies require. Nancy loves to sing, and I think of her healing approach as a duet. She can provide the sheet music and the orchestration, but the patients must sing along to keep everything in tune.

Nancy dispenses her wisdom with a dry wit. When we were discussing the "Love" Chapter of this workbook, I asked her if she had found it difficult to make her intimate relationships work until she got a handle on who she was? She replied with a laugh:

"Yeah, and that was last week."

Said with humor, Nancy does share, on a more serious note, that her recent break-up with a man she cared for deeply had, after the grieving, brought her tremendous growth. "I value who I am much more now, and make choices with greater awareness of what *I* want to do," she explains with assurance. "I can acknowledge my own skills, and I not only feel that I'm invited to the party of life, I'm aware that I'm throwing my own party. Now that's progress."

One of the great parts of working with my healing team is that we always find a way to bring in laughter. Not only does laughter balance out the serious moments, it also puts life into perspective, and it definitely keeps us from taking ourselves too seriously! Another wonderful bonus is that we remind each other that we are all works in progress. With every healing moment comes growth, insight and often inspiration, and that process never ends.

Before closing this chapter, I would like to acknowledge other members of my wellness team. First, a man who helped to save my life by falling in love with a woman that I had not allowed to live, my anima, my completely feminine self. That man is my husband, Jack.

My best friend, Susan, is also on the team. We help each other with laughter, heart-to-heart talks, unconditional support and love. Another dear friend, Jan, taught my husband and me Transcendental Meditation and inspires daily with her gentle, peaceful, loving life style.

Deepak Chopra gave me the courage of my convictions that I was, indeed, healing from MS as he looked into my soul, took my pulse and shared a private meditation with me.

Dr. Leslie Dornfeld has watched protectively over me to insure that my course is a safe one, unofficially sanctioning all that he reminds me science cannot prove.

Jael Greenleaf and her wonderful intensive course for adult children of alcoholics truly opened my eyes. She left me with a life-long gift, five women I have continued to meet with regularly since 1992, still following Jael's program format. We have a unique way of bolstering each other without criticism or judgment and with trust and truth.

A Women In Creativity Group, formed by Tobes, sparked one of my biggest breakthroughs. While we seldom see each other now that our work is through, I'm confident that any one of us could call on another at a moment's notice and be there. We have low maintenance yet highly dependable bonds.

All the 12-step programs I have attended, all of the authors I have read, all the lectures and workshop leaders and attendees, all the inspirational men and women who have shared their stories with me, all of the people who have come to my lectures, listened to my tapes and joined their healing spirit with mine — all have been part of my wellness team.

I encourage you to begin to pull together your healing team while acknowledging those who are already members. As you can see from my team, members can be authors, acquaintances, people who have inspired you along the way, as well as people with whom you have an active connection.

There is room in the wellness team directory below to list names, their team positions (i.e. doctor, acupuncturist, friend, counselor, masseuse, beautician, spouse, author, lecturer — be creative!), and phone numbers if you desire.

WELLNESS TEAM DIRECTORY

NAME	TEAM POSITION	PHONE#

How To Use This Workbook

First, let me take the performance anxiety away from the tasks within this workbook. There is no wrong way to use this workbook. You can pick it up, play with it, make it a part of your life. You can start in the middle or start at the end and work your way to the beginning. Read through the index and see what strikes you and start there. Whatever you *feel* like, just do it! There's the key — JUST DO IT!

And the second key is, do it your own way, because that's what this workbook is about, learning to find your own way as separate and distinct from ways you have learned from others.

There are three tools that will be most helpful in your work. The tools are positive ways of behavior that when used often enough will replace some old negative behavior. I concentrate on bringing this behavior into my life everyday with a breathing exercise before I meditate.

__NEGATIVE BEHAVIOR__	__POSITIVE BEHAVIOR__
BREATHE OUT JUDGMENT	BREATHE IN ACCEPTANCE
BREATHE OUT CRITICAL	BREATHE IN ADAPTABLE
BREATHE OUT REACTIVE	BREATHE IN RECEPTIVE

"How do I use this while reading this workbook?" you may ask. If operating from the first column when reading a phrase such as, "Study inherited emotional problems," you might have the following thoughts:

"Well, that sounds pretty stupid. Why would I want to look at a lot of garbage I've worked so hard to run away from? This author must be nuts and bent on getting me stuck in the past! I'll show my family what I think of their emotional problems — they can shove 'em up the chimney that Santa never came down!"

Now, let's try reading the same phrase while operating with behavior from the second column. "I'm not sure what my inherited emotional problems may be, but if finding them will help me feel better in my life now,

I'm willing to try. Perhaps what worked then, doesn't work for me any longer. Wouldn't it be interesting to discover that some of my problems were learned and that with new information and some effort I can change things that hurt me?"

By *acceptance* I mean the ability to take in new information willingly and without the filters people erect out of habit and compliance with societal or other-sponsored thinking. By *adaptable* I mean the ability to be open to trying things a new way and the inclination to look at and evaluate new information and thinking; the capacity to bring information into harmony with a new pattern, example or principle. By *receptive* I mean perceptive, sensible, sensitive to new information and thinking that is different from your own.

You may want to set aside a certain time of day to use the workbook. Each section is designed to be short enough to do in 15 or 30 minutes dependent on how long you take with the experiments or exercises presented within chapters. If you have difficulty with one section or lack interest in the content, go on to another section. Invariably something will send you back to complete what you haven't finished, or ignored because you were too bothered by the content the first time. Each part of this workbook builds upon every other part. The more work you do, the easier it will become to see how this work can change your life. You probably will want to repeat some sections when you are working through different problems or emotions or when you encounter memories from different times or family members. The information is very flexible.

What To Do With Emotions When They Arise

You must know from the beginning that this is highly emotional work. When you are feeling things you haven't felt or acknowledged before — it's working. Watch out for these big feelings and know you are successful when you bump into them:

> FEAR, ANGER, RESISTANCE, RESENTMENT, SKEPTICISM, JEALOUSY, DEFIANCE, DISAPPOINTMENT, DEPRESSION...

I'm listing the negative emotions first, because they are usually the first to come out. After all, they are the ones we've been stuffing out of view from ourselves and others. There are journal pages provided throughout this book. When you run into a strong feeling, we suggest you write a paragraph about it. Always note the chapter which prompted the emotions. Also try to trace the feeling to a family member who felt that way and/or other times when you felt this way, but perhaps didn't express it.

For instance: "Chapter 13, Recognize a Self Separate and Distinct from My Vocation — made me mad. I've worked hard all my life to achieve my position. I'm proud of who my job makes me. My mother always said, 'Make sure you have a job to depend on, because you certainly can't depend on other people. Don't be like me, worthless, because I didn't learn how to do anything.'"

Do I need to tell you that there was a lot for me to work on in the above paragraph before Health-Esteem could be discovered?

Another thing to do when you bump into an emotion is to feel it. If you're mad — scream. Walk it out, run it out but whatever you do acknowledge it and feel the feelings. After you've wallowed in it for awhile, say 15 minutes or so, then brush it off your skin like you're brushing off mosquitoes. Do a breathing exercise to center yourself. (See Chapter 25.)

Don't be discouraged. You're also going to experience some real highs when you're doing this work. Look forward to:

DISCOVERY, JOY, ELATION, SATISFACTION, LOVE, PEACE, COURAGE, CONFIDENCE, RESPECT, HEALTH-ESTEEM.

Don't worry. You won't experience all the downs and then all the ups. The pattern is random because it's dictated by everything that has happened in your life up to the point of starting this work. You are finally going to make sense out of the puzzle of your life, but the puzzle will fight back some times as you endeavor to reorganize it to suit your purposes.

Whatever you do, don't abandon this work. It will change the quality of your life from this day forward. When you hit a bump and fall into your own pit of self doubt, come back to this chapter. It's always waiting with some loving comfort to get you started again. Remember to function from Column 2 and be ACCEPTING ADAPTABLE, and RECEPTIVE. Also remember, it took (*your age*) years, in my case 35 years of the vicissitudes of life to create my unauthorized story and deliver me to a crisis climax. It will take more than a few days, weeks, months, or even years to rewrite your story, societal programming and learned and inherited thinking to achieve maximum wellness and the particular results you seek.

Finding your Health-Esteem is a rebirthing process. You are becoming your own mother, father or both. To become the self parent you hope to be, you must say good-bye to the inner negative guides who have been setting your course. Part of you is dying, just as part of you is born. Don't hesitate to feel what that engenders.

Helpers

Positive statements to help you along the way:

I'm happy to spend time on my own wellness and nurturing.

It's just as important to exercise and eat right as it is to work!

I am not helpless when it comes to my own health.

I love my body and I want to take care of it.

I acknowledge negative thoughts I may have and know what to do with them.

I am in charge of my own life.

I deserve to love and be loved.

I am connected to my life and the lives of those around me.

I am connected to the world in which I live.

I am worth being healthy.

Notes: _____

_____

_____

_____

_____

_____

_____

_____

_____

_____

_____

_____

_____

Chapter

6

How To Use This Workbook In Any Crisis

Before we get into the specifics, let's look at how the general behavior of a life lived with Health-Esteem will benefit any situation.

First of all, when you have Health-Esteem, you take care of yourself. That means you make conscious decisions to eat right, to sleep enough, to exercise regularly and to listen to what your body needs. It also means that you respect, nurture and bring into harmony the different levels of your being — physical, mental, emotional and spiritual. When you do all of these things, your thinking will be much clearer, thus helping you to evaluate a crisis and work toward its solution.

This workbook will teach you how to evaluate and break down a crisis so that instead of one huge incomprehensible thing, you have smaller, specific issues to work on, to solve and to be able to eliminate from your list.

Disease: For instance, the disease name multiple sclerosis was far too big for me to handle. It sent me into one year of denial and panic. When I broke the name down into my particular symptoms, however, and began the search for emotional scars that could cause or exacerbate this type of symptom, I was already starting to open my brain to a new way of thinking and possible healing.

Divorce: When I was 23 years old and facing a divorce from my high school sweetheart, whom I married in college, the "D" word was far too big for me to handle. I had no idea how to break down the crisis and face the issues that led to the divorce. Because of that, I repeated the same mistakes for many years and throughout numerous relationships in my life. These are some of the issues I could have broken my divorce down into if I knew then what I know now:

I'm afraid I'll never be married again.

What if I can't make it alone?

I worry that others will think of me as a failure.

How will I ever attain the perfect life of wife and mother?

I'm not lovable.

I wasn't good enough, I didn't try enough, I didn't give enough.

I'm not whole without him.

There is a lot of sick-making thinking to trace back to its roots in the above list. You will learn to do this in Chapter 17.

Job Loss: Much of the panic associated with a crisis comes with feeling that you have lost a part of you. When I finally closed my advertising agency, I felt dead inside. Who was I without my business? Another common way to lose ourselves is in relationships with others. The beauty and awe of Health-Esteem is to realize just how much goes into making you who you are. The whole is so magnificent that any one singular part, when isolated, pales by comparison. Family, peer-pressure, society, the news media tend to magnify certain aspects of our lives. The key is to separate from those perceptions and establish balance in life. (More on this in Chapters 12 and 17.) When you live life in a more balanced fashion, you will have a foundation which will give you the strength to survive almost any crisis. You will always have options, places to turn, numerous sources from which to give and receive life-sustaining connection.

Death of a Loved One: This is not to say that even when you have done all of the above that you will not experience grief. The questions are: Do you know how to grieve? Who taught you? How did your family grieve? Can you let out your sorrow so that it doesn't reside inside of you with the potential to make you sick? Can you maintain your sense of balance and wholeness even through this loss? Can you add the essence of whomever you lost into your life? Do you know how to say good-bye? How to really let someone go?

When my grandmother was dying, I could do none of the above. I was 30. She had been my mentor, my best friend, my role model. I stood by her bedside where she lay comatose from a recent stroke and held on to her hand tightly. How would I survive if she left me? Suddenly, she opened her eyes, looked straight into mine and said, "Let me go." She was ready to pass, certain she would be with her soul mate husband who had died eight years previously. She was only holding on for me. I kissed her, told her I loved her and that I would be all right. I said good-bye. Her eyes closed peacefully and two hours later her breathing stopped.

The truth is, I lied. I didn't know if I'd be all right. I was angry. I felt deserted. I was afraid. I went straight back to my work and shut out grief and all thoughts of my grandmother, Dee Dee. I couldn't stand the pain, so I ran from it. Almost a decade later, I had to go back and fix that mistake. When I began to heal from MS, I needed to find Dee Dee inside of me, and I could only do that by grieving. Then, I was free to love her forever and take all that I had learned from her into my life in an active, positive way. (See "A Note About Grief," Chapter 23.)

Financial Difficulty: Often when we're in a financial slump, all the doubting thoughts that were ever put into our heads come crawling out and begin to beat us up. The negative parts of our personality that we normally hide come out on a rampage during times of crisis. Jealousy, envy, greed, hate, lust, resentment, worry, bitterness, fear — the flip side of all our happy feelings reside within us, too. If we don't know what to do with them, they cloud our thinking and our ability to make a clear plan of action. Sometimes you've just got to sit down with your bad self and purge the gremlins. Believe me, that applies to any crisis.

In 1980, I left a great job in a medium sized city where I was a media star to follow my fiancé to L.A. Not long after we moved in together, the relationship ended disastrously, and I was left jobless and homeless. My belongings went into storage and I moved into a girlfriend's tiny mobile home. For a week I lived in isolation. One morning, after she had gone to work I was so depressed I threw myself on the floor and screamed out fear, anger, sorrow, bitterness and pain. I flailed my arms and legs and beat them on the floor. I cried myself tearless, and then I got up, picked up an Adweek and began to circle job opportunities while I dabbed at my remaining sniffles. At the time, the purging cleared the way for me to be able to take action — even though I did not completely understand what I was actually feeling and why. Years later, when the crisis of MS, compounded by the crisis of closing my ad agency opened all the old wounds again, I had to finish my work. Those emotional gremlins had actually presented themselves in physical symptoms this time. I did that by tracing my feelings back to my family's and creating an emotional family tree. (Chapter 24)

Positive Life Stress: Momentous occasions such as milestone birthdays and big anniversaries, holidays, vacations, engagements, and marriages can also lead to anxiety meltdown. What to do? Utilize some, if not all, of the same techniques previewed above. Take care of yourself, break down your feelings, trace emotions to their hereditary or learned root, determine what this situation is doing to the overall balance of your life, make a good feeling/bad feeling list, purge the gremlins. When a clearer head prevails, make a plan of action.

An important point for any crisis crossroads is to take your mind off of it for awhile. All of the above steps require work, but some of the best solutions come when we have access to our inner knowledge. The best way to tap into that is through some form of meditation. The good news about this is that the secret of meditation is to sit quietly and do nothing. (See Chapter 20.)

A thrilling advantage in doing all of this work is that when we function as truly balanced human beings with our physical, emotional, mental and spiritual planes working together, we no longer have to try so hard to achieve what we desire. When we are connected to our own wisdom and that of the healing universe, what we want and need begins to come to us. By telling the truth about ourselves, we can begin to embrace our lives and even guide ourselves in more fulfilling directions.

Just by reading this chapter, you have the tools to begin breaking down your crisis into manageable units that can be explored. We've listed prompters to get you started. Simply fill in the crisis name, i.e., illness, divorce, etc., and the sentences that we've started, then continue to let your own thoughts roll.

Crisis Breakdown List

Crisis Name _____

I'm afraid that _____

_____

It makes me so angry when _____

_____

I hate the thought of _____

_____

If only I could _____

_____

Why did this have to _____

_____

What did I do to _____

_____

How can I possibly _____

_____

I don't want to _____

_____

I should have _____

_____

I will never _____

_____

_____

_____

_____

_____

_____

_____

Refer to this list often as you do the work in the following chapters. Midway through this workbook there will be a CRISIS PROGRESS SHEET and at the end of the book a HEALTH-ESTEEM CRISIS RECOVERY SHEET. Remember, getting the problem written down so you can begin to see elements that require action is the first giant step. You have done that.

Self-Evaluation

At the end of each chapter there will be three prompters for self-evaluation. They are MOVEMENT, CONNECTION and AWARENESS. If during the course of a chapter you noticed a change in one of those areas, simply note what it was by the appropriate prompter.

MOVEMENT: This would be a noticeable shift from a shadow side, painful feeling such as pain, suffering, upheaval, anxiety and stress to a more positive feeling such as peace, calm, assurance, joy. When movement takes place you have allowed for or accepted a change.

Example: I moved from fear of being paralyzed to an assurance that I've increased my probability of remaining symptom-free of MS as long as I practice Health-Esteem. I changed everything about my life in the process from diet to career to entering into marriage. Most importantly, I moved away from entrenched thought patterns that were making me sick.

CONNECTION: This denotes feeling a part of the energy source around you, which means feeling connected with your environment and the people within that environment.

Example: Today I felt connected to the homeless children I serve through charity. I felt their need for love and my need to love them.

AWARENESS: This refers to a realization of the healing power that lies within you.

Example: Today I became aware that fear of not being perfect has barricaded my heart from giving or receiving true love. I will now embrace every part of myself, so that I can, in turn, embrace others.

Notes: _____

_____

_____

_____

_____

_____

_____

_____

_____

_____

_____

_____

_____

_____

_____

_____

_____

Movement	Connection	Awareness
_____	_____	_____
_____	_____	_____
_____	_____	_____

Chapter

7

8 Steps To Spark Your Own Healing Process

You may have deduced by now that finding your way out of crisis and stimulating healing in your life depends upon finding the truth in your life. We all have a story. Sometimes we must become detectives to find the details of our lives that make up who we are and why we act the way we do.

I'm a screenwriter. The success of a classic movie lies with the screenplay, the story. Movies are popular because we can sit in a dark theatre and have a character on the screen make us feel something. We are drawn to a particular characters when we can relate to what they are feeling. Sitting alone within a crowd, it is somehow safe to feel things that we are afraid to feel in our own lives. Truly memorable characters on the screen have a back story. That refers to all the details that go into making them who they are before we meet them in this particular story. Hints of their back story come out in the way they relate to other characters, the way they talk, their facial expressions, their walk and every action and reaction they make in the movie.

Great actors spend weeks developing back stories for their characters. By the time they begin rehearsals they know their character's favorite color, food, song and activity, what their parents were like, watershed events in their lives, their strengths and weaknesses, their politics and humanity, their inner most fears, anxieties, and fantasies, their sexual appetite, what prompts tears and laughter, what they were like as a child and how they are now with children, how they feel about everything and why they feel that way. It's safe to say, they know more about that character than they know about themselves.

It's been easier for me to write the back story behind any character than to write my own. When I became ill with MS, I was completely cut off from my own life's lessons. I'm willing to bet that you are also deprived of a working knowledge of your life's lessons.

How do we get cut off from our own stories? Part of the problem is that we are all embedded in pop culture, which does not help us find ourselves. Rather, it bombards us with images, looks, icons, bigger-than-life athletes and actors who substitute for role models. In today's fast-paced society people "surf the net," ride the waves, jump on the information superhighway and race to keep up with looks, styles, data, trends, and transitory relationships. People live for the day and stay on the surface. Their hearts become separated from their brains and their minds from their bodies.

We may be approaching a limit to the pace of entertainment. Psychologists and social critics worry about information overload, just as cardiologists worry about Type-A hurry sickness. While the evidence is anecdotal, the result is mirrored in fast-paced montages on commercial TV of people at home and at work talking about their hectic lives, their need for timesaving, their hunger for speed, their fear of overload.

The result? We discount the role of subjective factors, of the human struggle, in dealing with crisis and disease. To get to true healing, we must tap into inner feelings and deal with thoughts and emotions that may seem to have no outlet. We need to sit on the porch and daydream, share stories, muse.

In a dramatic example of women coming together to share their stories in order to heal, two Mayan Indian women, ages 32 and 39, in a poor region of southern Mexico have formed a theatre troupe called Fomma, which stands for Fortaleza de la Mujer Maya (Mayan Women's Strength, or Fortress). The goal is to teach young women, many who are unmarried mothers, to learn how to survive in a society where they have been traditionally subservient. They are provided with a safe haven in which to tell, and sometimes act out, the stories of their lives, while taking workshops in literacy, sewing and job skills. Now acknowledged as the country's first female Indian playwrights, one of their plays, "Ideas Para el Cambio" ("Ideas for Change") depicts two female coffee pickers who are fired by their lazy boss. They are directed to Fomma where they find new hope and direction to rise out of poverty.

It's important to again stress the difference between "a cure," the holy grail that medical science seeks, and healing, an on-going evolution into consciousness that includes awareness of the disease/or crisis process and the possibilities of living with or changing the outcome. Health-Esteem is the vehicle that gets us through the process. We can begin the journey the moment we can say and believe, "I am worth being healthy."

You are the character in your own screenplay now. It is your back story that must be written and brought into consciousness. The eight steps we offer to spark your healing process will also spark awareness of your own story.

8 Steps to Spark Your Own Healing Process

1) Find where stress hides in your life — and in your body.

2) Discover inherited emotional patterns.

3) Determine the emotional link, past or present, to physical symptoms.

4) Make sure your actions are based on personal motivations, not world, social and peer pressure.

5) Balance the good with the bad in your life. Recognize personal failures, bad feelings and disappointments. Everyone has them.

6) Recognize a self separate and distinct from your vocation.

7) Listen for voices inside, silenced by external pressures and roles.

8) Feel life's events as well as observing them.

Before beginning a detailed exploration of these steps in the following chapters, I'd like you to take 15 to 30 minutes to write a short story about your life that incorporates a memory from your childhood and present times.

Life Story Exercise

1) First, select three words commonly used to describe you — two positive and one negative. For instance, I might select: INSPIRING, VIVACIOUS, WORRIER. Select your words now.

Three Self-Descriptive Words

_____

_____

_____

Make sure that you use some form of all three words in the first paragraph of your story. There are a few more rules for your story.

2) Include these words and complete these phrases somewhere in your story.

My parents...

I had a big dream (may substitute goal for dream) in life...

I always loved to...

Now I've changed...

3) Include at least one feeling.

4) Try to use all five senses (taste, smell, sight, touch and sound) somewhere in your story.

5) Start with Once upon a time...

6) Think of this as a fairy tale taken from your true life story. It can be happy, sad, or both.

I know it's a lot of rules, but it's not so tough. Here's my example:

Short Story From My Life Experience

Once upon a time my very proud father, after ten years of convincing my very hesitant mother to conceive their second child brought me home and shouted to a neighbor, "Here she is, our little Parker baby named Judith Kay. My parents' lives were about to change for the worse financially, but they had brought a vivacious little girl into their lives, to inspire them and lift their spirits. Soon they would become her biggest worry.

Six years later, we were in a new house we couldn't afford, mom was crying a lot and dad was mad a lot. I had a big dream — to be a Mouseketeer, I could just see myself in the mouse ears, being loved by all the kids in America. I loved to pretend and that's what I had to settle for while I watched the Mickey Mouse Club on TV. One day I was trying hard to make Mom smile, so I was dancing right along with Annette, my favorite Mouseketeer. I could smell the spaghetti sauce cooking in the kitchen. Dad would be home soon. Was he going to be mean again? I felt afraid, but I didn't want Mom to know, so I danced harder and smiled bigger.

Then I <u>heard</u> it; Dad's brakes screeched in the driveway. He stumbled on the walk and threw the door open. Mom and I both stopped breathing. I clenched my teeth so hard that I bit my tongue and <u>tasted</u> my own blood. I <u>touched</u> my skin and it was all goose bumpy. Dinner was going to be scary again. Even the Mickey Mouse Club couldn't change that.

<u>Today</u>, if anger is shown or a loud voice is heard at mealtime, I <u>feel sick</u> inside. My skin gets all goose bumpy and I <u>feel like a helpless</u> little girl who can't make her parents smile. I just want to dance and make the world a happy place where every day has a wonderful purpose and every face wears a smile.

Now it's your turn. You may type the story if it's more comfortable for you, or write it in the space provided. If you type it, make sure you tape it into the workbook. As you read the following chapters, more memories and details may come to mind that you want to add to your story. You may also think of other stories you want to jot down or tape record.

VERY IMPORTANT: If a story does pop into your head, don't ignore it because it has a purpose, usually a message that can help in your healing. My message from the above story was to understand the immediate nervous, sick feeling that overtakes me, even in present times, when the slightest disturbance happens at meal time. I fight the reaction to gloss it all over with a smile and realize I have choices; to leave, to ask the offending party to stop, or to somehow not subject myself to the negative experience.

Short Story From Your Life

Title_____

Once upon a time _____

_____

_____

_____

_____

_____

_____

_____

_____

_____

_____

_____

_____

_____

_____

_____

_____

_____

_____

_____

_____

_____

_____

_____

_____

_____

_____

_____

_____

_____

Movement	Connection	Awareness
_____	_____	_____
_____	_____	_____
_____	_____	_____

Find Where Stress Hides In Your Life — And In Your Body

When I was 25 years old and already an established workaholic writing and directing 100 television commercials a week, I woke up one morning unable to move my neck from side to side. While I wouldn't consider missing work, I was completely hampered by the immobility of my neck. I thought if I forgot about it, the stiffness would disappear. To my chagrin, it got worse. At the end of the day, I called the only doctor I had, my gynecologist. He could see me the next morning.

I trusted Dr. Yolokovsky. He was an older man, sixty-ish, with a ready smile and an easy manner. He had nicknames for all of his patients that somehow made each of us feel special and attractive. My nickname was "Legs," undoubtedly because that was the one part of my anatomy of which I was proud. On this particular day, Dr. Yolokovsky walked out to get me, put his arm around my shoulders and questioned warmly, "What's the matter, Legs?"

"That's what I want you to tell me," I replied.

He guided me into his office, not an examining room and settled back comfortably. "This time, Legs, you're telling me. What's your life like? What's going on? Are you dating? Are you happy?"

More than a little confused, I stumbled around with a few answers. Soon I was reeling off my exhausting schedule, and he nodded knowingly.

"No wonder you've got a stiff neck," he interrupted, "all you do is work. When was the last time you went out to dinner — for fun? How often do you exercise?"

I avoided the first question and answered the second one defensively, "I get enough exercise through my work."

"Wrong!" He countered. "I've got a prescription for you. I want you to exercise until you sweat. In the morning or at night, I don't care, but exercise until you sweat."

"Can't you just give me a pill?" I whined.

That day in 1975, Dr. Yolokovsky had given me my first holistic advice. He had also probably saved me from a possible addiction. I was hinting for a tranquilizer. He knew better. Exercise was by best tranquilizer.

I didn't think much more about that encounter. I joined a Women's Gym and managed to get over there two or three mornings a week and sometimes for an aerobics class in the evening. My stiff neck disappeared, so I didn't have to give another thought to what Dr. Yolokovsky was trying to help me find — where the stress was hiding in my life; in my body. I was too busy to examine what the stiff neck was saying about my life and emotional state. I was too busy for ten more years, and then my body had to shout to get me to listen.

This time the messengers came in the form of numbness and visual problems. Exercise did not make these messengers go away. In fact, exercise was difficult. This time after seeing a barrage of specialists, I ended up in front of a neurologist who gave me the diagnosis of multiple sclerosis. When I made it past my denial and anger, I finally found various health practitioners eager to start asking me questions that would help me hook parts of my life together that I had worked diligently to keep separate.

I was amazed at how much pain I put up with in my daily life, just because I didn't want to think about it or spend time searching for a solution. Instead of dealing with my stress, I piled on more stress. My chiropractor, Natalie, told me, "Feeling bad isn't natural — feeling good everyday is!" That sounded crazy to me, but I was certainly willing to try.

To begin to get to the point of feeling good everyday, I had to pay attention to how I felt when I wasn't feeling good. Next, instead of searching for a quick, "make me feel better by masking the pain" cure, I had to ask lots of questions: Why do I feel this way? How often have I felt this way in the past? What is feeling this way connected to? What's happening in my life when I feel this way?

To answer any of the above questions, you have to start to get to know yourself better. That requires a series of inventories: How you spend an average day; How you divide your time among certain life areas; What emotions you experience in a day; How you feel about your physical being and more. Forms and tips on how to do these inventories can be found in Chapter 17, "Who, What, Where, When and Why of Wellness."

You may ask, "Why do I have to do all of this?"

Because you are putting a shape to the details of your past and present so you can give shape to your self. We are basically a container full of events, thoughts, actions and reactions that all carry either a negative or positive charge. Until we understand the motivations behind all of those events, thoughts, actions and reactions, we are merely acting like puppets dangling from strings. We are waiting to be pulled into action according to someone else's program, we are operating from reflex and release rather than reason and resolve. Once we categorize and understand our motivations we can either keep the motivation, discard it, change it or decide to create a new one, all designed to fit into a program of our own creation.

The key consideration in the creation of a healthy life program is balance. The ancient Chinese believed that everything in the universe is made up of negative and positive flowing energy, that opposites attract, thus creating balance. Balance results in harmony. Positive and negative when used by the ancients did not denote good and bad, but rather a life cycle complete in its duality. Opposite charges are actually dependent on each other for balance and wholeness such as active and passive, life and death, masculine and feminine, work and play, joy and sorrow, Yin (negative) and Yang (positive).

The body's energy is fluid and ever-changing. Everything that affects us — from the food we eat, to relationships and stress on the job — is taken in and processed by our internal organs which determine how our energy flows. This flow keeps information moving between the body, mind and emotions.

When you begin to understand something about yourself that connects a pattern or early life lesson to a current or chronic pain or crisis, you are taking the first step toward wholeness or healing. Your brain must understand before it can send out messages to your body to heal. It's taken me 45 years to find the root destructive pattern behind a chronic pain in my neck, located more specifically in my left shoulder. When aggravated, that pain spasms into my head and down my back. The feeling associated with it is, "I'm not enough!" That feeling goes all the way back to childhood. No matter how many A's I brought home, no matter how many speech or accordion trophies I won, no matter how I clowned to make my family laugh, it was never enough. They didn't stay happy, Dad didn't stop drinking and Mom didn't stop hiding behind Simplicity dress patterns.

Let's do a temperature check on how you're feeling regarding certain areas of your life. The scale on the next page starts at "**Oh No**," which means there's so much pain or discomfort you don't even want to think about it to "**O.K.**," which means it could be better or it could be worse, to "**Outstanding**," which means great, incredible, couldn't be better, WOW!

Use a colored pen or pencil and draw an arrow stopping at the point that expresses how you feel on most days about the particular category. Always start at "Oh, no!" and work your way up, because at some point in your life, even if you're "Outstanding" about a particular area now, you probably had an "Oh, no" moment.

As you make your way through this workbook, you may want to come back and take another colored pencil and add a new arrow to some of the categories. Remember, life is fluid, energy is flowing and you are seeking a balance.

Movement	Connection	Awareness
_____	_____	_____
_____	_____	_____
_____	_____	_____

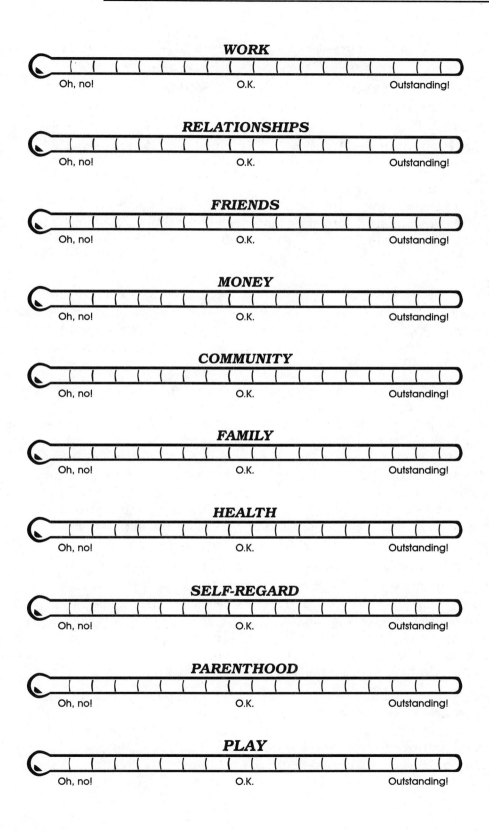

WORK

Oh, no!   O.K.   Outstanding!

RELATIONSHIPS

Oh, no!   O.K.   Outstanding!

FRIENDS

Oh, no!   O.K.   Outstanding!

MONEY

Oh, no!   O.K.   Outstanding!

COMMUNITY

Oh, no!   O.K.   Outstanding!

FAMILY

Oh, no!   O.K.   Outstanding!

HEALTH

Oh, no!   O.K.   Outstanding!

SELF-REGARD

Oh, no!   O.K.   Outstanding!

PARENTHOOD

Oh, no!   O.K.   Outstanding!

PLAY

Oh, no!   O.K.   Outstanding!

Discover Inherited Emotional Patterns

Let's talk about sex for a moment. Now that I've got your interest, have you ever wondered why in the middle of a perfect intimate moment your body suddenly sabotaged you? For instance, my husband Jack and I are hugging and kissing and I have to tear myself away to check on a roast in the oven. Without my knowing it, Jack has followed me into the kitchen where he tiptoes up behind me and pats me on the fanny. I cringe and say sharply, "Don't do that!"

He recoils looking hurt, and we both wonder what happened. Why could he touch me in the living room but not in the kitchen? Why could he kiss and hug me, but not grab my bottom? Why was his touch okay one moment and not the next?

After years of trying to remember my childhood, I found the answer. My mom cringed every time dad touched her and often would shout out disapprovingly "Don't do that," when she saw Dad touch me in certain ways, no matter how playful his intent. Mom would look down or away when any sexual display was enacted on TV or in the movies. She often shuddered with physical revulsion. I was programmed by her example to move away from a touch that I was not expecting or that was the *wrong* kind. I had to know what was happening and be in control of touching situations to not have a knee-jerk reflex revulsion overcome me. I had to separate my feelings from my mom's to ever be able to let go sexually.

Shelly, an attorney friend of mine, found herself "goofing off" at work one time under the most tragic of circumstances. Her boss, married only four years, lost his 53-year-old wife to breast cancer. While tremendously saddened herself, Shelly wondered why she was acting so inappropriately. Then she remembered that when things got really awful at home in her childhood, she would goof off in school. She had learned to use "goofing off" as her defense when life was too cruel to cope.

One very prominent executive I interviewed for my book, **Head Over Healing In Love**, seemed to have the perfect life and repeatedly said so. I allowed my questions to gradually take him back to his childhood and his early relationship with his mom and dad. About halfway into our conversation, he realized the pressure of living up to his highly successful father's expectations and the shame he felt when he didn't. He also related the pain he felt because his mother was unable to face anything other than perfection about him. He never received unconditional love, he received unconditional expectation. And that's what he continues to live under in all of his dealings, professional and personal — EXPECTATION and subsequent SHAME if he doesn't meet those expectations.

As we continued talking, a vulnerable voice surfaced that brought tears to his eyes as he realized he didn't know who to talk to about the "male" problems of having multiple sclerosis, including sexual problems. Secrets began to come out — things he considered shameful — things he had stuffed deep inside his body, out of sight from everyone's view — where it sat and brewed and made him sick. He wondered why he was telling me these things, because living up to those expectations had isolated him from talking to anybody about his innermost shame. His surprise gave way to relief at having the thoughts out in the open.

By understanding the patterning in our lives over which we had no control, we can opt to change it and the negative energy flow it engenders that can do so much damage to our bodies, minds and spirits. Why cringe from someone else's sexual revulsion? Why be ruled by someone else's expectations and sentence of shame?

How do you recognize when your thinking is coming from an inherited emotional pattern? And, if you suspect that it is, how do you isolate who in your family or history has passed on the pattern or the program to you?

First, you must write down a clear description of whatever crisis you may be experiencing right now. Don't be afraid. Whatever your crisis is, if you are reading this workbook, you are still alive. Which means you have choices to make. The key is to make sure that you are the one doing the choosing.

Example:

Step 1: Write your crisis definition.

Crisis Definition

> I am going through a financial slump. I've got a third mortgage on my home and I'm facing bankruptcy. I need to change my career direction, but I don't know where to start. I can't face anyone right now — especially if I lose my house.

Step 2: Think about your crisis and write down every thought that comes into your head about the situation you face — even thoughts you've been too ashamed to speak out loud. These sentences should be about how you are feeling as you face this crisis.

Crisis Thoughts and Feelings

You shouldn't have bought the house in the first place.

You don't deserve to live that nice.

If you hadn't wasted so much money years ago, you'd have it now.

You're a failure.

You'll never have another house like this.

Step 3: Who Owns the Thoughts and Feelings?

Go down the list and think about who in your family or circle of acquaintances felt that way about situations *they* faced. Write down their names next to the phrase.

You shouldn't have bought the house in the first place.	*Grandmother*
You don't deserve to live that nice.	*Mother*
If you hadn't wasted so much money years ago, you'd have it now.	*Father*
You're a failure.	*Aunt*
You'll never have another house like this.	*Sister*

Step 4: If, in Step 3, you're having difficulty deciding who in your family felt the way you're now feeling, you might try repeating the sentence out loud as you hear it in your head. It's really helpful to do this by saying each sentence into a tape recorder. Make sure you say the sentence the way it was said to you. Put the same emotion into the words that they were able to elicit in you. For instance, "You shouldn't have bought the house in the first place," is probably big on GUILT with a little bit of, "I never lived that nice so why should you," JEALOUSY subtext — and perhaps a pinch of "You made a mistake you bad boy or bad girl," DISDAIN thrown into the brew.

STEP 5: After you have identified the true owners of the feelings and put their names next to the respective sentences, do one of two things: If you still feel that way, put a check next to the sentence because there's still work to be done. If you don't feel that way anymore, cross the sentence off your list. Every time you cross a phrase off your list, give yourself a huge pat on the back because you have accomplished something major.

When one of these doubting phrases comes into your mind — you can even do this exercise in your car and get rid of it in no time. Don't worry, you won't look any more ridiculous than the person belting out a song in the car next to you. As you push out some of those learned responses, you may need to start a new list entitled **Health-Esteem Crisis Crunchers** because your brain will be coming up with new ways to handle your problem. Some sample crisis crunchers to the above problem might be: "I'm going to call my debtors and make out a payment plan with them that I can handle." Or, "I love this house, but there will be a better one waiting for me in my future." Or, "I'll move into an apartment and rent out my home, so I can concentrate on my new career instead of a big house payment." What a relief it is to find a self free from thinking you weren't able to respect in the first place — thinking that allows for change and options.

Now it's your turn.

Step 1: Write your Crisis Definition. Try to keep your description to 50 to 75 words. Be as descriptive as possible. Remember, this is only for your eyes, so you don't have to worry about what someone else is going to think.

Crisis Definition

_____

_____

_____

_____

Step 2: Think about your crisis and write down every thought that comes into your head about the situation you face — even thoughts you've been too ashamed to speak out loud. These sentences should be about how you are feeling as you face this crisis.

Crisis Thoughts and Feelings   **Who Felt That Way?**

1) _____

   _____   _____

2) _____

   _____   _____

3) _____

   _____   _____

4) _____

   _____   _____

5) _____

   _____   _____

6) _____

   _____   _____

7) _____

   _____   _____

8) _____

   _____   _____

9) _____

   _____   _____

10) _____

   _____   _____

Step 3: Who Owns the Thoughts and Feelings?

   Go down the list and think about who in your family or circle of acquaintances felt that way about situations *they* faced. Write down their names next to the phrase.

Step 4: If in Step 3 you're having difficulty deciding who in your family felt the way you're now feeling, you might try repeating the sentence out loud as you hear it in your head. It's really helpful to do this by saying each sentence into a tape recorder.

STEP 5: Either check or cross off every sentence on your list according to the instructions above.

Health-Esteem Crisis Crunchers

Write down new thoughts and possible solutions to your crisis that have come in to replace the old thoughts and negative programming. You may have one or two crisis crunchers now, but this list will continue to grow as you continue your way through the workbook. Be sure to come back and write down your crisis cruncher every time you think of one.

Health-Esteem Crisis Cruncher List

1) _____

2) _____

3) _____

4) _____

5) _____

6) _____

7) _____

8) _____

9) _____

10) _____

Movement	Connection	Awareness
_____	_____	_____
_____	_____	_____
_____	_____	_____

Determine Emotional Link Past or Present to Physical Symptoms

Jason Elias writes in his book, **In The House of the Moon**, "The journey toward wholeness — toward a balance of yin and yang, female and male, intuition and logic in ourselves and in our society's healing practices — necessarily begins with an understanding of what we have lost."[1] I maintain that we have lost a sense of who we are, of our family, of our family's family, of our connection to community. Our sense of kinship has been abandoned. The Information Age has caused us to value data over body, heart and soul; data bounced to us from satellites, beamed to us from the Internet, barked to us by news anchors, banged out to us on computer keyboards and ballyhooed to us by experts on everything and every event. We commune with computer, television and theatre screens instead of each other. We write to strangers in chat rooms with words that are transitory.

Event — that word and all it connotes lies at the heart of much of our isolation from our family and the world around us: We look at events not emotions; data instead of dreams; pictures rather than passion; words often separated from wisdom. We go to Event movies where spectacle, extravagant effects, and natural disasters erupt from the skies, the earth below, the high seas and from out of our own genes. These events are so big that we don't have to take them personally. They are out of our control. We just look at what's happening to those "other" people. Ever since the evening news brought the Viet Nam war into our living rooms to digest with our dinners, we've distanced ourselves from the significance of the content. We go on event dates and mark the passage of time through events — birthdays, anniversaries, births, deaths, marriages, divorces...

There is more to life than events, however. There is a river running through those events — a river of emotions that if unfelt, unchecked, and unattended will overflow when we least expect it and wreak great physical harm and even tragedy. Most of our emotional rivers are uncharted, their sources unrecognized. Those sources are families — our family of origin; our family of community; and our family of the world.

Later in this chapter you will begin to explore your family of origin. Now, to begin to recognize your community and world families, I'd like you to take a moment to do two experiments.

[1]Elias, Jason, and Ketcham, Katherine, In The House of the Moon, Warner Books, Inc., New York, New York, 1995, p. 30. New title for paperback, "Feminine Healing: A Woman's Guide to a Healthy Body, Mind and Spirit."

Your Community Family

On the grid following which is drawn like a city map, I'd like you to fill in places you commonly frequent. For instance according to your needs, habits and hobbies you might fill in grocery stores, shopping centers and boutiques, theatres, community meeting places, friend's homes, service stations, museums, restaurants, schools, parks, golf courses, recreation centers, attorney, accountant and health care offices and more. Think about what you like to do and where you go to do those activities. You may want to fill in some major street names to give you some landmarks. Start by marking your home, then reach out in a grid-like fashion to include as many places as you can think of that you frequent. Put a number by every place and an identifying letter if you choose. In the LEGEND provided below the grid write the name of the place and approximately how many people you know there — even if you only know them by face and not by name. There are many people we just smile and say "Hi" to — they are acquaintances — part of our community — waiters and waitresses, nurses, box boys and bus boys, clerks, attendants, perhaps a homeless person you help out every time you pass by his or her corner. Count as many acquaintances as you can think of. When you are finished total the places and the people.

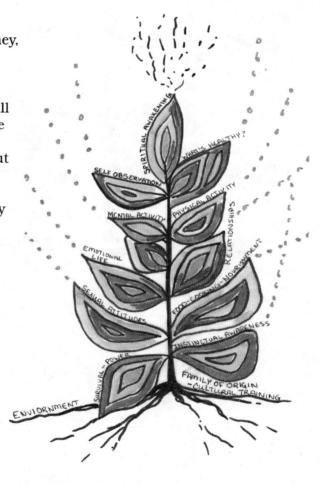

Emotional Family Tree process drawing: *A process drawing comes from the image of the feelings you are having at a particular moment in time. Tobes, a registered art therapist, drew this when our workbook team gathered and first began to define the emotional family tree concept.*

Your Community Connections

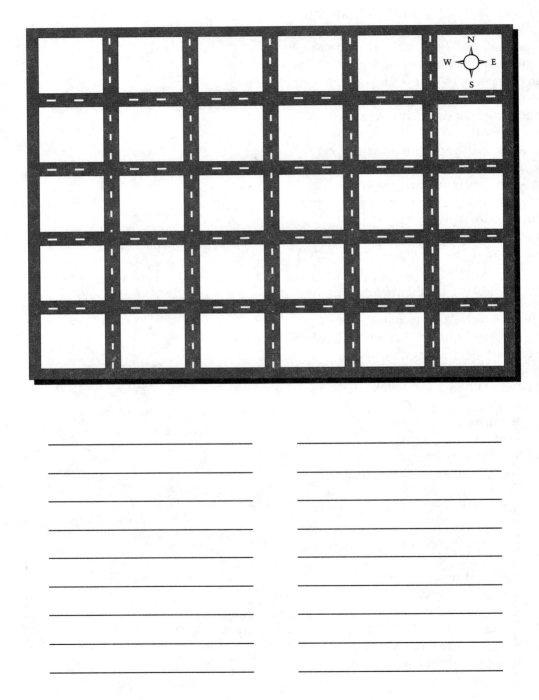

_____   _____

_____   _____

_____   _____

_____   _____

_____   _____

_____   _____

_____   _____

_____   _____

While we may often feel alone, you can begin to see from this exercise just how many lives we share a connection with and indeed touch in some way. As I took this information into my heart, I began to reach out a little more to my community connections, with a smile, a compliment, an acknowledgment of their work. I began to make eye contact instead of looking away to maintain my barrier of isolationism. I noticed that fear, distrust and some very negative emotions lessened as interest, curiosity and sharing and caring increased. I also noticed that I felt better — more energetic, more alive.

Your World Family

1) On the following maps provided, first draw a yellow circle where you currently live and connect that circle to the place where you were born and to other cities or countries in which you have lived.

2) Next, take a red pencil and draw a line from where you currently live to every world location in which you have a known relative either living or dead. Then, take a purple pencil and draw lines connecting you to places worldwide where you have friends. Go back as far in time as you possibly can. If you only know a country and not a city, that's fine, simply connect yourself with that country.

3) Take a blue pencil and draw a line to every city and country in the world where you have visited.

4) Take a green pencil and draw a dotted line to every country you somehow feel connected to and intend to travel to someday.

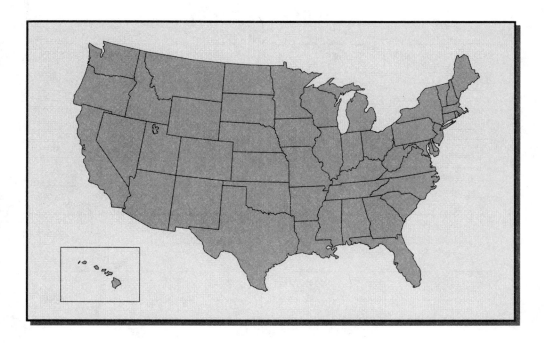

Your World Connections

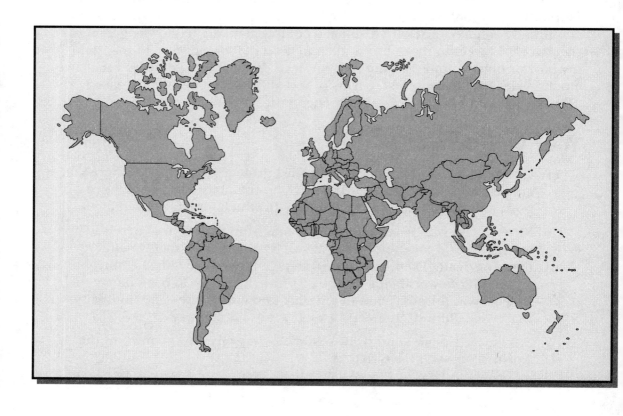

_____   _____

_____   _____

_____   _____

_____   _____

_____   _____

_____   _____

_____   _____

_____   _____

_____   _____

Now that you have more of a sense of community and global connection, let's take it to an even more personal level and begin to chart your own emotional rivers. "How am I going to do this?" you may ask. You begin by listening to your body because some very strong hints are provided through physical symptoms.

Years ago, when I enrolled in a movement course, I was surprised to discover that I start every move by tensing my shoulders. I was living in my head; and my aching shoulders were dragging my body along as if it were dead weight "hung on a hanger." My straight back was locking out fluid movement and functioning as my rigid defense against a world of sexual predators. Several of the above words — rigid, locking out, dead weight — served as indicators to help me search for the origin of my feelings and postures. They went straight back to my first sexual role model, my mother. I had seen her revulsion to sex every time she shrugged it off and tensed her body in protection or denial; I had heard it every time she would scream out, "Leave me alone — No!"; I had felt her revulsion every time she gave me a careful, partial hug, always pulling away quickly. By taking her revulsion in through my senses, I imprinted it in my body, so I automatically reacted like she did. I had to make an emotional connection to a physical reaction. In this case, I had to understand the emotions behind my mother's reactions, because they had been passed down to me.

Okay, it's your turn. On the body figures drawn on the next two pages, I'd like you to circle where it hurts. Is your body sending you a signal you've been ignoring? Later in the workbook, you'll be asked to keep a Symptoms Journal. For now, I just want you to make a quick assessment. Do your legs or toes cramp? Do you have headaches, eye strain, carpal tunnel syndrome, stomach aches, back aches — problems related to your eyes, ears, nose, throat or lungs? You name it — if some part of your body itches, aches or hurts today, or in your recent memory, circle the area of the body that is bothering you. Then, in the blanks provided by your aching body write down emotions you've been feeling lately. Feel free to refer to the glossary in the back of the workbook.

Where Does It Hurt?

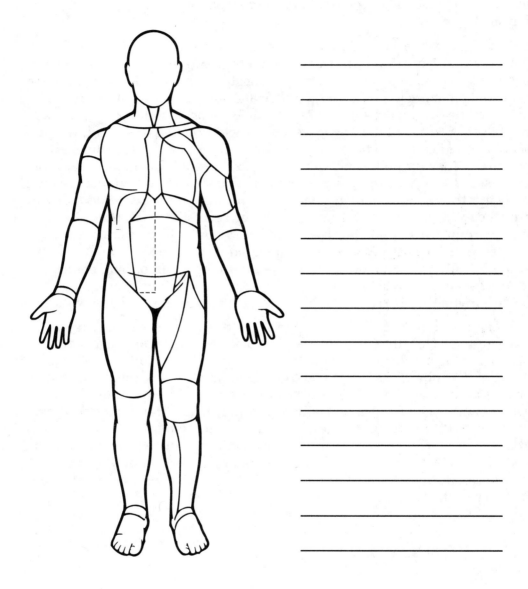

Where Does It Hurt?

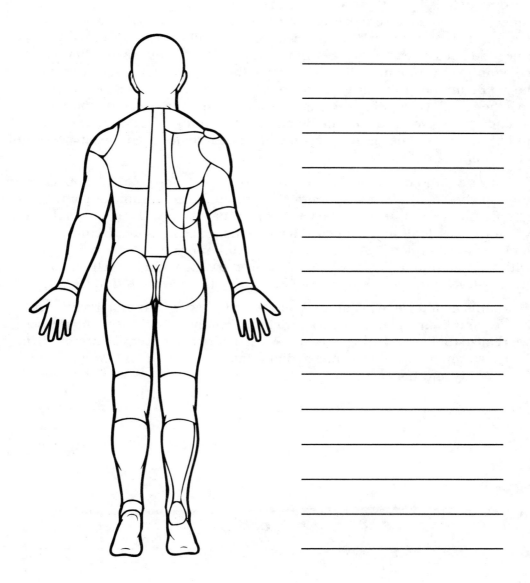

Sometimes you may be able to make an immediate connection between one of the aches and pains you've located on the body figures and one of the emotions you've noted to the side. For instance, if I circled my neck for the chronic pain I suffer there and wrote rejection in the side column, I could make an immediate connection. My neck pain is definitely aggravated when I'm feeling rejected or when I've been made to feel inferior. I can trace rejection back to every member of my immediate family. My mother was constantly rejecting my father. I felt my father was rejecting me every time he got drunk. My brother wanted to reject me from the household all together until we got older. Rejection was, indeed, my constant companion — enough to give me a chronic pinched nerve in my left shoulder. Even today, that nerve goes into a spasm when I experience even the slightest hint of rejection.

For now, if no immediate connections come to mind, please go forward in the workbook. You have done enough to begin focusing some of your attention inward. Carl Jung has written, "Your vision will become clear only when you can look into your own heart. Who looks outside, dreams; who looks inside, awakes." As you are able to link more physical symptoms with your emotional history you will indeed awaken and be well on your way to developing your emotional family tree. (Fully explored in Chapter 24)

As this chapter has begun to illustrate, when we get in touch with our bodies and their relationship to our emotional lives, both past and present, we realize that what happens to the self has a ripple effect. We are not living in a vacuum, we are interconnected and interdependent on family, community and the earth.

Movement	Connection	Awareness
_____	_____	_____
_____	_____	_____
_____	_____	_____

Chapter

11

Make Sure Your Actions Are Based on Personal Motivations Not World, Social and Peer Pressure

How Do You Measure Up?

_____

_____

_____

_____

_____

_____

_____

_____

_____

_____

_____

_____

There are spaces next to the above cartoon because I'd like you to think of all the ways you've *tried to be* to please a boy or girlfriend, husband or wife, mother or father, some other person who has expectations of how you *should* act. Did you try to be funny, adopt a love for football, pretend to love classical music, suddenly shift your passion from skiing to rock climbing, change your look, adapt your speech, convert your religion, stifle your style, dump a devotion, hide a hobby, invent a new past, create an abridged version of you?

I know that throughout the first 17 years of my adult life, when a new man would enter, so would a new me. I was a consummate shape-shifter. I waited for my significant other to complete my self-definition. It took me years to realize that every time I changed to please someone else, I was placing value outside of myself. I was giving away my self-esteem to the "other" person who obviously had a better idea of how I should be.

When you give away your value, your sense of self, you are giving away part of your spirit — your emotional strength. A hole is left behind, an internal void is created which can be filled up with stress or even illness. That's just what happened to me. To find my health-esteem, I had to go back and trace every step of my lifetime and find the points where value was either placed within myself or given away to some outside source, like a boyfriend, a screaming person or a demanding boss. I found myself very under-valued which left a huge internal void where illness could grow. And, that's just what happened. An illness for which there is no known cause and no known cure grew in the void — an illness called multiple sclerosis.

Remember, health-esteem engenders a rebirthing of yourself, independent from other's perceptions and completely tuned-in to your own wisdom: Wisdom that connects your mind and your body, your heart and your brain, your energy with that of the healing universe. In the previous chapter you spent time recognizing some connections with yourself as well as between yourself and the community and world around you. With those connections come even more expectations that can effect our actions and self-value. There are global images and perceptions that translate down to expected behavior.

When I was 25 years old and up for a raise after out-performing all of the other commercial directors at the TV station where I worked (who were all male, by the way), I was the only one not to receive a raise. The excuse was given that "Women don't need as much money, particularly single, childless women." I count three damaging mis-perceptions in that sentence alone! I also remember being told to "be grateful and don't expect too much," and to "beware of aggressive behavior that can offend those in charge." I was being pushed into an outdated role I didn't want to play.

Men, I'm sure that applies to you. Perhaps you remember being told to be forceful, determined, decisive and always right in order to earn the respect of others and not to cry or you might be considered weak or soft, not to complain or you'd be labeled passive.

The very same actions taken by men and women in our society are labeled with language that makes it acceptable for one sex and unacceptable for the other. A man is commanding — a woman demanding; A man is forceful — a woman is pushy; He shows leadership — she's controlling;

He's committed — she's obsessed; He strategizes — she manipulates. Just getting out from under negative labeling and outdated perceptions takes a lot of strength and commitment to our own sense of value.

The truth is we are all a lot of things, a combination of opposites. We can think and feel, control and accept, demand and give, be angry and forgiving, sexy and intelligent, handsome and soft, a boss and a lover. The point is, you must be the one to choose the way you're going to be and avoid giving that power away to an outside source.

When I got sick and began the process of getting well, I was shocked to realize that I had allowed everyone else to define who I was and how I felt about myself all of my life. To begin to take that responsibility into my own hands, I began with a simple exercise which I still do. I share that with you now.

Self Appreciation Exercise

Look yourself in the mirror everyday and appreciate yourself without judgment and criticism. Experiment with giving yourself this appreciation time every morning to start the day. Start with 30 seconds and work up to a couple of minutes. This exercise should be done nude.

Don't just stick to appreciating the body parts you've always accepted with pride. Work on the love handles, the tummy flab, the never-the-perfect-size breasts, the puny pecs, the new line or wrinkle on your face — appreciate every body part. Sure, you may still want to work out and improve certain areas. I did. But, it helps to work out of appreciation not self-loathing — out of self-pleasing, not other-pleasing.

This appreciation time can also include invisible thoughts and emotions that complete the wonderful, unique package that is you.

Soon, you'll find a whole person, not a bunch of parts to be analyzed, compared and measured by everyone else's standards.

Movement	Connection	Awareness

**Balance The Good With The Bad In Life
Recognize Personal Failures, Bad Feelings &
Disappointments**

I know everyone reading this workbook is a really wonderful person. You're bright, positive, happy, joyful, optimistic, loving, helpful, generous, sharing, compassionate, confident, peaceful, warm and courageous every moment of everyday. Right?

Wrong! Let's be honest now. Somewhere lingering in our psyches and buried deep in our bodies out of our sight and everybody else's minds is the flip side of some, if not all, of those emotions. Often referred to as the shadow side of our personalities, these darker emotions fuel the little gremlins in all of us that somehow manages to get out when we're having a really bad day! You know that side of you that comes popping out with teeth clenched and brow furrowed, spewing an assortment of negative emotions when we're feeling too weak, vulnerable or tired to hide them anymore.

The problem comes when we try to hide these emotions even from ourselves. If we're feeling anger, we don't have to act upon it, but it is important to acknowledge the feeling and trace it back to where it might have begun. For instance, a couple of years ago, I felt unappreciated by a little slight from my husband. He didn't seem to care "enough" that I was going to have surgery, and I felt he was belittling my anxiety. I found myself getting so angry that I actually wanted to hit him. What started off as a playful punch could have been a blow if I hadn't caught myself? Where was that coming from, I wondered?

I certainly didn't want to act out the anger I was feeling, but it was important to acknowledge the feeling and trace it back to where it might have begun. I wound up with a childhood memory of feeling sick, lonely and scared. I always felt that anything wrong with me was worse on my parents than on me, because they had too many big problems already. So I hid how I felt or downplayed it, and as a result I never felt nurtured. Now, I wanted Jack to make up for all of that. When I was able to trace my anger backwards, I could defuse it. Only then, was I able to explain it logically to Jack.

When you look at your current crisis definition from Chapter 9 and your Crisis Breakdown List from Chapter 6, you will find some feelings, symptoms or problems from your current crisis that you can begin to trace back to their roots. When you compare present reactions and behaviors to past reactions and behaviors you'll begin to uncover what I call EMOTIONAL SURVIVAL TACTICS. You will see *why* you learned them and *how* you learned them and also discover why they probably aren't working for you any longer. Mine were actually making me sick. I had to uncover those tactics and unlearn them. Then I was free to learn new lessons to make my mind/body healthy. I had to name and face my fears rather than give them the power of anonymity.

Now's the time to shine a light on your shadow side by making some more lists. First, list all the personal failures you have endured in your life that come to mind. In the next column, list how those failures made you feel. For instance, for failures I might list: closure of my agency; first marriage ended in divorce; never had children. In the feelings column I might list: Fearful, inadequate, rejected, shamed, lonely, empty, miserable...Remember, this list is not for publication, but for your eyes only!

Personal Failures   **How Does It Make You Feel?**

_____   _____

_____   _____

_____   _____

_____   _____

_____   _____

_____   _____

_____   _____

_____   _____

_____   _____

While we're on this shadow stuff, let's keep digging. Start a new list titled Disappointments. Again, you'll note a matching column for feelings. Sure to be on my list of disappointments would be: Receiving rejection letters for my writing; Lack of acknowledgment for hard work; Difficulty getting a movie produced; Birth family unable to love. Related feelings would include: Angry, jealous, frustrated, impatient, defeated, disturbed, defensive, unlovable... O.K., I'm being brutally honest, how about you?

Disappointments   **How Does It Make You Feel?**

_____   _____

_____   _____

_____   _____

_____   _____

_____   _____

_____   _____

_____   _____

_____   _____

_____   _____

_____   _____

There are a couple of ways to use these lists to continue our experiment. First, go down both "Feeling" lists and think about who in your family felt this way when facing failures or disappointments. If you make a match, jot down the person's name or initial to the right of the appropriate feeling. Second, put your list through a three-question self-test:

1)   Now that you have listed times in your life when you were facing a failure or disappointment, compare them to each other. In more recent bad times did your feelings and reactions change? Or, did they remain consistent with the way you felt and reacted during prior disappointments in your life?

2)   Are you growing out of some feelings and into new ones?

3)   As you study the list are there some feelings you would like to grow out of or replace?

Throughout most of my life, particularly as a young woman beginning my career in a Sacramento television station in the early 70's, I was like my counterpart on television, Mary Richards on the Mary Tyler Moore Show. I could turn the world on with my smile. I could also hide a lot of really bad, unbecoming emotions behind it. Sexual harassment? (grin and handle it) Passed over for another raise? (smile and keep on doing double the work) Boyfriend can't commit? (make light and cry later) You get the picture. I needed to outgrow and replace that behavior well before I was enlightened enough to do so.

Well into my healing from MS, I realized that all that smiling and stuffing of my feelings had done me no good and lots of harm. In the 90's, as we search for our shadow side to keep our bodies from betraying us, there is again an apt role model on television. She works at a TV station, too — a network this time, but she's no pussycat. She's Murphy Brown, a recovering alcoholic, openly conniving, selfish, jealous, tricky, vengeful, meanly competitive career woman. She's wearing her shadow side on the outside for all of us to see and revel in when it gets her into trouble. Murphy knows quite well what she's doing and can choose to use or not to use all sides of her personality. She's capable of moments of awareness and insight when she's willing to shift the focus away from herself. Murphy makes us laugh, because she's so out of balance toward the shadow side of her personality that we know we would never be like her. We might smugly say to ourselves, "Sure I've felt that way to some degree. But I would never do what *she* did — fortunately my feelings are under control."

Many of our edgiest comediennes are helping us laugh out our shadow sides. Satirist Eric Bogosian says of comic Chris Rock that going to one of his concerts is "an exorcism by laughter." Rock's 1997 HBO comedy special was titled "Bring the Pain," and he did: the pain of race relations, of being a man, of confusion. Bogosian calls it transforming "anger into entertainment." As we listen and laugh, we can take the next step and transform laughter into healing.

The secret is to recognize the good and the bad emotions that live within each of us — to seek a balance — to know that we are all a combination of opposites and a mixture of every feeling in the universe. It's imperative to learn your own history, to study your life story, to follow the path of your family's feelings to their origin. This will lead you away from your need to keep expressing feelings that don't work for you any longer.

Personal Negative Shadow Exercise

One of the best ways to keep from over-expressing negative emotions is to recognize why you are feeling them. The quickest way to do this is to write a letter to the person that is making you so angry, or jealous, or bitter or frustrated...

1) This can be done on a computer or in longhand. Simply start off: Dear _____:

   I am so angry at you, Dafney... I hate the way you... Every time you... You think you're so superior Dafney... I find your behavior toward me vengeful, selfish and juvenile.

   When you steal the spotlight, Dafney, it makes me crazy...

2) Write for as long as it takes to dissipate whatever emotions you're feeling. Write down every complaint you've ever had with that person.

3) Now take that letter and a magic marker and highlight every reference to that person, either by name or pronoun.

4) Ready for a big surprise? Take that highlighted letter and read it out loud. Only, every time you get to the highlighted name or reference, put in your name or I, whichever works.

While not every sentence may apply, I think you'll be surprised at how many do. Often, when intense, negative emotions are triggered, it's because someone or something has awakened something that lies dormant within our own personalities. When we realize what our trigger points are, we take away the other person's power to make us react in any other way than the one we prefer. It is also humbling to know that there is something within us all that resembles even those we most disdain. With that recognition we can begin to let go of a personality type that gets us all into a lot of crisis — the disdainful, critical JUDGE!

Movement	Connection	Awareness
_____	_____	_____
_____	_____	_____
_____	_____	_____

Chapter 13

Recognize a Self Separate and Distinct From Your Vocation

You are what you eat and you are what you think, but you are not what you do. Eighteen words that took me 38 years to learn. Let's see, so far in my life I've been a waitress, an actress, a public relations director, a commercial producer, a director, an account executive, a production company partner, an advertising agency owner, a movie producer, a writer, an author, a motivational speaker, a philanthropist...

Not one, nor even all of the above define who I am, however. I thought they did. I devoted every waking moment of my days to being indispensable to my employers and a consummate professional to others so that I could find self-definition. What could people possibly love about me other than how wonderful I was at what I did?

The fact is, the average person today will change their career 7.5 times. They will not change who they are, they will simply change what they do. I had to learn that fact the hard way, by almost working myself to death. My life was a tight rope, but I had no balance beam of activities, no connection to my community or the world around me. When I was diagnosed with MS, I had to get to know myself before I could help myself. I had to find what I was running from before I could finally win the race. If not outside myself, where was I to look for answers?

In an ancient folktale told to me, a fool, I've named him Jetta, was outside his house, down on his hands and knees desperately searching through the dirt. A neighbor walked by and asked if he might be of some help.

"What are you looking for, Jetta?" the neighbor asked.

"I lost my key," said Jetta.

The neighbor got down on his hands and knees to help Jetta and for quite some time they searched for the lost key. When it appeared that their search was futile, the neighbor turned to Jetta and said, "Think carefully, where exactly did you lose the key?" he asked.

"Why, I lost it in the house," Jetta replied.

"Good Heavens!" exclaimed the exasperated neighbor. "Then why are you searching for it outside?"

"Because the light is better here." said Jetta.

I was like Jetta. The light was better for me in the outside world of my profession. I did not know that the answers I sought were buried inside parts of me that I had abandoned with every disappointment in my life. I certainly did not know how to start looking inside for those answers. It took arriving at age 35 and having an illness overtake me for me to be willing to change my focus from outside to inside.

Once I was willing to try, the good news is, I found help quickly to speed me along my wellness path. My health-esteem team began to form without much effort. My media buyer sent me to a wise woman named Tobes. Tobes suggested a body therapist, Elizabeth, whose intuitive hands felt my sense of abandonment as a child. She suggested I take Jael Greenleaf's intensive course for adult children of Alcoholics. It felt like I was in a stream that had a life and a course of its own.

It was from Jael Greenleaf that I learned about 12 life areas, 11 of which were completely under-energized in my life. Before listing those areas, I'd like you to make a pie chart in the circle provided. Simply divide it up, preferably with different colored pencils, according to how you divide your time during an average week. Label each section's activity. My pie chart looked like this:

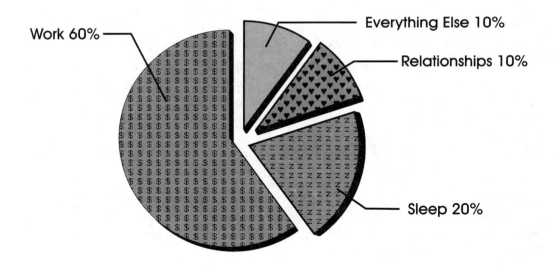

I didn't know it wasn't good to put all of my energy into one or even two areas of my life until I got Jael's list.

12 Life Areas:

1) Work	**2)** Money	**3)** Love/Spousal Relationships
4) Friendships	**5)** Community	**6)** Environment
7) Family Of Origin	**8)** Current Family	**9)** Parenthood
10) Play	**11)** Health	**12)** Spiritual/Religion

She actually recommended balancing all 12 areas. I thought, "How ridiculous." She then suggested a system for energizing forgotten areas. Select three areas a week in which you have spent little time, she instructed, then take three baby steps in each area during the week. Below are my original areas and a week's worth of baby steps:

Friends	**Health**	**Environment**
Write a letter	Do this work	Clean up desk
Make a call	See Tobes	Start on closet
Think about lunch	Read suggested book	Select one drawer to clean

Little by little, I began to see that work in each area improved the quality of my life in other areas. I also realized that life is constantly changing, thus the pie chart is always evolving. I highly recommend that you take up Jael's "3 life areas, 3 baby steps a week" system. You can keep records in your day book or keep a special journal if you prefer. Another really helpful hint is to find a buddy willing to do the same work with whom you can set your goals and report your progress. It formalizes your work and your decisions merely by having someone to share them with. Their job, and yours in return, is not to judge or criticize, but merely to listen and be supportive.

After several years of work, this is the way my WELLNESS life pie chart looks now: (next page)

Wellness Life Pie Chart

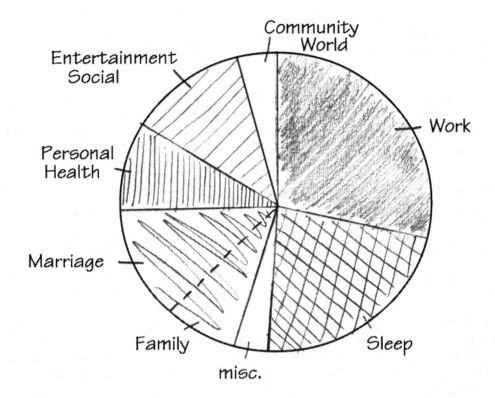

On the facing page are two empty pie chart circles. One is for you to fill in now using as many of the 12 life areas as you desire. This can be your "Work on it" or "Wish" pie chart to help you visualize the balance you wish to bring into your life while using this workbook as a tool.

The other pie chart is for you to come back to either after you have come through your current crisis, have finished this book, or are extremely happy with the balance of your life — or a combination of all three. Let's call this the "Wellness Pie Chart."

Wish Pie Chart

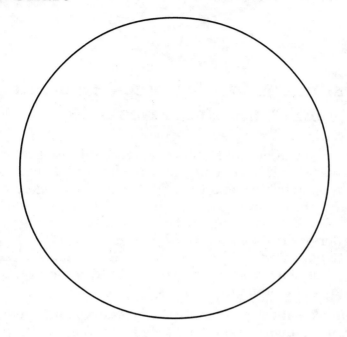

Wellness Pie Chart

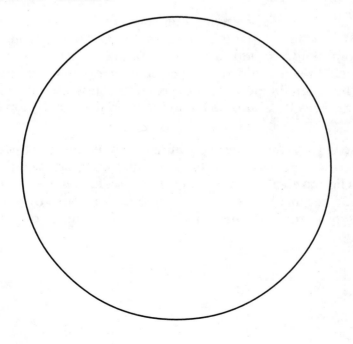

Chapter 14

Listen For Inside Voices Silenced by External Pressures & Roles

Don't worry. You will not finish this chapter and be talking in tongues. I simply want you to acknowledge the influence various voices have had on your life. We were all babies, children, adolescents, teenagers, and young adults once, and our bodies remember those stages of life in our cellular memories. We were all influenced by family members, teachers, community and world leaders, friends, mentors, pop icons, and, indeed, their voices are recorded in our minds, our thoughts, our emotions. They are all part of the chatter that influences us and makes us act in certain ways, sometimes in ways we don't understand or even respect.

There are universal voices as well. The classic woman's voice is said to be spiritually nurturing, harmonious, sensitive and a lover of peace. Whereas, the classic man's voice corresponds to their masculine ideals of competition, confrontation and conquest. Truthfully, both voices are in our heads and rather than being at war with each other, they need to be balanced and brought into harmony.

There are also voices of stereotyping, negative labeling and preconceived perceptions in our heads that were explored in Chapter 11. These voices may talk us out of applying for a certain job, dressing in a particular fashion, approaching some people or even aspiring to make a dream or goal come true. These are the doubting, pessimistic, spoil all our fun voices. These are the voices that hold us back and stop us from becoming all that we can be.

All of these voices sometimes combine to dig us into a pit when we're feeling depressed or to erect barriers around our hearts when we're feeling threatened. The pure voice of self-expression resides in our hearts, but sometimes our hearts are just too hard to get to because they are protected by a complex system of pits and barriers that have built up over time.

The I'm Not Enough Experiment

STEP 1. We all have different "Pits" protecting our hearts. You can determine your own by filling in sentences that begin with "I'm not" followed by an adjective of your choice and ending with the word "Enough." A few of the phrases I used to dig my pit were: "I'm not *deserving* enough. I'm not *lucky* enough. I'm not *lovable* enough."

1.	**2.**	**3.**
I'm Not Enough List	**Tone**	**Who**
I'm not _____ enough.	_____	_____
I'm not _____ enough.	_____	_____
I'm not _____ enough.	_____	_____
I'm not _____ enough.	_____	_____
I'm not _____ enough.	_____	_____

(Starter list: Do any of these apply? Thin enough, rich enough, busty, smart, pretty, handsome, tough, experienced, tall, short, funny, quick, young, old enough???)

STEP 2: Once you've filled in your pit blanks, wallow in the moat with your phrases for awhile. Say them out loud until they come out naturally, and then notice what tone of voice you're using. Is it angry? Judgmental? Critical? Disappointed? Fearful? Whining? Controlling? Fill in appropriate words to describe the voices saying the "I'm not enough" phrases in Column 2.

STEP 3: Listen to those voices. If you have a tape recorder handy, say the Column 1 phrases into the recorder using the tone you've selected. Do any of the voices sound like your voice? Mine certainly didn't. Can you identify the voices that don't sound like you? If so, please write down the names next to their corresponding phrases in Column 3. Sometimes I heard my mom' voice, sometimes my dad's. My speech coach from high school would crop up, a newscaster or an actor occasionally echoed through. My brother was represented and even an old boyfriend or two. Besides people you know, society mumbo jumbo is mixed in with marketing images that have been blasted into our heads since we were born with voices of beautiful people that are impossible to emulate.

With time this exercise will help you identify those often irritating voices in your head and determine which one's speak for your true feelings and which one's don't. This process gets you to the heart of the matter, your own heart, where you can free yourself from outside perception and definition by realizing that you are the author of your own thoughts. You must then make sure that the voice expressing those thoughts is your own. That voice ultimately is what makes us and saves us in life.

Once the loud protective voices are out of the way, you might find some soft voices that sound very far away. These are the voices that you have silenced over the years because you were too busy, too stubborn, too thoughtless, too self-absorbed, too fearful or too angry to listen.

I silenced two very important voices — my inner child and my grandmother. I didn't want to deal with my inner child's pain, so I silenced her pleas for playtime, for healing, for fun, for stability, for love and caring and unbridled creativity. I was angry at my grandmother for dying and leaving me, so I also shut off all the lessons she had hoped to pass on to me — her joy, her self-confidence, her passion were bottled up inside of me protectively. Every time one of their voices would start to sneak through, I would bury them with more work. To heal, I had to resurrect the wisdom of both voices. They each had answers for how to find and tend to my own needs.

In Chapter 24 we will do more work on Finding Your Voice and relating the work to your crisis definition and crisis breakdown list.

Movement	**Connection**	**Awareness**
_____	_____	_____
_____	_____	_____
_____	_____	_____

Chapter 15

Feel Life's Events As Well As Observing Them

The human being is truly an amazing creation. We are all programmed with automatic defense mechanisms to help us survive life. Adrenaline automatically pumps through our veins to enable us to fight or take flight in times of danger. Mothers report that their memories of excruciating labor pains fade with time, a definite aid in their decision to have another child. Soldiers recount having their minds clear of all thought, leaving them completely tuned to their own resources and truth when facing life-threatening situations in combat. Children, *especially*, are protected from pain too horrible to process: They have automatic shutoff valves that help them dull or bury feelings during times of abuse, that if experienced completely, might kill them.

No matter what causes us to put our feelings aside, however, there comes a time when they must be revisited. Feelings don't disappear completely. They wait to be processed. Unlike childbirth pain where women scream it out, breathe it out and then push out a new life; pain that is buried remains in your body, waiting to be understood, to impart it's message, to be shown a way out — to be treated and then expelled like afterbirth.

I was one of those children who buried pain in order to survive. I acted out some feelings with my dolls in convoluted make-believe and later, with my friends in costume fantasy games. I dreamed out some feelings in terrifying nightmares. By young adulthood, however, I realized that my mind had closed out most of the details of my childhood — in fact, the first 18 years of my life were little more than snapshot memories, most of them identical to the slides my family had shown on numerous occasions.

I came away from my childhood with a pattern of burying feelings that were too intense, hurtful or traumatic for me to handle. I was like a third party observing my own life. "O.K." my observer would tell my brain, "He's going to break up with you now. Smile and be brave. Whatever you do, don't stop long enough to feel the pain." One disappointment, betrayal, rejection, frustration, intimidation, terror, sadness, worry, failure or guilt piled up after another. They were all filed in my DO NOT FEEL drawer, deep inside my body behind layers of protective veneer.

As a result, I forgot how to feel. I knew how to pretend emotion, but my body always stopped short of really knowing how to feel. One classic warning of my mom's has been, "The woman who dines alone, dies alone." (A great example of a voice I needed to identify and purge from my memory — the voice of my mother programming her fear into my emotional data bank.) The alone fear is so engraved into my psyche that it came up in a recent conversation with Tobes, which I will now share.

Tobes: It's amazing how many people, when asked to name feelings, come up with perceptions or opinions — but not feelings.

Judy: In the old days, I wouldn't have thought of lonely as a feeling…it was a way of being. I put feelings into lonely — if I'm lonely, I'm feeling sad, rejected, afraid.

Tobes: That is "I'm alone."

Judy: To me it was lonely, perhaps because I couldn't stand even saying — I'm alone.

Tobes: Alone states the condition and lonely is the feeling.

Judy: I turned lonely into a condition because I couldn't allow myself to feel the feeling. I feel the loneliest in a big crowd, because I don't want anyone to see me being lonely. In a crowd, I feel like everyone *else* is having a good time.

Tobes: There are feelings wrapped up in that: Are you self-conscious, are you shy, intimidated? Why wouldn't you want to be seen feeling lonely?

Judy: Because that would indicate that I'm unpopular.

Tobes: Why?

Judy: (I thought for a long time and grew very uncomfortable before I blurted out an answer to avoid feeling painful memories.) Because if I wasn't lonely, I wouldn't be alone.

Tobes: That's a good rationalization. You slipped out of it. That's what I mean, people will give an explanation, or some kind of rationalization, instead of just getting in touch with their feelings. I could hear you say, "I'm scared in a crowd if I'm not doing something that feels like people will approve of me."

Judy: That's the bottom line for me — you got it. If people really liked me, they'd be around, and then I wouldn't have to feel lonely or be alone.

So you see, as far as I've come and as much as I've worked, there are still emotions that are scary enough to throw me into rationalization, unless I'm caught by my wellness spotters. They have helped me weave a safety net that will not let me fall through the cracks of my old sick-making habits.

There were several things that helped me get into the mode of feeling rather than just observing life's events. One was to realize how many emotions there are in life's palette. I was used to big swings; happy/sad, good/bad, mad/glad, angry/calm, weak/strong. Everything was polarized into a black and white world. I began to realize that there are many shades of gray, and that our everyday emotions run the gamut of that gray scale.

First, I encourage you to study the emotions list in the back of the workbook.

Second, I'd like you to keep a "Feelings Log" for one week and every hour or so check in with yourself to see how you're feeling; not how you feel physically, but how you feel emotionally.

For instance maybe you were driving to work and someone just cut you off and had the audacity to give you the finger — as if it was your fault. Chances are you're feeling angry. Acknowledge that anger, not by an outward expression that might put you in danger, particularly if you live in L.A., but by an inward notation. You might say to yourself "Ooh, that makes me angry." OK, you felt the anger and acknowledged it...now remind yourself to drive safely and hope the other driver does, too. Let the anger go and get on with your business. Throwing in a good thought for the offender helps your anger dissipate even faster (it's tough at first, but it gets easier over time). A half an hour later, you may walk into work and have a good looking new employee give you a completely unsolicited compliment, "Wow, every day you look great and happy — what's your secret?" Your feeling check-in now probably reveals flattered, maybe shy, perhaps elated, flirtatious, confident — there are just so many possibilities. A half an hour later, your boss may reprimand you, then anger, resentment, insecurity or nervousness may creep in. The point is to take note. You may think you're feeling one way all the time, when in fact you probably go through a gamut of emotions everyday. Naming your feelings allows you to be more tuned into your actions. It also helps you know that life is not all good or bad, black or white, sad or happy — it's a goulash, a stew, a melting pot. Most important, it helps you hold on to your memories.

When you feel an event as well as observe it, you own it. You can hold on to the good emotion involved or release the negative emotion triggered. Either way, your emotions become your partners in living life rather than saboteurs deleting memories as you run along the rocky path of experience.

Feelings Log

	Sun.	Mon.	Tues.	Wed.	Thur.	Fri.	Sat.
8 AM							
9							
10							
11							
12							
1 PM							
2							
3							
4							
5							
6							
7							
8							
9							
10							
11							
12							
1 AM							
2							
3							
4							
5							
6							
7							

What Is The Susceptibility Equation?

If there is one thing that all of us using this workbook have probably done when something really awful happens to us, it's to ask a two word question. _ _ _ _ _? Can you fill in the blanks?

Why would this happen to me? Why did she divorce me? Why did he fire me? Why did he die and leave me? Why did I get sick? Why did I have this accident? The most commonly asked, cried, screamed, or whined question in times of stress, sorrow or crisis is: "Why me?"

There are a lot of variables that go into answering "Why me?" questions. Add up all of those variables and you have what I call the "Susceptibility Equation." That equation includes everything that happens to an individual up to and including his or her point of crisis. The components are:

- Parental/hereditary/biological/genetic

- Spiritual/environmental/social/cultural

- Mental/physical/psychological/emotional

- Fate

- Family tree/personal details

- Reactions or actions to all of life's events

The part of that equation over which we can exert the most control is the way we act or react to everything and everyone that comes into our lives, and the emotional energy we invest in those situations. In other words, the one part of healing that we can take charge of is our thoughts and emotions. We must examine what thinking helped us to get into a situation. Then it's critical to ask how we can change that thinking to get out of crisis, to feel better, to come to peace.

My "Why me?" question was "Why would MS happen to me?" I slowly found that the answer was, "It had to happen to me." During the 35 years leading to my diagnosis, my reactions and actions to all of life's events, my thoughts and my emotions had thoroughly prepared me to develop a crisis like multiple sclerosis. Not discounting all of the other factors in the susceptibility equation, I had tipped the balance out of my favor and into the arena of potential illness or crisis by actually *learning* to behave in sick-making patterns. MS is different for everyone — as different as the life experiences of the person afflicted with the disease. To some degree, however, to whatever degree your thoughts and emotions play into your own susceptibility equation, there is truth in my experience for everyone in all types of crises.

MS was a perfect match for all the pain and travail of my youth and young adulthood. MS was the brick wall I could not leap over, chip away at, or avoid. MS simply took up residence in the body I had been ignoring, abusing and taking for granted all my life. It threatened me with lack of vision and numbness, so I had to stop and see and feel all the things I had been avoiding.

As you can tell from the workbook exercises you've completed up to this point, it is important to know what our thinking and our emotions have done to our bodies over the years. The following is a list of questions that will help you begin to explore your own "Susceptibility Equation," especially the parts over which you can exert the most control — your thoughts and emotions, your actions and reactions to all of life's events.

Your answers will help you determine where you have the most work to do in your life. Often the content of an answer can lead you to an insight that will help you change a crisis-making attitude. One thing is certain: For every area over which you have no control in the Susceptibility Equation, (fate, hereditary, genetic make-up...) exploring these questions will help you discover areas in which you can gain the powerful influence of healthy thinking.

Space is left below each question for any comments or feelings that may come to mind. At the end of the Questionnaire, there is room to write the three questions you would like to work on first and three things you would like to do in each area during the first week.

Questions to begin to explore Your "Susceptibility Equation."

1) Have you explored your mind/body connection? What does that mean to you?

_____

_____

_____

2)   Are you willing to look at where all the stress in your life went — how it was resolved — where it hid out? Can you name a few of your stress hide-outs?

_____

_____

_____

3)   Can you list one or two inherited emotional patterns?

_____

_____

_____

4)   Can you think of a major disappointment that you automatically stuffed out of sight which could be surfacing currently and manifesting in some type of physical health complaint?

_____

_____

_____

5)   Can you list three of your major motivations in life? Are they separate from motivations forced upon you by the world and people who are important to you?

_____

_____

_____

6)   Do you ever feel that your life is coordinated by someone on the outside? Who is that person or force and how does that make you feel?

_____

_____

_____

7) Is it possible that your life, so perfect and nice on the outside, needs to be balanced by recognizing the failures, the bad feelings and the disappointments? List one or two that you'd like to let go of.

_____

_____

_____

8) Can you see a self separate from the one created by your vocations, and by the expectations of your parents and significant others? Describe that independent self.

_____

_____

_____

9) Is there a voice inside of you that has been silenced all of these years by the role you were forced to play? What does that voice have to say?

_____

_____

_____

10) Is it possible that you observed a lot of life that you wouldn't allow yourself to *feel*? Can you describe a time when make-believe and wishing got in the way of feeling reality?

_____

_____

_____

Movement	Connection	Awareness
_____	_____	_____
_____	_____	_____
_____	_____	_____

Susceptibility Equation Experiment

Please select three of the "Susceptibility" questions on which you would like to do some work. Below each selected question, list three things you would like to do or explore during the first week. For instance, if I selected Question 9 - Silenced voice — I would have answered "Yes, my play voice was silenced — I didn't know how to relax and have fun." My list might include: Laugh more; Go to a movie; Take a bubble bath. In the following weeks you may stay with your original questions, or go on to another question that needs work.

Week 1

3 Questions I'd Like To Work On And 3 Little Actions

Q1)_____ Q2)_____ Q3)_____

1) _____   _____   _____
2) _____   _____   _____
3) _____   _____   _____

Week 2

3 Questions I'd Like To Work On And 3 Little Actions

Q1)_____ Q2)_____ Q3)_____

1) _____   _____   _____
2) _____   _____   _____
3) _____   _____   _____

Week 3

3 Questions I'd Like To Work On And 3 Little Actions

Q1)_____ Q2)_____ Q3)_____

1) _____   _____   _____
2) _____   _____   _____
3) _____   _____   _____

Crisis Progress Sheet

Crisis Name _____

Fill in the crisis name you chose in Chapter 5, and refer to your answers from the Crisis Break Down List before filling in the sentences below. Are your feelings changing since you listed your first thoughts about your particular crisis? Are you beginning to turn "stuck-in-the-past" thinking into action statements? As you compare this list with your original from Chapter 5, you will probably see that you are already breaking free of patterned behavior and sick-making habits?

If you remain stuck, don't despair. You've still got half the workbook to go, and a Crisis Recovery Sheet awaits you at the end of your work. You can always refer back to this Progress Sheet as breakthroughs occur from your continued reading.

My fear has _____

_____

I've turned my anger into _____

_____

I understand why I hated the thought of _____

_____

I'm replacing "If only I could" statements with _____

_____

One of the reasons this happened to me is _____

_____

I'm going to do these things differently now: _____

_____

I can possibly _____

_____

I want to _____

_____

I didn't do it before, but I will do it now: _____

_____

I will _____

_____

_____

Who? What? Where? When? Why? of Wellness

Like the detective with the magnifying glass pictured, when you begin the search for truth and answers in your life, you must find and study even the tiniest of clues. Then the challenge is to ask enough questions that the answers will guide you to the culprit, the perpetrator of a life-long wound. This workbook teaches you how to sleuth your way into slaying your own monsters of disease and dysfunction. Initially, your head will be full of questions every good investigator and investigative reporter must ask — Who? What? Where? When? Why? These questions must stay active in your mind and pour from your lips until you connect with the truth. Who am I? What has happened in my life to make me react this way? Where did I get these feelings? When did I learn to react like this? Why am I the way I am?

The more I talk to people either flirting with, close to, or in the middle of crisis (unfortunately that's just about everybody these days), the more I find we all have in common. Our bodies not only reacted the same way to similar emotional wounds we had suffered in the past, but also continued to hold on to those reactions and wounds. The big similarity is: NONE OF US HAD MADE THE CONNECTION! I'm talking about the connection of emotional wound and pain to physical symptom and pain.

> No matter what emotional wound you may have experienced or what physical symptoms you may now be suffering, if you will make the connection between wound and symptoms and hook that connection into your awareness, healing can take place.

Again, I remind you when speaking of healing, I'm not speaking of a cure. I'm speaking of a number of possibilities; awareness, acceptance, connection, permanent remission, change in attitude and action, new insight and direction, growth, movement, progress, letting go, peace, serenity, love... All of these possibilities and more have one thing in common, they disarm stress.

You are going to be asked to do a lot of truth searching in this chapter. Perhaps for the first time in your life, however, rather than focusing your magnifying glass on the outside world, you are going to focus on your inside world for answers. When I focused within, I found a world of extraordinary connectedness. One piece of data would lead to another — one answer to another question. I soon learned that:

Awakening Doesn't Just Happen Once, It's A Process.

My journey was not along straight lines that simply intersected with other straight lines; rather, it turned and revolved and brought dimension to what was now the circle of my life.

Before you take the plunge into some major inventory work, we would like you to do three warm-up exercises.

How To Become Self Aware Warm-up Exercises

1) Leave the room you are currently working in, and take your workbook with you before reading the rest of the directions.

Now that you are in another room, sit down, close your eyes, and mentally recreate the room you just left. Visualize the furnishings, the paintings on the walls, the windows and their coverings. What is on the tables or desks? Is there anything out of place? How many lamps, decorative items and knick-knacks can you place? Are there photographs? Who is in them? Are there books, magazines, flowers — see them? In two minutes of visualization, try to imagine every detail of the room.

After two minutes or so, open your eyes and write down your room description in the space provided.

Room Description

_____

_____

_____

_____

_____

_____

_____

_____

_____

_____

_____

_____

_____

_____

_____

_____

_____

Now go back into the first room. Was your description accurate? Did you leave out some obvious things? Were there any surprises in what you remembered and what you didn't? Many of us become so locked up in our own thoughts that we become oblivious to our environment and even to those sharing the immediate environment with us. This is also an interesting exercise to do after sitting in a lecture room for a few hours. It's often surprising to note that we can't describe the attire of the people sitting closest to us. Another manner in which we often become oblivious is in the way we listen to others.

Years ago, I had a small office just off the main hallway in the television station where I produced commercials. One Monday morning, I overheard an extraordinary exchange at the coffee machine.

George: Morning, Arnie. How've you been?

Arnie: I've been better.

George: Wasn't the weather great this weekend? Did you have a good one?

Arnie: Actually, no. My wife's been sick for months, and she died on Saturday.

George: (already walking down the hall & sipping his coffee) That's nice. See ya' later.

This is a true story, and the bottom line is, George was going through the motions, focusing only on his coffee and weekend memories and not listening to one word. Does this sound familiar to anyone? While perhaps not guilty to George's degree, I'm sure most of us have been accused of not listening.

An extremely busy publishing executive friend of mine is currently jobless for the first time in her life and facing a professional transition. She admitted to me, "It's the first time in years that I actually listen to my husband. Because I have more time, we can really talk about what he wants to discuss. Before I was dead tired, and I digested some of what he said, but I didn't listen. We've been married 23 years and we're having a better time now than in a long time. It's the best gift that has come from my career crisis."

We must not forget to listen professionally and personally. That is a key way to take in the gift of knowing another person's thoughts and feelings. You will know how well you have listened if you can repeat a conversation you've just had — immediately — one hour later — the next day. If you can recall the other party's content as well as your own the next day, you are a good listener.

2) Write down directions to your home using only landmarks. Pretend that there are no street names. You must depend on the number of stoplights or signs, interesting businesses or homes, memorable structures, parks, schools, you name it. Write them as if they were instructions given to numerous friends invited to a party at your home. You may use one major boulevard that everyone would be familiar with as your starting point, but after that absolutely no street names.

_____

_____

_____

_____

_____

_____

_____

_____

_____

_____

_____

I would have been a very lonely person if I had to rely on directions like these to have my friends visit. Besides having no sense of direction, my environment simply passed me by, because I never allowed it to enter my consciousness. I used the excuse of being in too much of a hurry. I was missing out on both information and a sense of connection with my community.

3) Tobes has used the following exercise to help many of her study groups gain self-awareness from an ordinary activity. When you wash your hands, look at them. How simple you might say, but how often do you do that? What's your thumb doing when you wash your hands? What are your fingers doing? Does it feel good to add a little extra pressure around the knuckles and the joints? Are there some nicks and bruises on your hands you hadn't noticed? How far can you spread your fingers apart? Can you still bend your thumb back to touch your wrist? Remember how we could do that as kids?

Now that your warm-up is complete, it's time to do some inventories:

Inventory of Physical Appearance

Mental: We will start with a mental inventory. When you close your eyes, how do you see yourself? Are you dressed? What are you wearing? Can you visualize yourself naked? Do you see one image of yourself or several? Are you fatter or thinner? Is your hair the same? Are you standing, sitting or reclining? What is your body language saying? What's happening with your posture? Your facial expression? Search for as much detail in your visualization as possible.

If you are so inclined, when you finish, draw a picture of your visualization — a self-portrait in the space provided.

Self Picture Page

Select a picture you like of yourself and put it on this page.

If you have them available, select a picture you like of yourself from different ages in your life — perhaps at 5 to 10 year intervals, kind of like a class reunion with yourself.

Complete these sentences:

I Dress to _____

Usually I look _____

I feel most comfortable in _____

When I look at myself naked, I see _____

List 10 ways you see yourself — i.e., I see myself as strong, cute, capable, a leader, insecure, too round in the hip area, friendly, lonely, etc.

1. _____
2. _____
3. _____
4. _____
5. _____
6. _____
7. _____
8. _____
9. _____
10. _____

List 10 ways you think that other people see you.

1. _____
2. _____
3. _____
4. _____
5. _____
6. _____
7. _____
8. _____
9. _____
10. _____

Face To Face: Now, go to your bathroom mirror and take a good hard look at yourself. What do you see? Does the person staring back at you look like your mental image? It's best to do this inventory naked, perhaps after you have showered. We've included a list of prompters on your inventory sheet. In the blanks simply put an arrow up or down, dependent on your attitude about that particular body part.

Visual Physical Appearance Inventory

HAIR	_____	FACTS/MEASUREMENTS
HEAD SHAPE	_____	Height _____
FACE	_____	Weight _____
EYES	_____	Bust (chest) _____
NOSE	_____	Waist _____
EARS	_____	Hips _____
MOUTH	_____	
NECK	_____	
CHEST	_____	PHYSICAL BODY GOALS
ARMS	_____	1)_____
HANDS	_____	_____
FINGERS	_____	_____
BACK	_____	_____
WAIST	_____	2)_____
STOMACH	_____	_____
HIPS	_____	_____
BUTTOCKS	_____	_____
LEGS	_____	3)_____
THIGHS	_____	_____
CALVES	_____	_____
ANKLES	_____	_____
FEET	_____	
TOES	_____	
MUSCLE TONE	_____	

Was your overall assessment positive or negative? Either way, step back and give your overall body, not the individual parts, an appreciative glance. Select one of the following phrases to say to yourself: I look great. I'm handsome. I'm beautiful. What a wonderful body I have. I appreciate my body. Say your phrase each day when you look in the mirror. Even if there are things you wish to change (and, who doesn't have a few of those), being appreciative of your body will put your body on your side during the change process.

You may want to note a few goals concerning your physical body at this time. Start with perhaps one to three physical areas, and remember three tiny actions each week add up to big results.

How Do You Feel Inventory

This next inventory is to get you to tune in to signals from your body or what we call "messengers." First, we want you to read the following words very carefully.

> Your body is designed to work and function perfectly and it will do just that if there is no interference.

This is the basic philosophy of chiropractic medicine. Nancy explains that aches and pains and some of the things we want you to start noticing are symptoms of physiology that is out of balance rather than symptoms that lead to only one conclusion, i.e., "I am sick." Even, "I am sick" translates to "My system is out of balance," among other things.

How you will react to illness or crisis presents the challenge. When I was told I had MS, my knee-jerk reaction was to panic and think, "I've got MS and I'm going to end up paralyzed." After all, I was already numb and partially blind, and the media stereotypically portrayed MS sufferers in wheelchairs. Many people, when diagnosed with cancer, automatically think death. We are programmed that certain diseases mean certain things.

I had to learn to slow down and ask a different question about my symptoms, "Hm-m-m-m, what does this mean?" My numbness didn't necessarily mean that I was headed for a wheelchair. It meant that I had numbed out my entire emotional system, and that I needed to go back and start feeling lots of things that I had buried in my body.

My chiropractor, Nancy, compares the process of tracking down the "why" of symptoms to being a 2-year-old. She gives the example of a woman with gallstones who says:

"Why do I have pain here?"

Because you have gallstones.

"Why do I have gallstones?"

Because you eat so many fatty foods.

"Why do I eat so many fatty foods?"

Because...

"Why...?"

And the questions and answers proceed until the woman finds the root of her problem.

It's extremely important here to change the way you react to symptoms. When I started asking "Why?" I began to have hope that I would find an answer that would bring some degree of healing.

It's also important to note that this is a very active "Why?" This is not a whining, passive, "Why me?" which finds you waiting for some outside source to magically appear with an answer or a cure. This is you deciding to become a partner in your healing by seeking your own truth and making whatever changes are required.

To begin, all you have to do is pay attention to messages your body is sending you. For example, a headache could be a messenger signaling that there is an imbalance regarding food — blood sugar — or an emotional disturbance. The next time you get a headache, ask yourself some "Why?" questions and see if you can decipher the message. Never hesitate to contact a doctor if the whys you discover don't eliminate the pain within a reasonable time.

A list of messenger prompters is provided on the next page. For now, just run down the list to identify familiar symptoms. Then note time and day, circumstance, frequency and any possible message associated with each. (Helpful information for your healthcare provider.)

Movement	Connection	Awareness
_____	_____	_____
_____	_____	_____
_____	_____	_____

How Am I Feeling Messengers

Symptom	Time/Day	Circumstance	Frequency Message
Headache			
Diminished eyesight			
Insomnia			
Hair loss			
Fatigue			
Congestion			
Chronic joint pain			
Bruising			
Allergies			
Nausea			
Constipation			
Diarrhea			
Gas			
Bloating			
Belching			
Waking with fear			
Fainting			
Dizziness			
Muscle cramps			
Itching			
Backache			
Indigestion			

Symptom	Time/Day	Circumstance	Frequency Message
Neck pain			
Shortness of breath			
Memory loss			
Weakness			
Achiness			
Pain (note area)			
Coughing			
Colds (frequency)			
Other			

Becoming more aware of your body's messengers will eventually introduce you to what being healthy feels like. Nancy notes, "People today know they're not sick, meaning they're not laying in bed, incapable of going to work — but they don't know that they're not well. It's a tragedy that a huge percentage of those with heart disease don't notice a problem until the first fatal symptom — a heart attack. It's essential, when experiencing a symptom, to ask what that symptom is saying."

Sometimes people feel bad for so long — tired, listless, grumpy — that they start to feel it's natural. Many say, I don't want to spend so much time focusing on myself. Believe me, that's an indication of fearing what you may find.

Focus on yourself, ask what your symptoms are trying to tell you, face the issues revealed, and endure the emotions that may surface. Your reward will be the discovery that feeling good everyday is natural.

As you go farther along in this work, you may want to take these inventories over again. I'm sure you will change, as I did, and most likely be delighted with the change.

Change — Become Co-Creative

Are You Willing To Change In Order To Feel Better?

If your answer is, "No," then you might as well close up this workbook and go on living out your particular crisis. For those of you unwilling to change, it's unlikely that you'll ever be able to sense when it's time to quit certain things you are doing that are bad for you. It's also quite unlikely that you would ever be willing to make short-term sacrifices for long-term gain. As for all those calls for help your body is sending out, the receiver who won't change is permanently off the hook. Time may find you more open to change in the future, however, so don't throw the workbook away, merely keep it on file. It has taken me a year and sometimes more to be able to absorb and act upon some of my literary purchases.

I hear another very large group who is at least a little bit willing to change, but busy chanting, "I just don't have time." For you with no time to change, one of the following reactions to crisis may be yours: Pretend it isn't there or that it didn't happen; Cover it up with some excuse or fabrication; Forget it ever happened; Hope it will go away or just take care of itself. I'm familiar with all of those excuses because I used each and every one of them when MS hit. For one year I practiced the denial game starting from the day I pulled my Vice President into my office and offered this ultimatum:

"While I've been diagnosed with MS, I'm only telling you because I may need your help on this client trip to Dallas. But, don't do anything for me you wouldn't have done before. And, whatever you do, don't ever mention my MS to anyone — even to me, or you're fired!"

How's that for a mind open to change? Totally closed! I didn't have time. I had to concentrate on my business, like I had all of my life. I didn't want to take time to ask the question, "WHAT'S THE WORST THING THAT CAN HAPPEN?"

If I had asked, "What's the worst thing that can happen if I don't pay attention to the MS messenger my body has sent?" I would have been answered, "It will resort to scare tactics." And, that's just what it did. My numbness got worse, my vision lessened, the tingle down my spine increased, my balance decreased. You get the picture. Denial didn't make anything go away or take care of itself. It didn't allow me to forget MS had ever happened.

So I ask all of you with too little time to change to ask the question. What's the worst thing that can happen if I don't change? I don't want to scare you, but the truth is whatever you answered will probably happen if you don't make the changes your particular crisis is demanding. Whether your answer is to find a new job; resolve marital strife; give up certain foods, alcohol, smoking or other recreational drugs; to let go of a loved one; to restructure financially; or to follow symptoms back to their original pain and feel them — you can see that change is required.

For those of you who are still on the fence about change, we may have something else in common. As long as I didn't change, I had lots of repeats in my life. Repeatedly familiar, unhappy relationships with men, repeat ailments such as bronchitis, nerve spasms in my neck, and lots of female problems, repeat loneliness, repeat anxiety, repeat stress... Fortunately, being a child of the television age, I finally realized that if I was tired of repeats, it was time for me to change the channel. I didn't come easily to that realization. My body had to mutiny on me first, but finally I switched the channel and invited change into my life.

Perhaps the pain has to be really bad to get us to be co-creators in something most of us have been willing to turn over to a third-party — our health. We're used to a diagnosis and a prescription that we can follow without having to think too much.

MS changed that way of thinking for me. In 1985 there were no treatments for doctors to recommend. I still had a choice; to passively accept that predicament and do nothing, or to become active in my own care instead of continuing in my own self-destruction. I chose to become active and to make whatever changes were necessary. But where to begin?

My healing team taught me to look to my own body for hints as to what needed to be changed in my life. Considering that one of my big symptoms was numbness, a big starting point for me was to look at my life-long sensitivity to touch. That led me all the way back to my mother's repulsion to anything sensual and my father's inappropriate behavior toward me physically and sexually. I had to understand, forgive, let go of their behavior patterns and teach myself to embrace my own sexuality.

When you begin to look to your own body for change hints, you are looking for habits, behaviors, actions and reactions that are memorized, learned, patterned and not of your own choosing. It was not my choice to flinch when touched in certain ways, it was a reflex action. I had to find who owned that reaction and give it back to the person or people from whom it had been learned. Please spend some time with the check-in list that follows. It will help you receive important messages from your body about areas of potential change.

What Truth Lies Hidden In My Body Waiting For Change?

1) Check in with your senses. Are you particularly sensitive to any one or all of the following? If so, list specifics that may come to mind.

sight _____

sound _____

touch _____

smell _____

taste _____

Look at where you're ticklish; sounds that make you have a quick, negative physical reaction; sights that you must look away from; smells that send your memory on a retrieval trip; tastes you dismiss for no reason.

Once you find a sensory clue, start asking the "Why?" question, followed by the rest of the Who? What? Where? When? wellness questions. Follow these questions all the way back to a precipitating event and/or the source of similar behavior.

2) Check in with your habits. Where did they come from? Who else had these habits? Do you want to keep these habits or change them??

Habits	Where	Who	Keep/Change
Closet upkeep			
Getting up procedure			
Going to bed rituals			
Personal grooming			
Favorite greetings and sayings			
Basic assumptions about how you're perceived in the world			
How do you automatically perceive others?			
Are you an introvert or extrovert?			

Habits	Where	Who	Keep/Change
How do you sit in a chair?			
Where do you head in a movie theatre?			
How do you react to lines? To traffic?			
How do you behave in a group?			
Work habits?			
Eating habits?			
Other habits?			

Once you begin to ask why do I act this way, feel this way, react this way, behave this way questions, one will lead to another and another. Just keep asking *"Why"* questions and you will arrive at the answers you seek. With the understanding you have gained, change will be much easier, because you most often are changing something that was not of your choice in the first place.

In the book **Why Aren't Black Holes Black?**, two scientists Robert Hazen an earth scientist and co-author Maxine Singer, a biochemist, reveal that there is a lot we don't know. Neither aging nor what causes death at the cellular level is well understood. Among many other things, how memories are stored, the nature of consciousness and the nature-versus nurture debate in behavioral genetics are also riddled with questions. What that means to me is, that anything is possible, and I have a role in finding the optimum possibilities within me. Not unlike the scientists, I start with my own *"Why"* questions.

Before leaving this chapter, I would like to share with you a positive/negative self-image exercise that brings about change in a most natural way. This exercise was taught to me by Mark Learner, a man who used illness to send him on a spiritual journey that now finds him the founder of two corporations, author of three books and a devotee to counseling others with serious illnesses and handicaps.

Ditzel/Darling Exercise

1) Think of the worst thing that ever happened to you and capture the feelings and experience in one word. (I thought PANIC.)

Write Worst Thing Word _____

2) Imagine the physical sensations that occurred when that worst thing happened to you. Give the self that felt those sensations a name. (I imagined the sensations of panic and chose a name for myself when I felt panic — DITZEL.)

Write Worst Feeling Name for Yourself _____

3) Concentrate on the best thing that ever happened to you and capture the feelings and experience in one word. (I thought of EUPHORIA.)

Write Best Thing Word _____

4) Imagine the physical sensations that occurred when that best thing happened to you. Give the self that felt those sensations a name. (I imagined feeling a blissful peace and gave the self that felt that way the name of DARLING.)

Write Best Feeling Name For Yourself _____

5)   Practice automatically connecting to the self you named in number 4 by feeling the pulse on the side of your neck and repeating, "I am _____, I am _____ every night before going to sleep. Repeat the phrase while concentrating/visualizing on images of yourself when you felt that way.

In my case, I concentrated on images of myself when I felt euphoric, moments of blissful peace while repeating "I am Darling, I am Darling," every night before dozing off.

After you have done this for awhile, when you feel the negative self you visualized in step 2 coming into action, you merely have to feel the pulse at the side of your neck and repeat your "I am _____" phrase to deprogram the negative and bring your positive self into action. Now that's what I call positive change.

Movement	Connection	Awareness
_____	_____	_____
_____	_____	_____
_____	_____	_____

Chapter
19

How To Start Receiving Your Body's Signals

"I'm mad as hell, and I'm not going to take it anymore!" were the words shouted out the window by a disgruntled television news anchorman in the movie "*Network*." I'm sure that is how my body felt when it kept sending me signals that I ignored. It sent endometriosis, chronic bronchitis, exhaustion, yeast and bladder infections, two automobile accidents — and still I didn't listen. Then my body got really angry and shouted with blindness and numbness. I finally had to listen.

Elizabeth remembers a patient that she and Natalie treated. She grew hundreds of fibroid tumors and eventually was diagnosed with breast cancer. The patient asked, "Do you think that 15 automobile accidents in less than five years has anything to do with all my tumors?"

The answer was "Yes." She was on a suicide track one way or the other, through cancer or through cars, unless she stopped to ask the "Why?" questions. Why was she so unhappy, anxious, angry...? What shadow-side emotions motivated her and where did they come from?

Fortunately for the patient, Natalie and Elizabeth sought the help of a hypnotherapist, who was able to take the patient right back to the point in her life where her emotional turmoil began. Together, the healing team helped the patient remember, process, and clear from her body toxic thoughts and emotions that stimulated tumor growth. Within three months her breast cancer was gone.

You may sit back confidently now and say, "I'm not getting any signals like that." Perhaps not. Do you have trouble sleeping? How's your appetite? Are you taking significantly more aspirin than usual? Are you reaching for the antacids more often? Ever have trouble breathing? Do you ever notice a bruise you don't remember getting? Do you find more of life to be a chore lately? How often do you find yourself short tempered, cranky, unable to cope? Have you found yourself zoning out in front of your TV more evenings than you care to admit? Are you finding foods you used to love to be suddenly disagreeable? Are certain emotions popping out inappropriately when you least expect them? Are you constantly late, consistently overwhelmed, frequently frenzied? Do you forget things a lot?

Are you hearing similar complaints or concerns about your behavior from several sources? Do you worry a lot, are you scared often, has uneasiness taken over? Or, are you just bored, listless, uninterested in life?

Am I hearing a few "So whats?" out there? "So what if things aren't perfect? I've got a life to keep running. I can't be stopped by each and every discomfort, displeasure, distress or dis-ease." I know that feeling, too. Before my sight and numbness problems were diagnosed and for sometime afterwards, I continued to keep *acting* as if everything was all right.

While my actions said, "So what?" however, my emotions were screaming to come out and be heard. I would wake up every morning with fear as my bed partner — always wondering what would happen to me that day. I wanted to talk to someone — but who? I had set myself up as the invincible one — the boss. I wanted to cry — but how? If I cried I would be admitting something was wrong, and then it might actually be true. If I weakened to tears, would my strength ever return? I felt sick inside — lonely and terrified. How long could I hide my body's rebellion?

Still, I kept up the act. God forbid, my work should suffer just because I was suffering. Then a multi-ton, stainless steel messenger was sent to help me put on the brakes to my self-destruction.

I was having a bad MS day. I could barely feel the right side of my body. Instead of the sporadic black hole in my vision, which I was used to, I had little squirmy things floating through my eyes, like tiny tadpoles. I kept blinking to make them go away, but they were still there, like a bad light show that wouldn't end. I was completely unable to concentrate.

Completely disconcerted by the light show in my eyes, I got in my Datsun 280ZX to drive to Tobes', barely able to feel the gas pedal, let alone shift. As I sat at one of the city's busiest intersections waiting to make a left turn, I rubbed my eyes nervously and watched the light. I was sure the light had turned yellow which, in L.A., means you can go like hell and make a left turn. I shifted into first gear and started my turn. Loud, insistent honking woke me up to the horror of a black Porsche bearing down on me far above the speed limit. I couldn't move my feet fast enough to shift and brake. I swerved to barely avoid a collision and spun into and over the center divider. On-coming traffic miraculously avoided me, while I guided my car to safety on the correct side of the road. I was in shock by the time I entered Tobes' home.

Finally, I stopped pretending with the woman who had been trying to help me for over one year. "I'm not all right," I cried to Tobes, "I'm scared to death that everyday I might wake up and not be able to walk or see. I face my future with terror in my heart." Tobes didn't act shocked or even worried. In fact, she was smiling. "I knew your health was a secret from even yourself. I was simply waiting for you to share. Now, we can do something about it. You had to recognize the problem, before we could start to heal it."

She looked at me compassionately and said, "You work on everything but yourself. For some reason, you don't like yourself enough to get well. It's a warning, dear. MS has come to you as a warning to change the way you see and run your life."

I've learned a lot over the years. It no longer takes automobile accidents to make me listen. Since learning that being well is not just the absence of being sick, I've committed to taking an active role in being better — thinking better, acting better and becoming a better, more balanced human being. I've been symptom-free from MS since 1990. Yes, in my case, healing started when I became sick, but it is now a part of my everyday life. When you are feeling energetic and healthy, that too is a time to check into your body and acknowledge what makes you feel centered and in harmony with your world. With balance in life as our day to day commitment, our bodies don't have to swing dangerously out of control to get our attention and bring us back to center.

Closet Check

One quick way to check out the balance in your life is to spend a few hours in your closet.

- Is your closet organized or in complete disarray?

- Are your clothes rumpled, neatly pressed or somewhere in between?

- How many items are hanging around that you haven't worn for one year, five years, a decade?

- What memories are you hanging on to with certain apparel?

- What percentage of your closet is taken up by business/work apparel, sports clothing, leisure attire, dressy duds, sleep wear, casual comfort, clothes, or messy, I-don't-give-a-damn statement threads?

- How many of your clothes are or were trendy?

- How many are hopelessly out of date?

- How many sizes of you are represented in your closet?

- How many moods of you are represented by your color selections?

- How many clothes represent something you gave up a long time ago?

- Bottom line — does your closet reflect a balanced you?

Mine certainly didn't! I had 80% working woman clothes, 10% evening clothes selected for the sexy, successful *working* woman, one pair of *working* woman jeans, sleep wear divided between sexy new romance and no-man-in-my-life-all-*work* frump, and some old tennis and ski clothes representing sports I gave up a decade ago.

It's a wonderful healing exercise to organize your closet and watch it become more diversified as your life branches out to embrace balance. Weed out the old, broaden your color spectrum, balance work clothes with play, sport, casual and dressy. Make sure that every item expresses a side of you who you respect, like and nurture.

Now that your closet has helped you become more tuned into the balance in your life, see if you can pick up on some body signals.

Signal Recognition Experiment

Using the list of prompters below or others, list five signals your body sent you over the last month indicating that you were out of balance. In the column to the right of signals, list the possible warning that signal was bringing. Try to keep the warning about you, not anyone else involved in your particular signal. (i.e., If you had a fight with someone, what does that fight say about *you*?) Avoid the obvious. (i.e., if you got a speeding ticket — the message is not just "I was going too fast." Why were you going too fast? Keep asking *Why?* until you get to the message, like we did in Chapter 17.)

Accident	Traffic Ticket	Anger
Depression	Lethargy	Fights
Drowsiness	Mistakes	Cravings
Urges	Longings	Memories
Family rumblings	Social ups & downs	Community
Stress	Discomfort	Illness
Sloppiness	Disrespect	No control

	SIGNAL	MESSAGE
1)	_____	_____
2)	_____	_____
3)	_____	_____
4)	_____	_____
5)	_____	_____

Every day of my life I look and listen for body signals. I'm aided in that search by meditation, the art of going inward, listening to peace, connecting with my own wisdom.

Notes: _____

_____

_____

_____

_____

_____

_____

_____

_____

_____

Movement	Connection	Awareness
_____	_____	_____
_____	_____	_____
_____	_____	_____

Meditation

There is two-way conversation going on between my body and my mind now every moment of every day. It happens naturally, with little thought required. If I'm after specific information, however, I can use tools, such as exercise, a quiet walk alone, yoga, stretching and meditation to stimulate answers from within.

Since MS entered my life, I have learned to use exercise as a kind of full body meditation to check in with my physical and emotional self. I'm often in search of warning symptoms concerning my MS. Are there tingles? Is there stiffness or soreness? I check in with stretches, some gentle yoga postures, and deep breathing. At one point, I lie flat on the floor, facing the ceiling. I close my eyes and perform a quick head to toe inventory, feeling my toes, my feet, my ankles, my calves, knees and thighs, my hips, waist, stomach and chest, my shoulders, back and neck, my chin, cheeks, eyes, forehead... According to what my body tells me, I adjust my workout accordingly and think about what the messages received are telling me. Am I feeding my body right? Sleeping enough? Drinking enough water? Have I been beating myself up again with anxiety or worry? It's like taking my own pulse — and as I get better at it, I get valuable information. When I'm not feeling well, breathing and stretching exercises allow me to check in with my body's message center. (Many breathing exercises are detailed in Chapter 25.) I once took my body for granted. I can never afford to do that again.

Before I walk or exercise, my other very important morning ritual is meditation. It truly prepares me for all the events that will fill my day. Tobes first introduced me to meditation. When I asked her to teach me, she said the only lesson necessary was to watch what she did and do it. She sat on the sofa, comfortably, closed her eyes, took a few deep breaths and did *nothing*. I was ready to *do* something. She said I could sit on the floor in a lotus position if I preferred, or anywhere, as long as I was comfortable. Most importantly, I was to relax and be very still while I simply observed whatever thoughts might pass through my mind. She said to start doing that for five minutes a day and then work up to twenty.

I was frustrated. I was used to taking action on my thoughts, not sitting and watching them float through my head like a school of floundering fish. Still remarkably work-driven, I devoted only sporadic attention to the sit-and-do-nothing type of meditation, until Tobes urged me to utilize my talents as a reporter and journalist to take note of my own inner life.

I began by using a tool, *The Power Deck* by Lynn V. Andrews, a world renowned author and teacher of modern mysticism. The deck contains 45 cards, each with a beautiful illustration on one side representing the physical body and a message on the other to help divine the truth of your spirit and power. Andrews explains that the deck works "by examining both the positive and the negative aspects of yourself, the pieces of your power and personal puzzle that are present and those that are missing."[1] I devised my own method of working with the cards; each morning, when I sat down to meditate, I would concentrate on a question.

During one morning's meditation, I saw an image of myself dressed in armor. I was covering up some horrible truth, hiding my vulnerability my nakedness. A thought flew through my mind, "I do everything out of duty — never out of desire." I felt very, very tired. The armor was too heavy to bear. The question I asked the cards was, "How can I strip away the armor and act out of desire, not duty?" With my eyes still closed, and the Power Deck cards spread out face down in front of me, I selected a card entitled "Grief." The illustration was of a person on a seaweed covered shore huddled into a tight ball next to a black rock with a wilted yellow rose on top. The tide had gone out. In an instant I felt that I was mourning for my lost innocence, represented by the wilting of my favorite flower, a yellow rose. Like the tide, my passion was gone. The words on the card read, "Through grief you can explore every aspect of your dark side — anger, pain, abandonment, terror, loneliness; and these are aspects of the secret wound that in our daily lives we usually try to ignore. Grief forces you to look at those parts of yourself that are not yet healed...The seeds of wisdom and enlightenment are planted within the wounds of grief. What is lost can only come back to us again in higher ways."[2] I took those words into my body and worked on them through journal writing and self-examination. All the ages of me needed to grieve. (You will find more on grieving in Chapter 23.)

Day by day, I explored question after question and used the cards to probe deep within myself for answers. I saw images of myself as a child choking back tears to the point of feeling suffocated. I remembered defending myself against my father's crude insults which shot into me like poison darts. I had been able to pull out the darts, but the poison had penetrated deep into my system. I shivered during meditation, as if to shake

[1]*Andrews, Lynn, V., The Power Deck, the Cards of Wisdom, Harper, San Francisco, Harper Collins Publishers, New York, 1991, p. ix Preface. Ms. Andrews' Medicine Woman series, published in 12 languages, and her School of Sacred Arts and training have reached people around the world.*

[2]*Ibid., Card #19 and p. 63.*

off the hand that was touching Little Judy (L.J.), the hand of my father. The shiver was familiar. It was a shiver that crept involuntarily into every relationship of my life.

The pained faces of L.J. came to me one by one. I saw them, I remembered circumstances and I felt her anguish, her anger, her fear, her resentment and sorrow. After some meditations, I would have to sit for awhile to find the strength to get up. I would take deep breaths, brush off my skin and then go in to exercise the places that had atrophied with emotional pain. Throughout this process, my body grew stronger — even cold and flu germs seemed to stay away. Any hint of MS came as flashback symptoms that I could quickly move through by altering my routine, diet, exercise, nutrients, thoughts, or emotional state.

This directed meditation was one I devised to help me find my forgotten childhood. I also used it to explore family issues when there were no family members with which to talk. I encourage you to be creative in using tools that will help you elicit answers from your own internal wisdom. One time, I bought the Inner Child Deck of Tarot cards with the thought of using them to tell my step- grandchildren stories. When I opened them and looked at the colorful, fanciful pictures they, instead, became an immediate vehicle to open up communication with my inner child.

When Tobes, Nancy, Elizabeth and I gathered for the first time to create this workbook, we began with a ritual to guide and focus our thinking. We held hands, closed our eyes, breathed as one, concentrated on our workbook effort and chose an inner child card to guide us. As the author, I was selected to pull the card from the deck. Out came #9, Hansel & Gretel. As usual, the message was perfect: "Realize that each person has a feminine/masculine balance and that it is now time for you to bring these inner components into a state of balance and equilibrium. Hansel is a symbol of the animus — the wind, the spirit, and male energy. Gretel signifies the anima — the soul, nurturing, and female energy. Together, hand in hand, their rapport indicates a preliminary form of the divine marriage. The old crippled witch in the tale signifies the dark regions of consciousness that must be recognized and purified."[3]

I use this example to show you how tools such as *The Power Deck* or *Inner Child Cards* help to stimulate our imaginations to find emotional memories and bits of our psychic lives that are universal, archetypal — principles of life. Our work in this book is to help you find a state of balance and equilibrium, to help you unite your male and female energies, to aid you in recognizing and purifying the dark regions of your consciousness. The traditional tarot archetype symbolized by Hansel and Gretel is The Lovers. The union of Gretel's soul and Hansel's spirit focuses

---

[3] *Lerner, Isha, Inner Child Cards, Bear & Company, Inc., Santa Fe, NM, 1992, pp. 66–7.*

on heart energy and inspires love. Our journey to Health-Esteem is aided by love of self, of each other, of the community and world around us. I urge you to take a heart-centered focus into your meditations and to use whatever tools will inspire your imagination to translate the messages your senses deliver. As you will see, my journey into understanding the power of meditation was an evolution. It took time to learn to be without effort, to receive without trying, to accept without judgment, to learn without struggle.

Meditation — An Internal Treasure Hunt

About halfway through my journey with card meditations, I was fortunate to have a mutual friend introduce me to Dr. Deepak Chopra. Considered a leader of the wellness movement with his unique combination of Eastern wisdom and cutting edge Western science, his books and tapes had certainly inspired me.

Told to meet Dr. Chopra at the Transcendental Meditation Center in Pacific Palisades, CA., I was warned that I would have only five minutes since he was a very busy man. On the way to see him, I rehearsed what I was going to say in my valuable but limited time. I also came armed with a notepad and tape recorder.

I walked in ten minutes early, and was immediately greeted warmly by Dr. Chopra who motioned me to sit down with him on easy chairs in the den-like lobby area. He asked how I was doing with my MS. I launched into a quickly paced history of how I became symptom free of the disease through holistic techniques. Dr. Chopra urged me to sit back saying, "We have time. Please, relax. I want to know all about your story." Forty-five minutes later, he smiled, congratulated me and said there was one thing he felt I needed to add to my regimen. He invited me up to his office where we sat next to each other in comfortable chairs. He reached for my arm, took my pulse, then commented on how strong and healthy it was. He, like other Ayurvedic doctors, can read a body's health chart from a pulse. Dr. Chopra then gave me a sound to repeat continuously and led me into a very deep twenty minute meditation, followed by ten minutes of relaxation before I could open my eyes.

After the meditation, I reported to him what it had been like. The construction noise outside became like background music. I smelled the room and saw a range of beautiful colors ending with a deep violet. I was plunged into infinity and visited by lots of thoughts that were sucked into a black hole. At times, I seemed to have wiper blades in my brain, sweeping away thoughts like rain drops. Coming out of the meditation, I felt euphoric and invigorated. Dr. Chopra urged me to add ten to twenty minutes of meditation to my schedule in the mornings and late afternoons.

As I walked to my car, I wanted to shout — "Finally, I understand what it means to be still and to merely observe my thoughts! Yes!! I've got it!" I immediately changed my meditation schedule and added ten minutes of Dr. Chopra's meditation, which I later learned was called the primordial sound technique. Eventually, a magical thing started to happen. I began to get answers without asking questions. Joan Borysenko, Ph.D. describes what was happening to me in her book, **Minding The Body, Mending the Mind**. "Meditation, through its ability to help us navigate the mind, restores that ability of inner listening, allowing us to make the best choices."[4] She explains that meditation's ability to calm the body "is the most important tool of self-healing and self-regulation."[5]

About one year after meeting Dr. Chopra, my husband and I both learned Transcendental Meditation (TM). Just as Dr. Chopra describes in his book, **Perfect Health**, we have both learned what it means to go beyond or transcend. My husband can lower his blood pressure by going beyond the pressures of the day to his own peaceful place. We can abort arguments by going beyond thoughts to loving silence.

I now do TM once or twice a day for 10 to 20 minutes. I relish the notion of simply *being*, because for the first time in my life, I have a sense of self. When I don't meditate, I notice increased stress and decreased concentration. TM sends healing wisdom and energy from deep within my soul to every cell of my body.

We would like you to leave this chapter only after trying a meditation. Please remember, there are many ways to meditate, there is not one right way — there is a right way for you. Enjoy as you discover the most effortless yet rewarding activity of non-activity in your personal healing realm.

---

[4]*J. Borysenko, MINDING THE BODY, MENDING THE MIND, © 1987 by Joan Borysenko, Ph.D. Reprinted by permission of Addison Wesley Longman, p. 35.*

[5]*Ibid., p. 36.*

Health-Esteem Meditation

⑦ The Pituitary Gland

⑥ The Pineal Gland

⑤ The Thyroid Gland

④ The Thymus Gland

③ The Adrenal Gland

② The Pancreas

① The Reproductive Glands

This drawing indicates the seven major energy centers (often referred to as vortexes or chakras) which are positioned around seven endocrine glands: 1) The lowest center is on the reproductive glands — representing survival; 2) The second energy source is on the pancreas in the abdominal region — representing sexual and personal creativity; 3) The third positions around the adrenal gland in the solar plexus region — representing emotional sensitivity; 4) The fourth revolves around the thymus gland in the chest — representing the heart center; 5) The fifth surrounds the thyroid gland in the neck — representing communication and expression; 6) The sixth flows through the pineal gland at the rear base of the brain — representing wisdom; 7) And the seventh, the highest energy center is located on the pituitary gland at the forward base of the brain — representing divine destiny and purpose. Each center is a powerful electrical field located around glands that stimulate hormonal output. Hormones regulate all of the body's functions, including the process of aging.

When our bodies are in balance, energy flows upward through the endocrine system giving us a sense of energy, vitality, and well-being. I would like you to visualize these energy centers as you meditate.

1) If you are comfortable in doing so, sit in a lotus position, as this drawing indicates, otherwise assume a relaxed sitting position in a chair with both feet flat on the floor.

2) Close your eyes and take five deep, cleansing breaths, bringing your breath upward from the first energy center and visualizing it traveling through all seven energy centers until it finally escapes through the crown of your head as you exhale audibly through your mouth. Repeat this five times: Breathe in through your nose, feel the breath travel through your energy centers. Then, breathe out through your mouth as your breath and all it carries with it is released into the atmosphere. Perhaps the breath carries a worry, a problem, a frustration, a bad memory — let it go as you exhale — the louder and more forceful your exhalation the better.

3) After the five cleansing breaths have opened your healing channel, silently fill the pathway with these words, "I am worth being healthy, I am worth being healthy..."

4) Repeat the phrase as often as you like while you settle into peaceful silence and calm. Let thoughts flow in and out of your mind without judgment, action or concern as you sit and observe and do nothing. If you feel a need to assist the departure of some thoughts from your mind, simply silently repeat, "I am worth being healthy, I am worth being healthy..." This will help your mind settle deeper into the peaceful calm of your own inner wisdom.

5) Maintain this state for 10 to 20 minutes. At the end of your meditation — stretch, breathe and smile. You have accomplished a wonderful meeting of your mind and body with its own wisdom.

Throughout the coming days, repeat this meditation or experiment with others of your choice. There is only one rule, and that is to MEDITATE AS OFTEN AS POSSIBLE.

Movement	Connection	Awareness
_____	_____	_____
_____	_____	_____
_____	_____	_____

Chapter 21

Sorry, This Call Can't Be Connected

Now that you are almost two-thirds of the way through this workbook, it's time to make a commitment check. Are you committed to doing the work? If your answer is yes, please go on to Chapter 22. If you're answer is no or any indecisive step in between yes and no, read on.

Perhaps you still have some saboteur voices in your head, feeding you excuses in the disguise of reasons why you cannot, must not, should not, will not do this work. Well, it's time to disarm those pesky saboteurs by taking away their ammunition.

First, fire back at those saboteurs with some positives. Here's a little speech you can try on for size.

"Listen up! I am worth being healthy. I am committing to the one part of healing I can take charge of — my thoughts and emotions — whether you like it or not. I am accessing the data bank of my own life, and you can't stop me. I made three Health-Esteem goals at the end of Chapter 2 and I am going to accomplish them. Health-Esteem can help me through any crisis. The author did it, and I CAN DO IT, TOO!"

Now, while you've got those saboteurs on the run with your positive attitude, steal their ammunition. The following is the SABOTEUR'S TOP 40 list of favorite excuses to keep you status quo and to prevent their biggest fear from happening — that you might change and grow away from needing them. These excuses are normally presented in a whining, defensive, self-righteous, nagging, guilt-ridden, totally offensive delivery. Here they are now, in the light of day where your mere glance can send them running for cover, since they've lost their job as your cover-up.

What's your cover-up? I know it's hard to come out from under all of the excuses that we have used to hide from ourselves and others. It's just as hard as coming out from under a warm comforter on a bitterly cold morning. It's so much nicer just to roll over and sleep for five more minutes...ten more minutes...

But, the bitter cold can also wake you up, invigorate you with fresh, new thinking and stimulate your movement toward fulfilling new directions in thought, action and accomplishment.

What happens in melodramatic movie moments when someone gets hysterical? They are *slapped* back into realistic thinking. What happens when our heart stops beating? It's given an electromagnetic *shock*. What happens when you've seen something so awful you can't get it out of your mind? You *shock* your senses with a splash of cold water to your face. When genteel ladies used to faint from distasteful news, what came to their rescue? A *shock* to their olfactory glands with a bitter sniff of smelling salts.

It's time to peel away your cover, *shock* your system, *slap* away your excuse or excuses. Check the ones you may have used on the list above (don't be surprised if you check all or most of them, we're only human). In the spaces provided write your favorite saboteur excuses that may not be on the list. Acknowledging and writing down your excuses begins to rob them of their power. It's like taking a giant can of RAID to the bugs that keep you running away in fear.

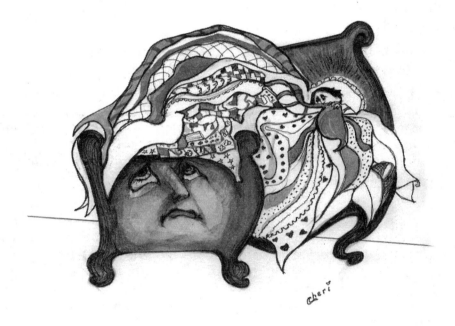

cheri

What's Your Cover-up?

1) _____

2) _____

3) _____

With your cover-up excuses fresh in your mind, let me give you two more examples of how those pesky saboteurs work. Tobes has a client with a bulging disc in her lower back. Divorced from a doctor, she's still married to his medical ways and so she goes to surgeon after surgeon to see if one can cut her pain out. MRI's keep revealing that surgery is not the answer, however. So, she gets cortisone shots which cover up the pain temporarily. Unfortunately, the long term effect of the cortisone, which only offers pain relief not a cure, is to cause actual degeneration in the area.

Tobes work with the woman has revealed several areas of exploration: 1) When working with a recommended masseuse, the woman will not allow her neck or head to be touched because she gets nauseous. She also doesn't want her hair messed up. She is so stiff and tight in this area, that she has blocked the energy all the way down her spine. Her defensive armor won't allow help in, however. 2) The woman is a therapist, who sits on a little hassock with no back support. She exacerbates the back tightness and tension daily by constantly leaning forward. 3) She's had eight pregnancies that didn't go full term.

The woman's attitude is: "I don't understand — my body's always been perfect." She's disappointed that there's no external fix. Tobes explains: "She wouldn't hear me until she got desperate. Certain people must get really desperate or frightened before they can process new information. Now we can make progress." Tobes' client is just beginning to ask the "W" questions that will allow her to connect her physical pain with all the other messengers/signals she's been ignoring, starting with "What's happening to my body?" The "Why" questions must follow: Why the miscarriages? Why won't I let my neck be touched? Why and what am I covering up?

Nancy recalls a patient that came to her absolutely convinced that she had diabetes, because she had a long history of diabetes in her family. Nancy's tests showed that while the woman was prone to the disease, she did not yet have it. She prepared a preventative diet and health plan that could possibly keep the young woman diabetes free and advised her, "Your history is not your destiny."

Certain she got through to the woman, Nancy was amazed when she didn't show up for her next appointment. Nancy called and was told, "I like you, and I appreciate what you did, but it's only a matter of time before I get diabetes." No connection could be made with such a strong fatalistic saboteur in place. She could not compute that her history was not her destiny — for her, it was, and unfortunately, it may be.

We've asked the question before in this workbook: What's the worst thing that can happen? Now, it's time to ask it again. What's the worst thing that can happen if I don't connect with my own Health-Esteem?

In the words of the 20-something woman who heard me speak and gushed, "I'm so glad I heard you, because I could have ended up just like you." To her, that was the worst thing that could have happened. She recognized my workaholic path of self-destruction.

My husband's 5-year-old great granddaughter Danielle put it a different way. I gave her parents my tape at Christmas time. Later that evening, Danielle was attracted to it, because my picture was on the cover. She took it to her room and started playing it. Half an hour later, she ran into the living room and said, "Mommy, Daddy, I'm going to make sure that my feelings have a place to go all the time to make me feel better, so when I get old, I won't be mean or sad."

On the opposite side of the coin, years ago a healthy, strapping young man came to Dr. Natalie and Elizabeth, extremely upset about his way of being in the world. He was gay and wanted desperately to find someone to take care of him. Within one year's time, he was in a wheelchair, yet he didn't have one physical problem that would have led him to the wheelchair. To him, the worst thing that could have happened was not being taken care of, so he put himself in a wheelchair.

We must never underestimate the power of our minds. Remember:

> No matter what emotional wound you may have experienced or what physical symptoms you may now be suffering, if you will make the connection between wound and symptoms and hook that connection into your awareness, healing can take place.

For all of you still battling a few very stubborn saboteurs, I close this chapter with a poem written years ago by Sydney Harris, former columnist for the Chicago Daily News:

The Difference Between Winners and Whiners

The difference between winners and whiners is —

The Whiner says, "I don't know, and I'm sure nobody else knows, either."

The Winner says, "Let's find out."

When a Whiner makes a mistake, he says, "It wasn't my fault."

When a Winner makes a mistake, he says, "I'm responsible, and I'm going to see what can be done to set things right."

When a Winner makes a commitment, he honors it.

When a Whiner makes a promise, he keeps it, if he doesn't change his mind."

A Winner feels responsible for more than his job calls for.

A Whiner says, "That's not my department."

A Winner says, "There ought to be a better way to do it."

A Whiner says, "That's the way it's always been done. Why change?"

A Winner paces himself and rarely bites off more than he can chew.

A Whiner has only two speeds — hysterical and lethargic.

A Winner says, "I could be a lot better, and I'm going to try to improve."

The Whiner says, "I'm not as bad as a lot of other people."

Movement	Connection	Awareness
_____	_____	_____
_____	_____	_____
_____	_____	_____

129

Looking Inside For Answers

If you're not convinced by now, I want to reiterate that everybody has places, way down deep inside that contain secrets that need to be revealed, places where they need to be seen and loved despite not being perfect — *because* they are not perfect. When those dark places are illuminated, pain is released and answers come forth. But how, you may ask, do you start finding those inside hiding places, and how do you find the courage to expose what's waiting there?

We often find the inside place by being in outside pain and realizing we've been there before. Remember the repeats in Chapter 18 — "Tired of repeats, change the channel"? That's what we're talking about. For instance, Nancy shares how a disappointing love affair helped her wake up to inside pain that was directing her into repeat relationship mistakes.

Nancy: *I remember when I broke up with Rod — he was a real different path for me — the first guy I dated that was older than me and not Jewish. I dated him for six months and it was bliss — then at six months he turned around and ran from me — frightened. For the next two months I just stood back and watched and waited to see what would happen. That was very different for me. When I realized the relationship wasn't going anywhere, I went through about three days of pain — my emotions were flat. I'm used to being engaged with the world, but now I was flat and mopey. On the third day I woke up and asked myself, "Who can live like this?" Being in that flat place was so much worse than facing whatever the pain was. I had to live the pain, move through it, and go on with my life.*

I went and talked to a friend about it — and I cried with this wonderful friend like I had never cried She was one of the first people in my life with whom I felt like I could really be seen — just naked — with all my raw emotions hanging out there unedited and without apology. I cried and cried and I said, Oh thank you for listening to me and letting me do this. She said, "Oh my God, I'm so grateful to finally be able to do something for you." And I thought Wow, you mean someone really wants to do something for me for a change. It was an awakening for me and wonderfully healing. To think that I could actually find a place inside of me that I wasn't aware of, bring it out and actually share it with someone. Everybody has those places and wants to be seen even in those places — seen and loved.

It was healing to accept that I was vulnerable, and to move away from being only who I thought I was supposed to be to the world. That allowed me to acknowledge information from deep inside of me and to move forward.

So, one way of dislodging answers from painful memories locked within is to repeatedly run into painful experiences in your outside life. Some other ways to look inside for answers are listed below:

Reading

There's a reason self-help and motivational books are so popular. They work! We do learn by example, and it is comforting to know what other's have experienced. One of the healthiest things we can do with our fellow human beings is to share our stories.

When a friend recently diagnosed with MS and still locked in denial first read my book, **Head Over Healing In Love**, she called me in tears. She said, "I could have written this book. I hope you don't mind, but I just forgot it was about you and put my own name in place of yours. It opened up so many things for me. I'm ready now to try everything you did. I'm so thankful. But, I'm sorry, I know your book's about you, not me."

By this time, I was crying. "Oh, no, Sandy," I replied, "my book is about anyone and everyone who relates to the words on the page. I encourage all of you to substitute your name for the subject's name whenever you are reading something that touches you deeply.

There is a complete list of recommended books at the end of this workbook. When you're on the healing path, you'll also find that recommendations will come your way, often with just the information you need at that moment. Synchronicity is a part of the process. Answers surround us, but they often do not become visible until we are able and willing to see and hear them. Books help open our senses to the information around and within us.

Listening

Answers can only be heard when we listen. Chapter 20 discussed the art of listening inward — meditation. I used meditation to help me reconnect with my forgotten childhood. I was aware that fears and anxieties from the time I was a little girl poured into my life daily. To heal, I needed to unite with that part of myself. I called her Little Judy (L.J.) and started attending to *her* wounds. After closing my eyes, taking my deep breaths, and sitting in peaceful silence, I visualized that L.J. was with me in my favorite place of escape - sitting under an oak tree gazing into a beautiful pond. She was always wrapped up tight in a ball, holding herself with her head down on her knees. She never looked at me. I held her, but she didn't respond to my touch. In one meditation I asked her about hugging. This was her reply.

I want to, but I feel too stiff. It might hurt. If you hug me now, you might hurt me later...or leave. What will I have to do for you in return? Hugs cost stuff. They get you in trouble. I just don't want to be touched unless I'm sure it's okay.

Listening and writing often go hand in hand. I would write in my diary or in my computer journal the answers that came to me in meditation. Then I would write down my interpretations without study or thought, but from my feelings. This is how I interpreted L.J.'s words:

No wonder that as an adult I felt I had to earn love, to prove myself, to be someone else or something in addition to myself. Since my youth, I had learned that "hugs cost stuff." I had buried the memories of what the hugs cost.

I recognize now that the cost was my ability to enjoy touching and being touched. I had to learn to enjoy my own touch and to allow my body to receive and enjoy the touch of others without feeling I owed them something. I started by mentally hugging L.J. each and every day.

Internal listening has helped me to recognize the many influences in my life that have always been there. When I have the courage to stand up for myself come hell or high water, it's my grandmother Dee Dee. When I'm feeling deprived and whiny, it's my teenager. When I'm feeling scared, lonely and frightened, it's my very young self. When I'm feeling self-critical, very sorry for myself and completely without confidence, it's my judgmental inner mom. I believe we all have voices of life-long influential people in our heads, guiding, chiding or deriding us. By matching names and ages to those voices, I began to understand their motivations, and thereby decipher helpful from sabotaging self-advice.

In addition to listening inward, I encourage you to practice your everyday listening skills. Meditation has also taught me to be a better listener. I am now anxious to learn from those I speak with, to learn, not only from their words, but from their tone, inflection, eye contact and body language. I can respond completely when I have listened to and taken in the whole person.

A third form of extremely important listening is listening to your body. When I got up this morning and went to my computer, I felt tired, achey and still bothered by yesterday's scratchy sore throat and a bit of congestion. Normally after two hours, I would break and exercise and take a walk.

Today, my body said, "No, I want to be pampered. I'd like some hot tea, a nourishing breakfast and I need to take it easy today." That message would never have gotten through to me years ago. As a result, a cold hung around for three weeks. Now a cold is out of my system in three days.

Writing

No matter how you felt about your skills as a writer in school, writing now can help save your life. This is writing for your eyes, body, spirit and soul only. Getting your thoughts on paper turns them into something concrete — something on which you can take action or make a choice to discard or keep. Writing can pull words directly from your heart that were literally aching to get out. Here are just a few of the ways that writing can help you:

1) Inner Child writing: I recommend the book, **The Self Parenting Program** by John K. Pollard, III. One of the first ways I contacted L.J. was to write down my questions to her with my right hand (I'm right handed) and answers from her with my left hand. (You would do the opposite if you are left handed) I had no idea if my left hand would be able to write, let alone be legible. It could, it was and the messages were enlightening. Eventually, I could write for L.J. on the computer, which definitely sped up our conversations. While I was doing this work, I kept a picture of myself at age seven by my computer to help me remember what it was like to be me at that age.

2) Perhaps nothing is more helpful than your own private journal. You can ease into this concept by designating a section of your Day Book for personal musings. The contents of your Journal can be very free form: How you're feeling that day; moments of awareness, movement or connection; memories that come to mind; events or interactions you want to record; exercises from this workbook or others. One of the most important things is to simply keep a daily record of your thoughts and feelings, so that you can begin to interpret the flow of your days. Your Journal, whether on the written page or on your computer is your way of communicating with yourself. It sounds so simple, but ironically, most of us are alienated from ourselves. That is one of the major reasons why our bodies act up — to get our attention. When you check in, you may be given some revealing, healing information to write down.

3) Write down interviews, memories and conversations with family members to begin to put together your emotional family tree. (See Chapter 24.)

Suggestion: I recommend that you buy yourself a very special Journal. The very act sends a message to yourself that you are worth the gift, and that your thoughts are deserving of being recorded.

Dreaming

While we're on the subject of Journals, another very helpful one is a Dream Journal. This is a notepad or book that you keep beside your bed to jot down what you remember about your dreams. Often when we begin the journey to self-awareness, health-esteem and self-healing, our subconscious provides directions through our dreams. I think of my dreams as neon billboards of my subconscious, flashing out another answer or life lesson that I'm ready to process. My dream interpretations reflect Jungian philosophy, in that all the characters in my dreams mirror something about my personality. I also put my dreams into the context of whatever happened in my life the night of and the week of my dream. Writing down the dream helps me to better analyze its content when I'm ready.

I've had many dreams that relate to my healing from MS — none more telling than this one.

The week before my dream, I was experiencing several unsettling confrontations regarding my MS research. I was beginning to contact other MS patients for possible interviews; some were quite hesitant to embrace the concept of "healing" relating to *their* disease.

The resignation and negativity in these conversations caused me to doubt my own wellness convictions.

My vision started to become blurry for short periods of time. As uncertainty crept into my purpose, both of my legs began to ache, and dare I say it — to tingle. I hesitantly told my husband about the return of my symptoms, hoping for some comforting words. Instead, I had to bring it up three times, and each time he changed the subject. A fight ensued in which I called him uncaring and insensitive to my needs. Shortly afterwards, I went to bed and had this dream:

A gorgeous male doctor checked me into a spacious, private hospital suite. He sat by my bedside, holding my hand, stroking my hair and looking comfortingly into my eyes. I felt warm, nurtured and safe until he got into my bed saying, "Now, I'm going to make love to you."

I cringed, pushed him away and yelled for him to get out of the room. Simultaneously, the nurse walked in and said my husband was outside. I was relieved, but soon horrified to see that the man who walked through the door was not my husband, but instead, the worst memory of my father.

He was weaving from the effects of alcohol. His clothes were disheveled, his face menacing and mean, and his eyes beady. I shook awake with an exclamation of, "No!"

I was too upset to interpret this dream immediately, but with time, I learned many things. The doctor in the dream was my animus — my internal embodiment of a male being. He was a healer. In the dream, I was comfortable with him as long as his love was expressed in the form of nurturing and healing. However, I was enormously uncomfortable with him when he expected me to be a receptive, loving woman. When the doctor started to make love to me, I cringed and flashed back to my first female sexual role model — my mother. She felt men demanded sex when they were drunk and *uncaring*. I fell asleep that night feeling Jack had been *uncaring*. When faced with a sexual aspect to my dream, I became my mother, and so — in walked my father.

This dream reminded me that until I resolved the sexual issues within myself, I would revert to my original sexual role models — my mother and my father. On the positive side, I could now confidently call upon the healer within my own body.

Dream Exploration

1) Keep a dream diary or tape recorder beside your bed. Upon waking from a dream, change position as little as possible, and don't get out of bed. Immediately write down or record as much as you remember about your dream.

2) What was the mood of your dream?

3) Who was in your dream?

4) What actions were taken?

5) Did you see colors?

6) Were there symbols of some kind?

7) How did the dream make you feel?

8) Write down the dream like a story, recalling as many details in the order they occurred as possible.

9) Try to remember if you were preoccupied with anything before going to sleep.

10) How was your body/health/physiology represented in your dream?

The next day while the dream is still fresh in your mind, try some interpretation. Ask yourself what the characters in the dream are saying about you and your life? What do they represent? If you are having a recurring dream, look for some aspect of your life that hasn't been sorted out or a problem that is unresolved.

Remember: ***Dreams Represent Our Feelings In A Visual Way***. Try to attach feelings to the events and characters in your dreams, and think about what those feelings mean in your life.

Connection

Just as I had allowed my workaholism to cut me off from all the other aspects of myself, I also allowed it to cut me off from my environment and the world around me. I had no understanding of community, which I define as "the sense of knowing that my life matters to someone else beyond myself." I did not realize how things happening to other people impacted me, how community and world events touched me. I viewed the rest of life like it was coming from a television. I could turn it off and on at my discretion. It was not personal. It was outside of me, and I didn't have to let the outside in. Right? Wrong!!

The world gets in, but when unacknowledged it enters subconsciously through stress, anxiety and negative reactions. When I didn't recognize energy outside of myself, I often felt tired and found it difficult to simply push myself up out of a chair.

When I sought to protect myself from outsider invasion by not making eye contact with strangers, I found myself increasingly isolated. I have now learned to take in other people with a look, a smile, a word or acknowledgment. I see so much more about myself and others and realize I am not so alone.

This very simple lesson of connection was extremely hard for me to learn — primarily because I didn't have to do anything to learn except accept that I'm connected. We are not separate from our community and world around us; we are innately connected. Acknowledging one connection leads to many connections that give our lives purpose, direction, meaning, fulfillment, enjoyment, energy, answers, awareness and most of all "the sense that our lives matter to someone beyond ourselves."

Perhaps part of our need to cut ourselves off from community comes from the distorted way media insists on pumping it into our lives — through murder and mayhem. The June 15, 1997 "New York Times Magazine" reported that on February 26, 1997, there were no major catastrophes anywhere in America. There was time, they noted, to "explore the local economy, or the performance of government, or cultural attractions, or the good works of volunteers and the needs of the poor. Yet 72 of the lead stories at 100 stations in 35 states were about crime and violence, mostly murder." One third of all the news on local TV that night dealt with crime. We do not have to take in the distortions of the media. We have a choice. I suggest that it's far better to make your own connection with life and participate than to sit passively and absorb one image after another of homicidal violence.

Connection Exploration

1)   Eliminate watching the late night news before going to sleep.

2)   Experiment with a "Media Fast." For one week, listen to music instead of news or talk radio in your car. Turn off the televisions in your house and explore other pursuits — family, friends, hobbies, movies, theatre, sports, reading, museums...Do not read the newspaper or news magazines for one week. Stay off the internet if possible. SIMPLIFY YOUR LIFE!! You may have accomplished these tasks when on vacation. Now you are allowing yourself a vacation at home — free from media anxiety, canned laughter, overly loud commercials, and a barrage of images being fired at you to trigger false needs, impulse buys, and hyped expectations of life.

You may want to incorporate a "Media Fast" in your life monthly or quarterly, dependent on how often you need to flush media-created anxiety out of your life.

3)   Go back and take a look at your community and world connections in Chapter 10. For five days, become more conscious of the secondary relationships in your life, sales and service people, etc.
Make eye contact with the grocery checker or bagger.
Notice the names on sales clerks badges, and call them by name.
Smile, wave or say "good morning" to the jogger you pass every day.
Compliment the waiter, waitress or busboy who has gone out of his or her way. Better yet, connect with the waiter or waitress who is ignoring you, perhaps because they're having the world's worst day. You may turn it around. The point is to come out of your protected space and connect with some of the people you may take for granted.

For just one of the five days, jot down the number of people you come in contact with during every activity. When possible list their name and a brief description.(Example: Lancome sales girl, Jackie, perky brunette)

People Pad — 24 Hours Of Connections

Who	Name	Description

Movement	Connection	Awareness

Chapter 23

Learning To Have A Disease/Crisis

Lessons of example, lessons of action, lessons of living *do* speak louder than lessons of books and words. I was always a good student of whatever I studied, but all of the various classroom hours and all the stimulation of my absorbent intellect could not overpower the lessons that were absorbed by my body — silent, secret lessons etched into my body from my early life at home. Those lessons would color my actions, make my choices, shade my relationships, mold my workaholic career, and predispose me to work myself into a disease before I had my 35th birthday.

Everyone's childhood lessons are different. I will give you a few examples of lessons of action and living from my early home life that led to some sick-making behavior and patterns in my life. I remember being a little girl and repeatedly hearing my parents screaming at each other late into the night. My father was drunk, angry and vulgar, screaming accusations at my mom as he demanded sexual attention. My mother was sad, helpless and disgusted. I heard his grunts and her groans. Lesson learned: To be very still, not to breathe, to be horrified, to feel shameful whenever I heard screaming or when I was exposed to the sights or sounds of sex.

I learned to smile and put on a happy face to hide shameful secrets at home. After countless shameful scenes in public, I learned that screaming is vulgar and humiliating and that when something terrible was happening to me, mind over matter would make it go away. After stopping my father from committing suicide at the age of 12, I knew I was responsible for my parents' lives and happiness. I also learned the meaning of drama in my life and began to see things polarized the way my parents did. Life was either good or bad, happy or sad, black or white. There was no middle ground.

There were also positive lessons from my childhood. I learned to be an achiever and a performer. I learned to be a survivor — strong, self-sufficient, and versatile — and somehow, I picked up a sense of humor.

Later in my life, when embarking upon my healing journey, I learned from authors and teachers such as Dr. Deepak Chopra, Dr. Harold Friedman and various alternative healing professionals that all those emotional events in my childhood had corresponding physical components. I began to understand that thoughts turn into chemicals that can cause feelings of heartache, panic, weakness in the immune system, and numerous physical complaints. I then started to question where in my body had I stored all the fear, sadness, guilt and secrecy of my childhood. What were they doing to my immune system? What could that mean to my physical health?

I not only had to go back and find what I had not allowed myself to remember, I had to examine those thoughts to find out if they were even mine to own. In many cases I was playing out my parents' thoughts, beliefs, emotions and patterns. I had to separate myself from their thinking which had embedded itself deeply enough in my system to make me sick. Why continue to live my parents' pain or to abide by lessons they never intended to impart to me in the first place? Understanding the answer to that question led to even more questions which I recommend you ask of any life crisis you may now face. Why me? Why this crisis/disease? What do I need to understand? What do I need to learn? What have I been doing to damage myself? What can I do to stop damaging myself? How can I learn to live a happy, healthy life?

I also learned to ask those same questions and more regarding the environment in which I was raised and my cultural background.

You will find as you ask these questions that it's all about perspective and the way you were taught to see, feel, hear, and think. Tobes explains the importance of understanding these perspectives when dealing with diversity in a group.

TOBES: *A word that means nothing to a Caucasian can be loaded for a Black person. There was an Indiana woman in one of my groups who talked about the way her family communicated. It would more accurately be described as non-communication unless someone offered something. For instance, she had a brother who had gotten divorced a year before, but she couldn't ask him about that because he didn't tell her he got divorced. The family knew about the divorce indirectly — but everyone knew not to talk about it unless he brought it up. 50 to 60 percent of the people who participate in my groups from the midwest are from this kind of background. They've grown up in an intact family with no communication except the superficial. They never answer how they really are. The answer to how you are is "Well, here's what I did today." They talk about what they're doing but not about how they are.*

In terms of cultural background, I was born in 1950, the start of a decade summed up in one word: suppressed. Americans lived through three recessions in the 1950's. Following the lead of President Eisenhower, who maintained a calm American exterior by avoiding political change,

Americans simply ignored the financial and psychological toll of the Cold War, how extensive and hidden America's disadvantaged population was, and the silent shame of race relations.

The 1950's were happy days, because things people didn't want to look at were simply swept underneath America's new multi-blend carpets. In those "simpler" times, everything was black and white. There were good or bad girls; communism was the enemy of democracy; failure was the alternative to "Keeping up with the Jones's." Mothers could stay home rather than work, and 60% of Americans attended church regularly. From the perspective of the media and popular television shows like "*The Mickey Mouse Club*" and icon mom and dads like "*Ozzie and Harriet*," violence and drug abuse were unknown. Bad things didn't happen.

I know that I learned to have a disease by absorbing the pain, disappointments and actions of others while I scripted my own actions to be perfect. Like the '50s into which I was born, I suppressed and repressed to look good on the outside, no matter the cost.

Since my health crisis in 1985, however, my research has been inward, to understand the one part of healing I can take charge of — my thoughts and emotions. For me, finding emotional prescriptions for my MS symptoms has been exhilarating and health-preserving. It is a very personal journey that will enable all who undertake it to discover their own answers in life rather than living by someone else's rules.

Lessons From Your Decade

Take a moment to work with the *Lessons From Your Decade* chart on the following page. Fill in the decade in which you were born and think about some of the major events of that time and how they affected your thoughts, feelings and actions. List two or three major world events, heroes, cultural happenings and communications breakthroughs such as TV in the '50s and fax machines in the '80s. Then put some of the pivotal people in your life into the context of their birth decade. Think about three marker events that froze a moment in time for you. (i.e., assassination of President Kennedy, the Berlin Wall coming down, the death and world mourning of Princess Di.) Contrast those events to a parent perhaps born in 1920. (i.e., the Depression, WWII, FDR's death)

For baby boom and Vietnam era women, the following are questions that came to my mind when judging society's impact on personal satisfaction.

How many of us, going for it all, lost the basic ability to feel? How many of us, with our new liberating opportunities in hand, determined to make it right for our sisters and lost sight of ourselves? How many of us, born into the sexual revolution, sacrificed trust, nurturing, intimacy and love? How many of us, driven to break down barriers and smash through glass ceilings, had to crash in order to come face to face with a self we didn't know? How many of us were so *out there*, waging the fight for equal pay, status, recognition, and rights that we abandoned our insides — abandoned our selves? How many of us left home for careers and found ourselves butting heads with our male bosses and counterparts until we took up the masculine way and sacrificed our feminine selves? How many of us, besieged by female ailments, shut down our womanhood, and then found ourselves crying for someone, anyone, to take care of us, so we would have more time to compete and accomplish?

Lessons From Your Decade Chart

	Major World Events	Heroes	Cultural Music, Dance Movies	Communications
Your Birth Decade				
Parents' Birth Decade				
Grandparents' Birth Decade				
Boss/Co-workers' Birth Decade				
Spouse/Partner's Birth Decade				
Other				

Baby boom and Vietnam era men have lots of questions, too, including: How can I be strong and sensitive at the same time? Is it so bad to want to take advantage of the Old Boy's Network? How do I nurture and provide at the same time? What do women want from me? If I appreciate or compliment a woman am I going to get slapped with sexual harassment? Can I love and accept love from a woman who's more successful than I am? If I'm not the strong one, am I not a man? Is what I've been working for all my life not really me? My dad wasn't there a lot for me and I turned out OK, so why should I be different? How do I balance and achieve and grow and change and keep up all at the same time? Do I really have to learn to talk about all the things I was taught and worked so hard to ignore about myself? Do I have to get in touch with my feelings to find love?

I know countless men and women in their 40s who come to a crossroads of catastrophe. It could be relationship, family, or employment-oriented, but often it's illness — a cry for help from abused, ignored, disassociated bodies. A cry that led me and is now leading you to Health-Esteem.

As we approach the Millennium, radical change is occurring at breakneck speed — Generation X, hip hop music juxtaposed with the revival in popularity of country western music, the internet, Bill Gates, HMO's, mega-mergers, the national budget deficit, Timothy McVeigh and the Oklahoma City bombing, diversity, wellness, and the rejection of accepted systems. Practically every socio-economic structure that we have considered to be definitive of our culture and heritage is coming under question, scrutiny, upheaval and restructuring including our political, judicial, medical, welfare, governmental, educational, defense and free enterprise systems. To make matters even more complicated, all of this is happening on a global scale. We can have E-mail conversations with a few of our new, close international friends as easily as having a cup of coffee with our next door neighbor.

To handle all of this we must be grounded in self-knowledge. We must know where our thoughts and feelings are coming from and if they belong to us or someone to whom we'd like to return them.

Memories Have Feelings, Too

On the following chart are places for you to list good and bad memories from your childhood and associated feelings. The purpose of this experiment is to find lessons you learned as a child that you may either now want to rewrite or discard. For instance, I have a memory of my dad getting drunk on major holidays. My lesson was that good times can suddenly turn into bad times, and that I must be vigilant. I am rewriting that lesson now as I learn that good times stand alone, and bad times are not inevitable. I am learning to simply enjoy and not to wait for the boogie man. Now, it's your turn. Following the chart is a prompter sheet that may help a few memories and feelings fall on to this sheet.

Good Memories/ Lessons	Feelings	Bad Memories/ Lessons	Feelings

Memory Prompters

1) Birthday parties, celebrations, recognitions, presents — what comes to mind?

2) Major holidays — were they good, bad, boring, dreaded, anticipated, everything or nothing like you expected...

3) When was the first time you were punished and how, for what?

4) What was your first big accomplishment? How did your family react?

5) What was your first big disappointment or failure? How did your family react?

6) What was the first thing you did that made your mom and dad angry?

7) What was the first thing your parents did that made you angry?

8) Brother and sister memories — their birth, any competition, relationships, jealousies, ???

9) Who was your first girl or boyfriend?

10) What was your first knowledge of sex? How did you learn about sex?

11) What, when and where was your first sexual encounter?

12) When was the first time you were: Scared? Fearful? Anxious? Sad? Curious? Angry? Shameful? Guilty? Proud? Embarrassed?

13) When did you experience your first broken heart?

14) How did you learn to play? To exercise? To enjoy life?

15) Did you sing as a child?

16) Did you like school?

17) What was mealtime like in your family?

18) Did you go on family vacations? Did you like them?

19) What was the best part of your childhood? The worst part?

20) How did changing schools, graduating, moving away from friends affect you?

21) Were your parents happy? Did they teach you about feelings?

22) Did you feel loved as a child? Did you feel secure?

23) When was the first time you wanted to get away from home?

24) Were you prepared to leave home when you did?

25) What warnings did your parents give you?

Childhood Memory Meditation

If you are having trouble dredging up memories — try to visualize your childhood home with the help of this meditation.

Sit in a comfortable chair, completely relaxed with both feet flat on the floor. Close your eyes, take five deep breaths and imagine your mind as a blank screen. One by one, bring on the rooms of your family home and explore them. What was your kitchen like? Was there tile on the floor? What color were the cupboards? Were there windows? Curtains? Was there a table or kitchen counters where you ate quick meals? What does it smell like? Where's the refrigerator, the stove? Now travel from the kitchen to the living room, dining room, family room, bathrooms... and visualize each room? Put in the furniture, the wall coverings, the paintings, pictures and decorative items. Go into your parents room? How does it look? How do you feel being there? Go into your siblings rooms? Finally go into your own room. Jump on the bed. Look at your stuff. Remember what it was like to be there in your own little world or the world you shared with a brother and sister. What did you think about in that room? What did you plan, dream about and want out of life? Slowly walk out of your house and across the street and look at your house from afar? Imagine the people coming and going from your house. Imagine the last time you left the house. Slowly take five deep, cleansing breaths and open your eyes. Now, try the prompter list, and in the spaces below list some of the lessons you remember taking with you from that childhood home into your adulthood.

Some of my lessons were:

1) _____

2) _____

3) _____

4) _____

5) _____

Movement	Connection	Awareness
_____	_____	_____
_____	_____	_____
_____	_____	_____

A Note About Grief

When you bump into some of your memories, you will probably experience pain. Remember the words from Lynn Andrews' *Power Deck* that "grief introduces you to parts of yourself that are not yet healed...It is said that the seeds of wisdom and enlightenment are planted within the wounds of grief."

Sadness is triggered by past memories when they represent unfinished business. Young minds have defense systems against pain too intense to bear. The system buries the pain in our bodies. Unfortunately, the pain lingers in our bodies where it can make us sick, until we find a way to release it — and there is only one way. We must find and feel the pain.

I'm sure you've noticed after you've had a good cry that you suddenly feel more free, less burdened — better. It's a travesty that so many men have not been allowed to cry. It's a natural release that is neither masculine nor feminine — it's human. Allow yourself a good cry. I visualize pain floating out of my eyes on tear boats. I am glad to see the pain depart. You can cry alone. But, don't be ashamed. Rant and rave if you need to. Flail your arms, kick your legs, LET IT GO!!!

You may be frustrated to still be carrying around pain from past wounds. Perhaps you'd like to talk about it to the people involved, but they may not be available. Write them a letter. It's not the letter receipt that matters, it's the action of getting your feelings out.

Perhaps you feel sad, but still feel blocked. Meditate about the event. Imagine yourself at the age you experienced the event. Be that age, visualize what you did, where you were, who you were with, what your life was like. Concentrate on how you felt.

Remember, by experiencing the sadness, you are actually saying good-bye to the pain. Until I was 40 years old, I never said good-bye when relationships ended in my life. I used euphemisms: "See ya' later; ba-bye; so long; until we meet again; it's been great; see ya' around; here's lookin' at you, babe." I was leaving the door open and refusing to close the chapter. The result was, I didn't have to accept the ending, the sadness, my fear of being alone, my panic that there would never be anyone else. The irony is, that saying good-bye would have actually cleared the emotional garbage out of the way much faster, so that I could start fresh, open the way for new people, and even learn to like to be alone for awhile.

During intense periods of grief, it also helps to talk to professionals; therapists who can help us through the difficult passages of life. In addition, grief recovery groups and groups dealing with your particular loss or crisis are also available. It's always simultaneously surprising and comforting to know just how many people are also experiencing the pain you felt was so unique. Their ways of dealing with the pain may illuminate an idea that was dormant in your brain.

Please, don't be afraid of grief or of reaching out for help when you are experiencing grief. It is truly a vehicle for rebirth.

Chapter

Emotional Family Tree

Everyone has an emotional family tree. It is the root system of all of your thoughts and feelings, and it branches out in unexpected ways. My grandmother was a passionate woman, and she had a string of husbands to prove it. My mother resented the parade of partners my grandmother brought into her life and became withdrawn, shy and even disgusted by anything sexual. Both of those attitudes were imprinted into my psyche and had quite a conflict with each other, until I established my own feelings about sex and intimacy. I had to find where my feelings came from, from whom I learned them, and whether or not I wanted to keep those feelings or find a new way of behaving and thinking.

Your emotional family tree is made up of all the relatives and influential people who taught you ways of thinking, feeling and behaving as you grew up. The key is to know when you're feeling fear, is it your mom's or is it yours? To whom do your feelings and thoughts belong? Your dad? Your grandmother? Your school teacher? Societal peer pressure? Find the sources and either give them back if they don't work for you, or own them. Take it from me, thoughts and emotions that we live with, even though they make us feel uncomfortable, can also make us sick. They throw us into sick-making patterns.

The reason you need to chart your family emotional history is to change hurtful, negative patterns in your life. The work is not about finding family members to blame, however. It's about discovering some "Ah ha! moments" when you suddenly understand, "so that's why I don't like peas." Or, more importantly, "so that's why my mind goes numb when people shout at each other — so that's why I think or feel that way." Those moments help us all to become accountable for ourselves rather than victims of somebody else's thinking.

Unfortunately, while we may become conscious of why we think or feel a particular way, our bodies don't automatically follow along at the same pace. For years I've known about my mother's sexual disgust and frigidity, but as much as I wanted to, I couldn't stop my body from shuddering when touched a certain way. My mind wanted to say yes, but my body said no.

According to my chiropractor, Nancy, that's where chiropractic and homeopathy come in:

They can actually shift emotional patterning in your body. Every event that happens to you whether it's physical, emotional or chemical is imprinted on your nervous system. Without your nervous system creating a record of an event, you have no clue that it happened to you, or that you're supposed to do anything about it now or when it happens again. Being essentially conservative, the central nervous system will take similar events and send them through the same pathway, which eventually directs your actions or reactions. Over time that creates patterns of behavior. The problem is that you lose the individuality of particular events, since your reaction will be the same even though the events are slightly dissimilar. That's when you might take someone's remarks a certain way — only to have them say, "Wow, that's not what I meant at all." Chiropractic and homeopathy can erase those patterns and allow you to have new responses that are owned, created and delivered by your individual conscious thinking, without being tinged by the thinking of Aunt Matilda, Uncle Edward, Granny Grace, or most frequently your own mom, dad and siblings.

It's important to get as much understanding of key family members who had a lot to do with your emotional imprinting as possible. The rest of this chapter will be devoted to methods of getting and evaluating that information. But first a warning: If while charting the emotional currents in your family, you bump into a memory or topic that is big and painful, don't hesitate to get help deciphering the information. While sometimes painful, the insights you gain from doing this work can change just about everything in your life.

A 35-year-old woman, Diana, after listening to my Health-Esteem tape wrote to me, "Now, I understand how my life was affected as a child and how I was repeating the same patterns. This knowledge has helped me get to know my friends better, too. Like me, they all have issues. We just never discussed them before because we were scared and ashamed to bring them up in a friendship. We feared being judged and not accepted. We just talked about fashion and fun. Then, at a dinner party, I played your tape. We used it to find a new way of talking to each other filled with honesty instead of patterned responses that were safe and based on *what we should say*. We're not only getting to know ourselves, we're also helping each other."

Interview Your Family

The quickest way to put together your emotional family tree is to interview your family members. I simply told my family that I didn't want to rely on my aging memory to contain all of our stories. I also encouraged them to talk about their associated feelings in order to really bring the stories to life. I wrote down all of my questions beforehand, so I wouldn't get lost when I became drawn into the memories. I tried typing the answers to my questions, but the keyboard noise separated me too much from my interviewee. So, I asked my family if they minded me using a tape recorder. Videotaping family interviews creates a record for future generations.

When you interview your family, remain non-judgmental and avoid a critical voice or tone. Stories will be more forthcoming if you are an interested listener showing empathy, sympathy, amusement or whatever is appropriate. Be responsive, make eye contact, show that you care with a nod or an understanding, "Hm-m-m-m." Have a pad and pen ready, so that if a comment jogs something within you that you want to follow up on later, you won't forget. Concentrate only on the person being interviewed and not how it affects you. There's plenty of time for evaluation later. If you can, interview only one family member at a time. That way you won't get involved with conflicting memories and the ensuing arguments those can bring. Be sure and follow a line of questioning through to its natural conclusion. Don't feel that you have to stick to your planned format. Be prepared for surprises, and listen carefully so you'll know what to ask next. The following sample questions are merely to get you started. Be creative.

TOBES

Self Discovery process drawing: A process drawing comes from the image of the feelings you are having at a particular moment in time. As Elizabeth, Nancy and I discussed the many roles in each of our lives and the importance of self-awareness, Tobes drew this reflection.

Sample Interview

1) What was the happiest time of your childhood?

2) What's the most important thing in life to you?

3) What's your greatest accomplishment in life?

4) How did you learn about sex?

5) What's the worst thing that ever happened to you?

6) What's the best thing about love?

7) What would you change about your life if you could?

8) What or who has disappointed you most?

9) Who were your role models?

10) Did you feel loved as a child?

11) How did you feel about your parents? Were they happy?

12) What is the most important thing a person can accomplish in life?

13) When have you been the happiest?

14) How do you feel about your health?

15) How do you express anger? Disappointment? Frustration? Joy?

16) Have you ever been jealous?

17) What are you afraid of?

18) What will happen to you when you die?

19) What do you want to be remembered for in life?

20) Is spirituality important to you?

21) How did you feel about having children? How did children change your life? Are you happy with how you raised your children?

When doing your interviews, get into values, morals — the ethical issues of life. How do they feel about capital punishment, gay rights, equality of the sexes, health, abortion, assisted suicide, politics? Ask how they felt about key developments in *your* life.

Do not respond to any of the answers no matter how they make you feel. During the interview, it's not about you, it's about them. Do not argue. Any answer is acceptable. If possible, don't interview your subject for over two to three hours, as the process can be very tiring. Split up your interview sessions over a few days or even over a few weekends. Test your tape recorder first, and make sure it's picking up your subject's voice.

How To Evaluate the Interviews:

1)   I found it very helpful to transcribe the interviews so that I could see the words on paper as well as hearing them.

2)   Listen over and over for the intonations, the pauses, the things that are said between the lines.

3)   If you have videotaped the interviews, watch for facial expressions and body language. Often the words and the bodies will be giving you different answers. You can also do this during the interview.

4)   Notice what you are feeling when you hear or read the answers.

Does the interviewee trigger the same feelings or different feelings in you? Is it a feeling you recognize? Is it a feeling you want to keep, or would you rather change your own behavior?

5)   Do you detect patterns of behavior in your family?

6)   Can you begin to follow those patterns back to where they may have originated?

7)   Does it make you feel better to know that you learned your feelings and thoughts and that you have a choice to unlearn or relearn them to suit who you are today and not who you were then?

8)   Can you begin to see places where there need to be boundaries between your feelings and theirs?

What If You Don't Want To or Can't Talk To Family Members?

Many people are more visual than verbal and can't stand the thought of interviewing anyone. That's fine. You can still create your emotional family tree.

1)   Go back and locate memories that have pictures. Go through as many family photographs as you can — particularly those relating to your childhood. Look at your family house or houses and car or cars. What was it like where you lived?

2)   When you look at the pictures ask several questions:
      What does the picture make you feel? What does it bring up?
      Check the picture against your senses...sight, sound, smell, touch,
      taste — does anything come to mind?

3)   What was communication like in your home? Who taught you about
      communication? Did you spend a lot of time talking? Did you share
      feelings about things?

4)   Do any pictures bring lessons to mind? What were you taught about
      physical activity, food, cooking, nourishment, sexual attitudes? What
      was your emotional life like? Who did you perceive as powerful? What
      was your relationship like with these people? Who, if anyone, taught
      you about spiritual matters? Who taught you survival, self-esteem and
      self-awareness? What comes through instinctually about yourself and
      others in your family?

5)   What does the entire picture activity bring up for you? If it's
      resistance, and only resistance, that's a very powerful message, too.
      Don't push too hard when there's huge resistance because resistance
      to that issue may have saved your life once. Perhaps you're still not
      ready. This can be another clue to seek and accept guidance through
      this activity, as well.

6)   Take the List of Feelings Appendix in the back of the workbook and
      see if you associate any of them with a particular family member. If
      you do, jot their names down beside the emotions, or make a list of
      family members and related emotions.

How To Interview Parents/Family Members If Deceased

On the following chart indicate how your mother and your father felt
about the areas listed. Whatever you write is actually the strategy you
learned from that parent in areas that affect your entire life.

	Dad	Mom
Work	_____	_____
Money	_____	_____
Love/Spouse Relationships	_____	_____
Friendships	_____	_____
Community	_____	_____
Environment	_____	_____
Family Of Origin	_____	_____
Current Family	_____	_____
Parenthood	_____	_____
Play	_____	_____
Health	_____	_____
Spiritual/Religion	_____	_____
Ethics	_____	_____
Self-regard	_____	_____
World Regard	_____	_____
Social Interplay	_____	_____

Study your answers and then check the parent whom you resemble the most regarding each category. You can also apply this method toward other family members.

If you are having trouble imagining a family member's feelings or attitudes, try meditation. You may find the childhood memory meditation from Chapter 23 helpful.

Another useful device is the journal. Ask the questions as you would if you were actually talking with them. Then answer the questions as if you were that person. Surround yourself with family pictures during this exercise. Look at the person you are imagining interviewing — remember how they talked, what they sounded like, any vocal patterns or idiosyncrasies they might have had.

Sometimes it works very well to meditate about the person you are going to interview first. You are accessing voices already imprinted on your cellular memory. You are not conjuring anything out of thin air, you are coaxing something to come forward out of your subconscious, where every person and event that comes in and out of your life remains.

Find Your Voice

Now isn't it easier to separate your voice from the other voices in your head? This work may give you a different perspective on the "Crisis Definition" you wrote down in Chapter 9 as well as the ownership of the related crisis thoughts and feelings. Try once more to follow them all the way back to where they originated. You are actually separating the emotional content from the actual crisis symptoms. Feel free to make changes and to write down thoughts relating to your crisis in your own voice now:

My Own Crisis Thoughts and Feelings

1) _____

2) _____

3) _____

You may also have a few new health-esteem crisis crunchers to add to your list.

New Health-Esteem Crisis Crunchers

1) _____

2) _____

3) _____

Now, go back to Chapter 14 and the "I'm Not Enough" experiment that helped you identify phrases with which we dig our own self-defeating pity pits. You may be able to silence most of those voices now as you name the owners of the self-sabotaging thinking. Once the pity voices are gone, you'll be able to hear your own voice emanating from your heart. This is your voice of wisdom that combines all the lessons of truth you have learned in your lifetime.

I didn't start to find my own voice until I was faced with a crisis — diagnosis with multiple sclerosis. One of the healthiest things I did on my search for wellness was to follow all those voices in my head back to their source — to find where they were in my body and what they had done to me — what pain they were holding on to that I had to release in order to get well. I literally learned to live and to stop separating myself from the world around me. As I did that, the numbness I experienced from my waist to my toes gradually improved and feeling began to return. The blind spots in my eyes cleared to reveal free vision, unfettered by others' perceptions. I could now embrace the world on my own terms.

Movement	Connection	Awareness
_____	_____	_____
_____	_____	_____
_____	_____	_____

Notes: _____

_____

_____

_____

_____

_____

_____

_____

_____

_____

_____

_____

_____

_____

_____

_____

_____

_____

_____

_____

_____

_____

_____

_____

_____

_____

_____

Breathing

Before beginning the work in this chapter, I'd like you to take in a deep breath. Breathe in as slowly and deeply as possible, then breathe out through your mouth until there is no air left to expel. Do that three times. Then, take a fourth big breath, the biggest of all; take in enough air to fill your chest cavity and diaphragm. Now, hold that breath as long as you can.

When you absolutely cannot hold the breath a second longer, expel it from your mouth with a big sound. Did you notice what happened to your body when you were taking deep breaths as opposed to how your body felt when you stopped breathing?

It's important to become conscious of what it feels like to *not* breathe. I notice my heart pounding and a sense of anxiety that I am stopping time and in fact, existence. Indeed, if I stopped breathing long enough, time would stop for me on this earth because I would die. When my healing began, it was amazing to me how often I stopped the life-sustaining act of breathing out of fear, sadness, anger, disappointment, embarrassment, shame, stress, anxiety or any number of emotional disturbances. I'd even run out of breath from business. How many of us have used the old cliché, "I don't have time to breathe!"?

Whether you blame it on the industrial revolution that moved us off the farms and into offices and factories, or the information age that sped up the movement from physical exertion to brain strain, one fact is clear. We've forgotten how to breathe — deep, healing cleansing breaths — conscious breathing that requires a dedication of time and thought.

Why, you may ask, do I have to pay attention to my breathing? That's just something that naturally takes care of itself. The fact is, many of us exist on shallow, minimized breathing. That's not the kind of breathing that makes us feel connected, that bathes our brains with food for creative thought, that allows our emotions to flow while cleansing our over-wrought minds and over-stressed bodies, that brings in energy and pushes out fatigue and negative thinking. Sadly, while many of us are starving ourselves nutritionally, we're also starving ourselves for breath. Baylor College of Medicine notes that for some people, regularly doing 10 to 20 minutes of deep-relaxation exercises and breathing relieves chronic back, head and arthritis pain as effectively as surgery.

From the body therapist perspective, Elizabeth reminds us that breathing practices are the foundation work for the movement arts of hatha yoga and all martial arts. She explains, "whether someone is a winning athlete or diagnosed with a 'big label' dis-ease, eventually deep breathing returns us to our source."

Throughout the workbook, we've been suggesting various breathing exercises. This chapter is dedicated to helping you establish a healthy breathing regimen. If you are sitting or confined to a chair when doing these exercises, simply concentrate on your breathing and upper body movements and whatever lower body movements are possible or feel comfortable to you. The important part is to breathe, and to notice the breath's passage through your body and how it is affected by movement and your concentration.

First, let me give you an example of how breathing can hold back emotions. Years ago I went on a Women In Creativity retreat led by Tobes. On the second night, we were told to try to remember our dreams. I went to sleep hoping I would dream and remember. A death-defying yell woke me up at 5:30 a.m. I had heard a one-word scream of "MOTHER!!!" With my heart racing, I held my breath and listened intently, to determine whether someone else had screamed "Mother," or whether it was me. I held my breath just as I had learned to do as a child whenever there was trouble. I tiptoed to my door and looked out. There was no sound coming from any of the other rooms. I hurried back under my covers. Did I have a nightmare and wake myself up with a scream?

Soon a cacophony of doubting voices filled my brain with worries about my work with the other women at the workshop: none of them really like me; I don't measure up; I'm not as good, as quick, as interesting, as dedicated, as on track... Soon I was shivering in my bed as the old icy feeling of being the outsider came in again. Why?

The next morning when we gathered in our circle, Tobes started with our dreams, and I anxiously volunteered to go first. As I told of waking up to this horrible scream, Cynthia gasped and said, "Oh no, I thought no one heard me." She had dreamed that her mother was killing her, and she woke up screaming to escape her mother's stranglehold. Tobes said the dream event was no accident, and asked what I had done prior to falling asleep and after the dream. When I related the negative feelings of the night before and the self-deprecating tirade brought on by the dream, Tobes kept probing. "And whose voice is that within you?"

Slowly the answer dawned — it was my mother. "Does your mother love you?" she asked. I felt tears coming, but I held them back by holding my breath. Slowly I answered, "She loves me, but she loves me more for what I do for her." Tobes asked me to scream just like I had heard the scream earlier. I did scream and the scream forced me to breathe, but the group said it wasn't enough. I screamed again — again — and again; then the scream turned into agonizing sobbing as I realized the negativity from the night before was my mother's — nothing I ever did had been enough. I wasn't enough to be really loved. I held myself, and my hands rubbed my arms so hard I practically scratched away the skin's surface as I rocked and tried to stop crying by holding my breath. But it didn't work, I just kept crying, gasping for air and exhaling my pain in choking sobs. I cried until I was exhausted.

When the tears were spent, Tobes and the group helped me get my breath back, and then they hugged me. The same breathing that let out my pain also helped me regain my composure.

That entire dream experience brought up the neediness of my childhood years and reminded me of feelings that, while different in adulthood, still needed to be purged from my emotional memory. Tobes explained that many children suffer from the feelings of "not being good enough for their parents" (to make them happy or to make their lives better) no matter how much they accomplish or how hard they try. She stressed the importance of letting go of those "old" feelings that, when buried deep inside, continue to be unwittingly acted out.

Breathing is the highway on which our thoughts and emotions rise and fall, ebb and flow, come and go. Conscious breathing allows us to remember, to know, to be connected to the truth. It keeps our system in tune.

Breath is life. We need to pay more attention to our exhalation of breath, periodically making it longer than the inhalation. This will allow the lungs to get rid of old, foul air that has accumulated in our air sacs. As long as our air sacs are filled with old air, no amount of strength or deep breathing applied to the inhalation can bring fresh air and life-giving oxygen from the atmosphere into our lungs. The very act of breathing, getting rid of the old to make room for the new, is actually a metaphor for what we are doing in this workbook.

Have you ever thought about taking a breath break from your work? Probably not. After all, we associate food with all of our break times in America. We program coffee and snack breaks, but not breathing and movement breaks. Yet, as we become more sedentary, many of us sitting for hours in front of a computer screen or on the phone, movement and breath breaks are essential to keep our creative juices flowing. The following are breath breaks we would like you to program into your life for at least two weeks and perhaps permanently.

Morning wake up breathing: Before getting out of bed in the mornings, lie on your back, close your eyes and take a long, slow deep breath that starts from your toes and works its way up your entire body. Take at least five of these breaths and imagine each time that you are pulling energy into your body. Perhaps the breath has a white light with it that turns on all of the energy centers in your body. When the energy breath gets to your head, breathe out audibly, expelling any residual sleepiness and dream thoughts that might be bothering you. After the fifth breath with your body's energy centers fully alive, exhale as you exclaim, "Yes!" Behind that exclamation is the thought, "Yes, I'm ready for this day." You can fill in as many adjectives about that day as you like...wonderful day, busy day, challenging day, joyful day, relaxing, peaceful, day of opportunity. I'm sure you've got the idea.

Pre-exercise breathing: Before performing any exercise routine, it is recommended to stretch, and breathing is stretching's twin. Besides waist bends with my arm raised and arched over my head as I stretch first to one side and then the other, full body stretches where I stand on my tip toes and reach both arms up toward the sky reaching as high as I can, and leg lunges where I bend my left leg and take a giant step forward with my right leg and hold the stretch for a couple of seconds before alternating the movement for my right side, I also perform several yoga postures. While holding each posture and stretch, I breathe with the exertion to help me get as far into the position as possible. Here are some wonderful floor stretches to orient your body right to left and left to right.

Lie on your back flat on the floor. Sink into the floor as far as possible. Spread your legs into a V. Spread your arms into a V over your head. You are like a Giant X on the floor. As you take a deep breath, feel the energy go from your right leg, diagonally across your body to your left arm and then from your left leg, diagonally across your body to your right arm. Repeat this three times for each diagonal — feeling the energy flow as you breathe.

Now bend your knees and bring your bent legs into your stomach. At the same time, roll up from the waist and touch your forehead to your knees as you wrap your arms around your legs. You are now curled into a ball. Allow yourself to rock on your buttocks as you hold this position.

Straighten from the waist as you cross your legs in front of you Indian style. Your arms are relaxed at your sides, your hands in your lap. Take a deep breath. While sitting with your back straight, release your legs and spread them into a wide V about six inches off the floor. At the same time, allow your hands to move out from your diaphragm using the breath to sweep your arms out into another V in front of you. Bring your leg and arm

V's back into center. Sit straight and begin again. Take a deep breath and on the exhale sweep your arms and legs out into V's before you. Repeat this five times.

Finally, while still sitting on the floor Indian style, your legs crossed in front of you, sweep your arms out like you're holding a giant beach ball, and then complete the circle as you bring your arms out to your sides. Keep your arms slightly curved as if still holding that ball. Taking a breath with each movement, shift your weight, first to the left side, allowing yourself to lean on your left elbow, then to your right side, leaning over onto your right elbow. Twist your body and look over your left shoulder, then your right shoulder. Feel the movement in your waist. Feel the momentum in your body and move all around. Straighten your right leg, as you lean back on your left elbow, then do the opposite. Experiment with the moves, keeping them fluid and your arms round, always holding the ball. In a sense, you are a ball, rotating from side to side as you float on the energy of your breath. There is no wrong way to do this exercise. Simply be conscious of each movement and recognize your body as an energy source, full of information and intelligence. Make sure that each movement begins with a breath. You are free form, floating, multi-dimensional and connected to the energy around you. Feel a movement in your arm connect to your toes as it ripples all the way through your body.

As I do these stretches and my morning aerobics that follow, I check in with my body. Is there stiffness or soreness? Am I feeding it right? Sleeping enough? Drinking enough water? Have I been beating myself up again with anxiety? I adjust my body accordingly and think about what it's telling me.

10:00 AM Stress Relief: Formerly known as a coffee break, we would like you to think first about this break as a breathe and stretch break. Get up from your desk, computer or work station. Stand with your feet and legs hip width apart. Bring your hands in front of your waist. Raise your hands and arms upward as you breathe in. Then turn your palms down and push your arms back to your waist as you exhale. Repeat three times. Now do a cross crawl walk to get a glass of water. Bring your right arm up and your left leg up simultaneously, Your leg is bent at the knee. Step down on your left leg as you bring your left arm up and your right knee to your waist. Step down on your right leg and repeat these steps ten or twelve times. Breathe in as you raise your arm and leg, breathe out as you step. This serves to wake up your brain and get the diagonal energy flow going again.

Noon Breath Break: Before going to lunch, relax your brain with a great neck and throat stretch. Stand or sit with your feet and legs hip width apart. Clasp your hands into a fist and place your fist under your chin, elbows together. Inhale raising your elbows up. Let your head roll back gently as you open your hands. As you exhale, close your hands like a bellows while bringing your elbows together in front of your chest. Repeat five times.

If you can, on your way to the lunch room, your car, a restaurant or wherever your lunch break may be, walk briskly with a wider stride than usual. Exaggerate your arm swing and stretch your neck from side to side. (For those of you who remember the "Charlie Girl" Revlon commercials — that's the walk. Guys, simply catch up to the beautiful "Charlie Girl" in front of you.) Be conscious of the movement rippling through your body from head to toe and the breath that goes along with each stride. Don't hesitate to smile when you walk this way. It feels good! Make this your lunch walk — before and after.

3:00 P.M. Stress Relief: This would be a great time to get up and cross walk for an 8-ounce glass of water. Before you take off, however, flap your wings with this butterfly breath break. Stand or sit with your feet and legs hip width apart. With your arms relaxed at your sides, begin inhaling and raise your arms out and up. (Like flapping your butterfly wings or making a snow angel in the air) Extend your arms from your shoulders upward until they form a "V" for Victory above your head. Hold the "V" and your breath as you stretch your arms skyward. Exhale while lowering your arms to your sides. Repeat five times. Now you're ready to repeat the cross crawl walk you did at your 10 A.M. break.

** Toxic Energy Breathing (anytime of day): During the course of any day or evening if someone has a hostile/negative impact on you, practice this technique. Take a long, deep breath and send it down through your diaphragm, concentrating on its journey and arrival. Exhale slowly, and concentrate on letting go of any hostility or negativity that was foisted upon you by the offending party. Breathing like this brings you back to yourself. Negative verbal exchanges, insults and accusations are attacks — bursts of someone else's toxic energy hurled at your system. You must separate yourself from that to avoid the invasion of their negativity into your system. Simply take the offense, and throw the toxic energy right back to the sender with the very breath that brings you back to yourself. This centering breath will also help you formulate the correct response and time for comment, if any is needed.

The Institute of HeartMath, a nonprofit organization based in Boulder Creek, California, has a unique technique to help students across the nation deal with the rising sense of isolation, decline in community and interaction tension they face. Seventh graders and their parents are taught to tune into the heart to defuse tension, anxiety and anger. Called HeartMath, it works by focusing attention on the heart instead of the mind in order to achieve balance, so kids don't waste their energy on people and events they can't control. Children are taught to freeze frame tense moments and then recall positive feelings. This helps to smooth out the electrical impulses of the heart that contribute to stress, anger and high blood pressure. Breathing helps to center the energy around the heart so they can ask the question, "What's the best way to handle this?" The brain is then capable of calmly answering the question. One 13-year-old gives this description, "When you're really mad at someone, you chill out, breathe through your heart, and you start relaxing."

End Of Day Transition Breathing: Your work day is over, and you are ready to change gears and prepare for your evening activity. It's time to shut the cares of the day behind a locked door in your brain, where they will remain until tomorrow. You can do this next breath ritual while riding home, or wait and do it as you change from work clothes into play, rest or going out attire. Concentrate on the words as you take a long, deep cleansing breath and breathe in relaxation, breathe out tension; Breathe in calm, breathe out anxious; Breathe in carefree, breathe out problems. If there are specific issues you would like your breath to help you blow behind the door in your mind, do that now by breathing in the opposite of whatever stress-maker you are breathing out. For instance: Breathe in ideas, breathe out writer's block. Or, breathe in understanding, breathe out anger.

Good Night Dream Breathing: To insure that you wake up anxiety free, do a mental checklist to release unfinished business or concerns to your higher power just before you turn out your light and roll over into slumber. There's a saying in 12-step programs, "Let go and let God." That's basically what I want you to do. If there are any unpleasant thoughts hanging around, open that door in your brain, just a crack, and with a deep exhale, blow those thoughts behind the door where they will be locked up safely for the night. Now take three deep breaths and feel each one moving through your body from your toes, up through you ankles, thighs, hips, stomach, chest, arms, shoulders, neck, face, and out the top of your head. Let the breath roll through your body on a wave of warmth, like a soft, down comforter being pulled up to tuck you in at night. As each breath rolls through your body, visualize any particular desire or goal that you may be working to realize. Repeat an affirmation if you have one. There's always, "I am worth being healthy!" Just before you drift into slumber, close your eyes and smile gently, because a smile on the lips goes directly to the heart.

Scarcity Mentality vs. Abundance Mentality Breathing: The chart on the next page was introduced to me by Elizabeth when I was feeling shut down by feelings of not being "enough" — good enough, sucessful enough, pretty enough... I felt depleted in every way. The chart is a wonderful tool to use when you're feeling deprived in some way, such as through fear, anger, despair, perceived danger or perceived lack of something you want. Find your feeling on the scarcity side of the chart, then follow the arrows through the cycle that feeling engenders. Next, go back to the original feeling, turn the chart over and find it's opposite on the abundance side. Follow the abundance cycle through, and take in the feelings abundance engenders. Enforce this exercise with your breath. Breathe out the scarcity feelings from which you want to be freed, and breathe in the abundance feelings. For example: Breathe out fear, breathe in love; Breathe out suffering, breathe in joy; Breathe out "I'm not enough, breathe in, "I am enough." When you're in a crisis mode, you may want to copy this chart on two sides of a single page, and post it where you can turn the page and breathe into consciously turning away from scarcity and into abundance.

To complete the breathing chapter, we mimic the breathing cycle by ending as we began. Take in a deep breath. Breathe in as slowly and deeply as possible, then breathe out through your mouth until there is no air left to expel. Do that three times. Then, take a fourth big breath, inhaling enough air to fill your chest cavity and diaphragm. Now, hold that breath as long as you can.

When you absolutely cannot hold the breath a second longer, expel it from your mouth with a big sound. Did you notice what happened to your body when you were taking deep breaths as opposed to how your body felt when you stopped breathing?

Cherish the feelings of breath through daily conscious breathing.

Movement	Connection	Awareness
_____	_____	_____
_____	_____	_____
_____	_____	_____

Scarcity Mentality

The Law of Deprivation

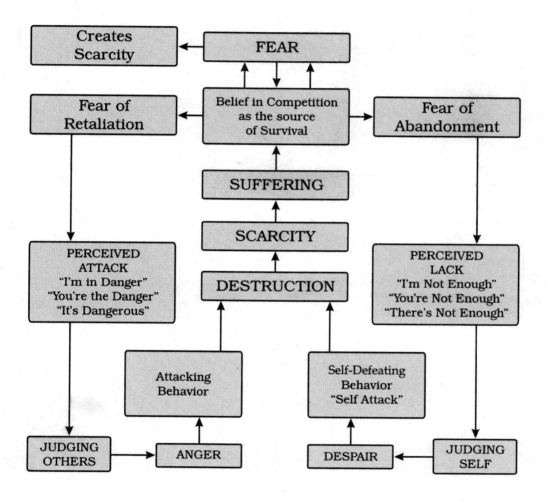

Abundance Mentality

The Law of Extension

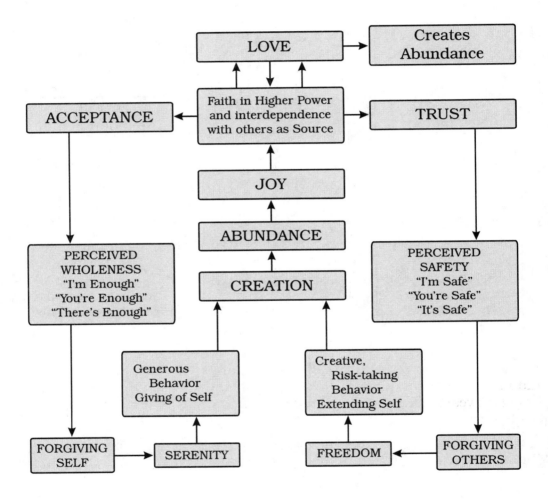

Nutrition

My mother says to me, "I ate all the wrong things all of my life and I'm 80 years old with no major health problems, so why should I have to be so careful now? And," she goes on self-righteously, "your grandmother was worse!" At first I found it hard to respond to my mom, because I would certainly like to eat all the things I grew up loving. With a little thought, however, I could give her four big reasons why we should be more conscious of the food we eat.

> 1) First and foremost — How we eat has everything to do with how we feel and function. We are what we eat and what we assimilate or don't assimilate. Food is our best medicine.

When we ignore the above nutritional laws and ignore the needs of our bodies, they get even. First, however, a body will send out all types of warning signals to avoid eventual disease manifestation. Nancy defines all disease as "Physiology gone awry to an extreme extent." Usually, there are messengers sent out to help us avoid that worst possible outcome. Those messengers are often cravings to eat certain needed foods.

2) Considerable speculation and resultant research is ongoing concerning what over-population and over-planting is doing to the vitamin and mineral content of our soil. Some fear that the same foods we've been eating for years simply may not contain as many nutrients to properly fuel our bodies.

3) We know that the industrial civilization has released chemicals into our eco-system that can affect us in our households and may be harmful to our bodies. New theories and information surface daily on how to make the nutritional adjustments necessary to live healthy in our ever-changing world.

4) Stress! Life is definitely more stressful with every passing year as we approach the Millennium. Today's 20-year-olds often live older lives than we did when we were 20. By their late 20's more and more young men and women are senior executives, buying homes and cars, having kids or facing

infertility and wondering how they're going to be able to do it all without having the carpet pulled out from under them. Numerous surveys report a high level of discomfort among this age group regarding sex, money, relationships, marriage, street violence and job security? Living with stress requires nourishment of both the mind and body.

Just like the majority of this workbook has centered on becoming conscious of what we are feeling, the food chapter begins with helping you become conscious of what you are putting into your bodies. In addition to the "what" question regarding food choices there are "why" questions. Why are you eating? For hunger? Or, for solace? It's important to realize that every time you are hungry there is a reason for being hungry. You are actually getting a message from your body saying you need certain things — sometimes the message is simple; you just need to eat. The key is to learn to observe messages from your body such as feeling tired or irritable, having a headache, getting suddenly giddy or experiencing a runny nose. Notice if your body symptom is occurring before or after eating. With time, you'll begin to see a pattern to your cravings. Before meal cravings may be a sign your body needs certain foods for specific functions. After meal symptoms may be a sign your body does not want the food you chose to feed it. The goal of this chapter is to help you receive and decipher those messages. All you have to do is simply observe what your body's feeling in relation to food. Eventually, you'll be able to interpret those observations either on your own or with the help of a professional.

As usual, it's important to start at the very beginning. When I was a kid the meal I loved to eat more than anything else on earth was French fries dripping in catsup washed down by a thick chocolate malt. Everything else paled in comparison. Dinner was always served promptly at 5 p.m. at my house and was often strained because of my dad's alcoholism. Because I hated vegetables, I had to eat my meals in a clockwise fashion — a bite of meat, followed by potatoes, followed by salad, followed by dreaded mushy peas or broccoli, or carrots, or heaven forbid, okra. Before I could start again, I had to eat that awful vegetable. Perhaps it wasn't the clock thing, but it has taken me until the age of 40 to begin to like certain vegetables, and that's because I simply didn't want to try them.

What do you remember about the what, where, when and why of eating as a child?

Childhood Eating Pattern Brain Tinglers

1) What were your favorite foods? Do you ever eat them now?

_____

_____

2) What foods did you absolutely hate? Were you forced to eat them anyway?

_____

_____

3) Were you punished if you didn't eat right?

_____

_____

4) What was explained to you as the "right way to eat"?

_____

_____

5) Did you talk about nutrition? Did you know about balanced meals and food groups, and if so did you eat accordingly?

_____

_____

6) Where did you eat most of your meals?

_____

_____

7) Were meals served at regular times? Did your family often eat together? How did you feel about mealtimes in your home?

_____

_____

8) Were there any rituals built around mealtime?

_____

_____

9) How do your eating patterns differ from your parents? Your grandparents?

_____

_____

10) Do your comfort foods have anything to do with your childhood favorites?

_____

_____

After I looked at my childhood eating patterns, I realized that eating was often a chore for me. It was no wonder that as an adult, I liked to eliminate eating from my schedule as much as possible, particularly if it got in the way of my work.

Nancy explains that my childhood cravings for meat above everything else on my plate reflected my need for protein. She says: *There's always a reason why you're hungry. You're getting messages from your body saying you need certain things. Your body is saying, "I need fuel, I need to create more skin cells — I need to create more eyeball cells. I need more hormones..." People need to learn to listen for the cravings of nourishing. What people actually think of as a balanced diet may not be balanced for them. Body type and physiology must be taken into account to determine the appropriate balance of food for each person. It's important to get out of the rut of what food manufacturers with a vested interest declare as a balanced diet. It is every person's option to decide what the right diet is for him or her.*

How To Listen For The Cravings of Nourishing

We're all familiar with growling tummies, hunger headaches, and the weakness that comes from skipping a meal. There are also planted cravings that media gives us by bombarding audiences with delectable images of donuts, pizzas, burgers and countless ooey-gooey desserts. Sometimes a food pops into our minds and stays there until we obey our brain's command to consume that food. These are all cravings, some planted, some natural, but all leading to choices that we can make. The key is to make informed choices.

In Chapter 17 you were asked to keep a MESSENGER chart that allowed you to note the time, frequency and surrounding conditions of any symptoms you might experience in the course of a day, week, or month. Many of those messengers may relate to food cravings. For instance, the weakness and anemia I would experience every month during my period was my body crying out for the proper raw materials to create more red blood cells. My body wanted food containing protein, blood builders, B Vitamins and iron so it could do its job. Long distance runners, bikers and marathoners' bodies seek carbohydrates to increase stamina.

Nancy calls the symptoms/messengers we're asking you to observe "your friends" because they give you valuable information about what your body needs. "Symptoms are not just about being sick," Nancy explains, "they help us identify a need before it becomes irrevocable or before our physiology goes awry to an extreme."

172

The definition of nutrition is: *"The process of nourishing or being nourished, especially the process by which a living organism assimilates food and uses it for growth and for replacement of tissues."*

To understand your own body's nourishment cravings you must get to know your body's hunger, rest, exertion and stress cycles, and combine that with knowledge of what foods do in your body. Sounds like a big job doesn't it? Actually, you only have to do one thing — PAY ATTENTION! Be present and observe what your body is feeling and, therefore, telling you. Don't be frightened or confused, simply be open to observation. "Use your common sense," says Robert Christensen, M.D., a family physician in Carroll, Iowa. "Usually, we have a pretty good idea of what we ought to be doing to protect our health. We just have to get ourselves to do it." When you listen to your body, you will receive a lot of information that will help you to:

> **Combine Knowledge With Cravings To Make Informed Choices That Lead To Healthy Nourishment.**

A friend of mine drinks eight cokes a day and wonders why she's hyper, bossy, aggressive and restless. A simple substitution of eight glasses of water would help solve the problem and cleanse her body.

When I was seeing a movie a week, accompanied by a box of saturated-fat-laden-popcorn I began to gradually gain weight. By carrying a baggie full of non-fat, garlic and herb flavored corn puffs or rice puffs into the theatre, my cravings were satisfied and my weight returned to normal.

Find out what foods are associated with your physical complaints and make a choice: Change or suffer. Remember, if you're not sure how to change, you can consult a professional such as a chiropractor, homeopathic doctor, or other alternative medicine professional. Don't let denial ("I don't want to know") or a dreaded imaginary diagnosis keep you away. Uninformed imaginations can be our enemies, symptoms can be our early-warning friends. Nancy stresses, "There is always help for these things." She explains:

When a system is out of balance, there can be as many as 25 to 50 foods that are not OK to eat. That's a scary thought. The fact is, however, there are usually one or two foods underlying all those sensitivities. Those normally come down to the basic five: wheat, soy, corn, dairy, sugar. Food sensitivities also change just like the circumstances in our lives. So we must always stay tuned in to how our bodies are reacting to what we eat. The secret is to eliminate a food from our diet that is bothering us, for as long as it takes to notice how good our bodies feel without that food. Often, we don't realize how good we've begun to feel until we put the offending food back in our diet and begin to feel shaky and sweaty and to have a headache or some other REALLY awful symptom. Your new attention level says, "Wow, I remember this. I don't want to feel this way and I know what to do." Sometimes foods can be gradually reintroduced into your diet without bad side effects, if done so in moderation. However, if a symptom is felt again, the offending food goes back off the list.

Notes:

_____

_____

_____

_____

_____

_____

_____

_____

_____

_____

_____

_____

_____

_____

_____

Ten Key Components Of A Healthy Diet

Nancy LaPidus, D.C.

1) Eat natural foods. The more natural, the more vitality.

2) Eat seasonal and indigenous foods to increase protection from environmental changes.

3) Eat fresh foods. The fresher the food, the less chance there is of it containing chemicals and additives to prolong it's shelf life. And the less chance there is of microbial activity.

4) Eat nutritious foods — protein, carbohydrates, fat, and the accessory nutrients. These contain the nutrients that provide fuel for energy and raw materials to make our body parts.

5) Eat clean foods. This means washed and free of chemicals and additives.

6) Eat tasty and appealing foods. When we desensitize our taste buds to the high concentrations of salt and sugar found in highly processed foods, as well as to chemically produced tastes, we can re-experience the rich, full flavors of whole foods in their natural state.

7) Eat a variety of foods and try to rotate your foods regularly. This assures a full complement of nutrients and is also a good way to prevent food allergies and sensitivities from developing. The most common food sensitivities are cow's milk, wheat, eggs, soybeans, corn, beef, coffee, chocolate, tomatoes, peanuts, yeast, shellfish, and mushrooms.

8) Learn to combine foods properly. This helps to reduce stress in the digestive tract and supports optimal processing and assimilation of the foods we eat.

9) Eat in moderation. Learn to read your own appetite and let it be your guide, **NOT** emotions, not social get-togethers, not cultural customs.

10) Above all, balance. Balance all the nutrients, the food groups, the flavors, the colors, etc.

Health-Esteem and Nourishment

Tobes remembers how wonderful it was to cook and to feed her family. She says, "Even when I'm alone now I still cook, because I'm still coming from that place that it's wonderful to cook." Tobes grown daughters all love to cook for themselves as well.

Tobes had high health-esteem, so she felt it was wonderful to feed herself. I, on the other hand, was living alone, and I thought it was a pain to have to feed myself . That thought was tied to an underlying *learned* perception that there was something wrong with me because I didn't have a husband in my life to feed, therefore, I didn't need to eat (or deserve to) so I would just have junk food.

I remember, years ago, having a craving for homemade Mexican food. I came home from a 12-hour day at the TV station and fixed myself a gourmet meal. I then sat down at my TV tray and promptly began to cry. Instead of relishing every bite, I was mourning the fact that there was no one with me to share my meal. I was not enough to enjoy a meal in my own company. I nibbled at the meal, but it made me nauseous. I went to bed lonely and hungry.

Years later, to heal from MS, I had to learn to be enough. I had to learn to fill that emptiness inside me with emotional and nutritional nurturing. The question became: Am I worth feeding myself? Nurturing myself? Are you?

As we approach the end of the twentieth century there are lots of young men and women who haven't even learned how to cook. I include males, because cooking is not a gender thing. It's a wonderful gift to cook for ourselves and each other.

All of us have witnessed many changes in our lifetimes, yet we remain industrial society eaters. When the whistle blows at noon, we have to eat. Our bodies instinctively know better, however. The challenge is to return to our instinctual knowledge. Tobes notes that when her daughters were young, she would sometimes let them choose their foods for an entire week. They wouldn't just be drawn to sweets, she noted. One child might start with rice and beans and then switch when her body needed something else. They all naturally went to high protein foods when they needed it, and then switched to starchy foods when they were feeling tired.

One way Nancy recommends to get back to the instinctual knowledge of our bodies is to keep a food diary. During the first week, concentrate on awareness. Simply write down what you eat normally. Don't change out of not wanting to admit bad eating habits. During weeks two and three, you might experiment with eating when you're hungry, and with selecting foods your body seems to be craving. You might also want to jot down in the margins how you are feeling, emotionally and physically, after eating your food choice during the course of the day. Simply be aware of when you eat, what you eat and why you are eating.

Food Diary

After you have completed your three week food diary, go back and compare it to the "Messenger" Diary you kept in Chapter 17. Do any of the messengers connect with the types of foods you were eating prior to or at the same time of day or night? Next, compare your food diary to your feelings chart in Chapter 15. Do you notice any emotional food cravings happening routinely? Once you become conscious of what you are putting in your system and how your system is reacting, you may have further questions about how to improve your nutritional routine. Don't hesitate to seek professional advice to maximize the most fundamental part of your health-esteem — nutritional balance.

A lot of diet problems can be solved with common sense. Nancy explains that the reason why breakfast is so important to us is because we've used up all of our glycogen stores overnight. "Why was I storing Glycogen in the first place?" a lot of you may ask. The human brain requires blood sugar or glucose 24-hours a day. The body is so smart that it stores sugar in the liver, where it's called glycogen. When we are asleep, the hungry brain sends a message to the adrenals for sugar, the adrenals signal the liver to crack out the supplies, and there goes the glycogen. So, when we wake up in the morning, our sugar supplies are completely depleted. The reason so many people have a blood sugar problem in our society is because they get up, have a cup of coffee, and then go until lunch without food. Often sleep related disorders are simply blood sugar problems. Many times in our culture, the last thing we eat before going to sleep is a big, sugary dessert. When that sugar zaps our sleeping brain it goes into hyper-drive and signals the pancreas to shoot out tons of insulin in search of body stability. Thus signaled, the body obeys by efficiently using up all the sugar, causing another big drop in the supply, which in turn wakes up the brain again, this time because the brain's hungry and in search of the depleted sugar supply. All of that internal activity leaves us wide awake. We won't wake up, however, if the dinner we consumed had a strong protein base to neutralize the negative effects of the sugar. When our blood sugar is stabilized, we will sleep through the night.

1ˢᵗ Day	**2ⁿᵈ Day**

Date: _____ Date: _____

BREAKFAST: **BREAKFAST**:

Meat & Dairy Foods: Meat & Dairy Foods:

Vegetables & Fruits: Vegetables & Fruits:

Cereal Foods: Cereal Foods:

Candy & Other Sweets: Candy & Other Sweets:

Drinks: Drinks:

BETWEEN BREAKFAST & LUNCH: **BETWEEN BREAKFAST & LUNCH**:

LUNCH: **LUNCH**:

Meat & Dairy Foods: Meat & Dairy Foods:

Vegetables & Fruits: Vegetables & Fruits:

Cereal Foods: Cereal Foods:

Candy & Other Sweets: Candy & Other Sweets:

Drinks: Drinks:

BETWEEN LUNCH & DINNER: **BETWEEN LUNCH & DINNER**:

DINNER: **DINNER**:

Meat & Dairy Foods: Meat & Dairy Foods:

Vegetables & Fruits: Vegetables & Fruits:

Cereal Foods: Cereal Foods:

Candy & Other Sweets: Candy & Other Sweets:

Drinks: Drinks:

BETWEEN DINNER & BEDTIME: **BETWEEN DINNER & BEDTIME**:

3ʳᵈ Day	**4ᵗʰ Day**

Date: _____ Date: _____

BREAKFAST:	**BREAKFAST:**
Meat & Dairy Foods:	Meat & Dairy Foods:
Vegetables & Fruits:	Vegetables & Fruits:
Cereal Foods:	Cereal Foods:
Candy & Other Sweets:	Candy & Other Sweets:
Drinks:	Drinks:
BETWEEN BREAKFAST & LUNCH:	**BETWEEN BREAKFAST & LUNCH:**
LUNCH:	**LUNCH:**
Meat & Dairy Foods:	Meat & Dairy Foods:
Vegetables & Fruits:	Vegetables & Fruits:
Cereal Foods:	Cereal Foods:
Candy & Other Sweets:	Candy & Other Sweets:
Drinks:	Drinks:
BETWEEN LUNCH & DINNER:	**BETWEEN LUNCH & DINNER:**
DINNER:	**DINNER:**
Meat & Dairy Foods:	Meat & Dairy Foods:
Vegetables & Fruits:	Vegetables & Fruits:
Cereal Foods:	Cereal Foods:
Candy & Other Sweets:	Candy & Other Sweets:
Drinks:	Drinks:
BETWEEN DINNER & BEDTIME:	**BETWEEN DINNER & BEDTIME:**

5th Day

Date: _____

BREAKFAST:
Meat & Dairy Foods:

Vegetables & Fruits:

Cereal Foods:

Candy & Other Sweets:

Drinks:

BETWEEN BREAKFAST & LUNCH:

LUNCH:
Meat & Dairy Foods:

Vegetables & Fruits:

Cereal Foods:

Candy & Other Sweets:

Drinks:

BETWEEN LUNCH & DINNER:

DINNER:
Meat & Dairy Foods:

Vegetables & Fruits:

Cereal Foods:

Candy & Other Sweets:

Drinks:

BETWEEN DINNER & BEDTIME:

6th Day

Date: _____

BREAKFAST:
Meat & Dairy Foods:

Vegetables & Fruits:

Cereal Foods:

Candy & Other Sweets:

Drinks:

BETWEEN BREAKFAST & LUNCH:

LUNCH:
Meat & Dairy Foods:

Vegetables & Fruits:

Cereal Foods:

Candy & Other Sweets:

Drinks:

BETWEEN LUNCH & DINNER:

DINNER:
Meat & Dairy Foods:

Vegetables & Fruits:

Cereal Foods:

Candy & Other Sweets:

Drinks:

BETWEEN DINNER & BEDTIME:

7th Day

Date: _____

BREAKFAST:
Meat & Dairy Foods:

Vegetables & Fruits:

Cereal Foods:

Candy & Other Sweets:

Drinks:

BETWEEN BREAKFAST & LUNCH:

LUNCH:
Meat & Dairy Foods:

Vegetables & Fruits:

Cereal Foods:

Candy & Other Sweets:

Drinks:

BETWEEN LUNCH & DINNER:

DINNER:
Meat & Dairy Foods:

Vegetables & Fruits:

Cereal Foods:

Candy & Other Sweets:

Drinks:

BETWEEN DINNER & BEDTIME:

And, here's a big piece of common sense advice that makes all your systems work better: DRINK MORE WATER!!!!! Water acts as a delivery system to carry nutrients throughout the body, helps all organs to work more efficiently, absorbs shock in your joints, muscles and bones, and keeps glands and hormones in top shape. You really do need eight to 10 eight-ounce glasses of water daily. Now that you're listening to your body if you notice your mouth is dry, your skin is flaky, you're frequently constipated and infrequently urinating, that you seldom sweat after even strenuous workouts or that you have a racing pulse —YOU MAY NOT BE GETTING ENOUGH WATER. Water can also help you lose weight. Here are a few tips:

1) Keep a glass of water by your side constantly — on your desk, on your bedside table.

2) Drink one or two glasses of water immediately after you get up — a cleansing way to start the day.

3) When you get up for your stretch or exercise breaks, drink water. Substitute water for coffee, tea, soft drinks, etc. when possible — or instead of a refill, have water.

4) Every time you start a new activity, have some water. Drinking water before each meal will help you eat less.

5) Carry water with you on hikes or trips. Make water your constant companion. Your life will flow much more smoothly.

Feeding Our Life Cycles

If this chapter has helped you become more aware of anything, it should be the many cycles that must be paid attention to in the human body and how they influence each other. Women's monthlies, sleeping and waking periods, productivity peaks, relaxation respites, emotionally sensitive intervals, even nutritional cravings run in cycles. Blood, oxygen, nutrients, impurities all cycle through our systems. What regulates all of these cycles?

According to Chinese medicine there are 12 primary energy flows in our bodies, each associated with certain organs, and certain organs are associated with emotions: Heart with love and confidence; Kidney with fear; Gallbladder with control issues; Liver with anger; Lungs with grief; Spleen with worry. The flow from organ to organ not only transports energy, but also emotions through our bodies.

If energy is blocked and therefore trapped in an organ (i.e., tears or grief that a man was taught to restrain stored in the lungs, or anger that a woman repressed stored in her liver) bodies may compensate with an emotionally suppressing addiction such as smoking, drinking or over-eating. The compensation eventually can work its way into an illness. When people try to fill emotional holes with relationships, things, greed, power, or selfishness they're at risk of a body backlash.

References that categorize people as either right brain or left brain in behavior are becoming quite familiar. Emotions originate in the right hemisphere of the brain which controls the left (Yin or female) side of the body. Mental thought and action comes from the left side of the brain which controls the right (Yang or male) side of the body. Throughout my workaholic years, my life was abusively directed by my left brain. That abuse caused the side of the body it controlled, (the right side) to go numb. I had to resuscitate my right brain by becoming more comfortable with my feminine self, and feeling all of my emotions. Gradually every cycle in my body changed. I slept more, ate differently, and began noticing patterns to my energy highs and lows My body was crying out for balance. It was in search of something — perhaps its natural programming.

I have learned that health is about balance, just as the health of nature's ecosystem depends on balance. Naturally, the Chinese philosophy relates the systems within the human body to the five elements which they call Nature's Transforming Powers; fire, earth, metal, water and wood. Western thinking centers on four elements; water, earth, fire and air. These four elements are then related to our four levels of being; emotional, physical, spiritual, mental.

I touch on all of this only to illustrate the multi-faceted lesson of balance and interconnection. The balance or lack of balance of the elements in our bodies actually affects our cravings, nutritionally and emotionally. I was driven by fire. I burned intensely with my need for action, movement and fulfillment. I was consumed with relating to the outside world. I needed to balance myself with the water qualities of silence, patience and introspection. By achieving balance, I would discover my health-esteem, and I did.

For more on how the elements relate to your system, personality traits, mental and physical strengths and weaknesses and particular dietary requirements, I recommend two books found in this Workbook's reading list: **Woman Heal Thyself** and **Feminine Healing: A Woman's Guide to a Healthy Body, Mind and Spirit**. You will begin to notice how the diverse yet intertwining cycles in your life can be used to your advantage to create your maximum health potential. As you keep your food diary and complete the following exercise, begin listening to the many cycles of your body and see how they flow in and out of each other to effect your daily choices about living. Mastering this knowledge puts a great deal of wellness information at your fingertips.

We leave this chapter with one more exercise to help determine if you are eating instead of feeling. We've talked about comfort foods, and we know we often eat them to make ourselves feel better emotionally, not because we *need* the food. If you find yourself doing that a lot, you may want to tape this exercise to your refrigerator:

Don't Eat When You Need To Exercise

1) Before you eat the chips and dip or the gallon of ice cream you are desperately craving — STOP!

2) Note the time — identify a feeling and write a short paragraph about the feeling. For instance, if you are mad — at whom are you mad? What happened? Did it trigger something you're mad at yourself about?

3) Is there another activity besides eating, that you could do right now to work out your feelings? (i.e., walk, call a friend, write in your journal, indulge in a hobby, read, learn a foreign language, plan a trip, take a night course, beat on a pillow, sing/scream at the top of your lungs, watch a silly movie and laugh...)

4) If you still want to eat — do it. Then write down what you ate.

5) Did you change your mind about what and how much you ate? How did you feel after eating?

Chapter

27

Music, Singing, Dance

When interviewing a renowned neurologist, Dr. Wallace Tourtellotte, a scientist quite unwilling to discuss mind/body medicine and various wellness techniques, he humored me with a question: "In what profession do people have the greatest longevity?"

Without pausing for my guess, Dr.Tourtellottee answered his own question, "Orchestra conductors."

I immediately replied, "I can think of two reasons for that. Besides the cardiovascular workout, they literally have beautiful music running through their bodies — a tremendously healing force."

"There you go again with that new age mumbo jumbo," he grumbled.

I countered, "I believe in music's power to heal..."

Dr. Tourtellotte interrupted, "There's no question that music makes us feel good. It's a mathematically oriented routine that the brain likes, but I think the longevity is mainly due to conductors' getting physically conditioned through their arms."

As author of this workbook, I have the last word, and I say it's a combination of the two; exercise and healing through music — mind and body working in harmony, in rhythm, in sync. Why do soldiers sing themselves off to war? Why do ship wreck victims sing themselves down with the ship? Why did slaves sing themselves through their travail? Why does every feeling have a song — thousands of them? Why do the oppressed raise their voices together to sing for their strength? Why does every nation have an anthem? Why does every school have a song? Why does every church have hymns? Why does every couple have a tune that can bring romantic stirrings back long after the relationship has ended? Why does every generation have a beat that can bring back the decades faster than any recounting of historical data? Why can a song bring back memories long buried?

The answer is that music makes a soul connection and that connection is universal. At the deepest level of your existence lies your soul. When your soul understands, it sends essential truths to your brain. Then your brain can communicate with the rest of your body, to heal, to accept, to change, to embrace the root of the problem or illness. In **Woman Heal Thyself**, Jeanne Elizabeth Blum writes, "Yogis don't chant for the fun of it or because they have nothing better to do with their time. They chant because chanting certain sounds (such as OM or A-E-I-O-U vowel chants - in as low a tone as possible) raises their inner vibrations to a higher spiritual level."[1] She goes on to exhort, "Shout, sing, laugh, groan, weep, or wail your way to health and clear out unwanted *bad* stored organ energy!"

Well, that's what I've done quite naturally many times in my life. I may have had trouble crying each time I had a broken heart, but I sure didn't have trouble belting out sad love songs. I didn't know anything then about Chinese medicine based on twelve energy flows and associated emotions. I didn't know then that a kidney full of fear and terror would rob energy from the heart, so that joy, self-confidence, compassion, and love associated with heart energy could not be felt.

When I looked back on my life through the filter of Chinese medicine, however, it all made sense. Fear and terror had been my silent partners through most of the first three decades of my life. I didn't know how to have fun due to my obsessive fear that it would be taken away and replaced by my constant worries. I put up a facade of confidence while I shuddered inside with terror that my act would be revealed. And, the love that I so longed to experience could not be felt due to my frightened certainty that I was not "enough" to love. My kidney fear certainly seemed to be stifling my heart love.

The very cliché of "singing my heart out" helps me to understand now that my body was naturally trying to purge my heart from the fear that was incapacitating it with one break after another.

Another great thing about singing is that you've got to take in more air in order to do it — you've got to BREATHE! The Chinese have a name for this breathing energy, too. It's called *Shen* energy and it is said to be stored on the heart and associated with the spirit, the mind and emotions.

Roberta Schweitzer, a research nurse and post-doctorate student at UCLA, is adopting a form of mind-body prayer into physical therapy courses for patients with severe arthritis and breast cancer. She feels that inner peace and strength are excellent tools for coping with chronic illness. The mixture of prayer, modern dance movements and ancient Hebrew chanting was developed at the Stephen S. Wise Temple in Los Angeles, Ca. Participants report that being in a holy place with a whole group of people doing similar movements and meditations provides a real sense of connection.

It becomes more clear all the time why singing, whether off key or on, is a very important thing to do!

[1]*Blum, Jeanne Elizabeth, Woman Heal Thyself, Charles E. Tuttle Co., Inc., Boston, Massachusetts, 1995, p. 102.*

On a recent Caribbean cruise, my husband and I took a day trip to Cozomel on a beautiful Catamaran. We were with about 40 other passengers. The day was balmy, the water was aquamarine blue, and the ocean's rolling was gentle and soothing. Just as we set sail, the captain put on rock n' roll hits from the '60s and '70s (my favorite music) and his crew began passing out margaritas. I could hardly contain myself. I wanted to dance. I looked around and was amazed that no one else was moving to the beat — not even slightly. I began to sing under my breath, so no one would hear and to sway slightly with the music. I noticed that the woman next to me was also caught up in the music. Her husband had agreed to watch their five kids so she could totally enjoy the afternoon, and she was starting to do just that. Soon, we were having a party for two, soaking in the rays and the notes. My husband's allergic to the sun, so he watched from inside the cabin, smiling at my nirvana. We arrived at our snorkeling destination, had a marvelous dive, then with all passengers completely exhilarated, took off for the sail back to port. This time, people had indulged in enough sun, fun and margaritas that one by one everyone started to shed their inhibitions and do what came naturally — sing and dance. For over one hour, forty strangers partied like long, lost friends. We sang, we danced, and all shreds of self-consciousness were tossed out to sea as we finally established a feeling of safety and trust with each other that allowed us to be ourselves, even in a group. We were able to join with nature in an incredible celebration of the senses. We were touching, seeing, smelling, breathing, tasting every moment and expressing our JOY through song and dance.

Song and dance give voice and movement to our emotions. The internal flow in our body is externalized and connected with the environment and all around us. "Indeed," says Nancy, "music is important because it will change your physiology. It changes your breathing (deeper from the diaphragm), your circulation, your energy — music makes you want to get up and move."

Choreographer Anna Halprin became a dramatic example of how music and dance can change physiology when she was stricken with cancer 25 years ago. She tells of lying stricken in bed and having a vision of a black bird, which she interpreted as a messenger of death. Anna told the bird she hadn't finished her work on earth, and the bird relented, promising her she could live if she used dance in the service of peace and love. Anna went on to have surgery and, as a visualization to speed recuperation, drew a picture of herself looking healthy. She tried to dance in response to the drawing and couldn't. She then drew an angular and distorted self-portrait, which inspired her to dance like a wounded animal. It was then that she could create a dance of healing. Her cancer was soon found to be in remission and Ms. Halprin, now 76, has devoted her work as a teacher and choreographer to causes promoting peace and love.

Another testament to dance comes from film star Michael Kidd, who danced his way through many an MGM musical in the '40s and '50's. He feels that the choreography that used to go into great screen dance numbers now goes into plotting the action in today's disaster-filled, pyrotechnic blockbusters. In his acceptance speech for a special Academy Award for career achievement in 1997, Kidd said, "Perhaps this award signifies an awareness that we have been missing something, namely the vitality and joy in living that movie musicals can express in song and dance."

For those of you who want the vitality and joy, but who don't want to get up and move, or can't even bring yourselves to sing softly in the shower, do not despair! Participation can happen internally, as well. Listening to music can be enough to evoke certain feelings. The important part is to let those feelings flow with the music. Stuffing them back or shutting them down once they've come to your attention, is like pulling a needle across an album. You're putting a scratch into your system. Needles caused scratches on our record albums of old, which precipitated songs getting stuck in the groove. Don't let your emotions get stuck in the scratches of your internal system. Let them flow and clean out whatever wounds you may carry so that healing can take place.

Another magical thing about music is its ability to defuse anger. Elizabeth had a singing coach once who had her sing every time she was having a fight with her boyfriend. Elizabeth noted, "You can't sing what you're angry about and stay upset." Just the thought of a couple singing out their doubts, misgivings and accusations in their own custom-designed opera brings a smile to my lips. It certainly helps sift out what's petty and silly from what's real and needs to be talked about calmly once the grandiose, operatic emotions have passed.

Which brings us full circle. Singing opens up the heart. It's hard to stay angry if you're reminded that you love your sparring partner. It's nice to know we have a sure fire way of getting to our heart energy by putting a song in our hearts.

One of the best blind dates I've ever heard of was experienced by Nancy not long ago. She was expecting to meet Fred for the first time at dinner. Then a friend told her about sing-alongs held at the Jazz Bakery in Santa Monica every Sunday afternoon. A true singing enthusiast, she didn't want to miss the event, but she didn't see how she'd fit in dinner with Fred on the same day. So, she called Fred and asked him to accompany her to the Jazz Bakery. To her delight, he also liked to sing. To her embarrassment, the program that afternoon was Irving Berlin love songs. They walked in strangers, sang some of the most beautiful love songs in the world to each other, and walked out with the hearts open enough to talk and share without the nonsense and game-playing often associated with first dates. The honesty that joined them in music remained a strength in their relationship.

How To Put A Song In Your Heart

1) If music has slipped out of your life, do a little music history: What were your favorite songs as a kid? Did you sing at home? Were you ever told not to sing? Who told you not to sing? When do you first remember dancing? Did you like it? Were you inhibited?

2) List some songs that made a difference in your life (i.e., first love, wedding songs, music associated with memories).

3) When was the last time you listened to your favorite music? Do you have CDs of your favorite songs? If not, get some.

4) Have you ever danced all by yourself? You don't need to have a partner. Put on one of those favorite songs and MOVE! Move, anyway you feel like it, sway with the music, let it go through you and guide you. There's nothing to feel self-conscious about, because it's just you.

5) If you have a headset available — listen to a song of your choice on the headset. Lay down. Close your eyes and listen. Pay attention to the music traveling through your body. How does it make you feel? What thoughts come to mind. Picture a blank movie screen in your mind, and see what images the music puts there. Where does the music take you? Try this with different types of music.

6) Change the station on your car radio. For one week, listen to a different channel every day. Who knows what you may discover.

7) Take a talk radio break. Let music take you away rather than exposing yourself to more arguments and diatribes on talk radio. We're already stressed out. Who needs more stress programmed into us? Alternate talk and music radio. Believe me, the opinions will still be there when you get back to the talk.

8) Sing or hum a melody that may be going through your head. Perhaps you have original lyrics to add to your tune or someone else's. Try this after a 5-minute meditation. Who knows what type of ditty may be born!

Movement	Connection	Awareness
_____	_____	_____
_____	_____	_____
_____	_____	_____

28

Exercise

Exercise was always something I did with an express purpose in mind: Lose five pounds; Fit into my old jeans; Impress a man; Look better on TV... I exercised to get it over with, so I could get back to what was really important — my work — or anything else for that matter. I especially took walking for granted. Then MS came along and numbed my limbs so much that I couldn't feel my feet touch the ground. In the shadow of my career-track, numbed-out existence, I realized I had more than a physical problem. I had never taken the time to deal with the emotion of movement. I didn't know how to *feel* what my walk was saying about me to others, as well as to myself.

One day, as I sat complaining to Tobes, about my stiff neck, the pains in my back, and my difficulty walking up inclines, she suggested I do some movement work. I had my doubts, but a week later I ended up in an INTELLIKINETICS™ class, created and taught by Tobes' daughter, Megan Reisel. Megan defines the process as "exploration designed to give back the full scale of movement available to you as a human being."

We Are More Than The Sum of Our Parts

I walked into Megan's class prepared to dance, move vigorously, and get a good cardiovascular work-out. That was not to be, however. After a few, gentle warm-up exercises, my five classmates and I sat in chairs and raised our arms over and over again, until Megan determined that we had actually felt the arm movement lift our waists and sensed how that movement was connected to the rest of our bodies. I was baffled, but I tried to have a profound feeling of movement. Then Megan had us walk around the studio, experience its space, and contemplate how we felt as part of the space.

I looked at my classmates and realized I was supposed to feel connected to them and to this strange little studio and wondered how I was going to accomplish that. One middle-aged piano teacher was learning to move to music for the first time after decades of sitting rigidly in accord with her mother's reprimand "not to show off." A professional mime had been unconsciously limiting his movement to the upper half of his body and now

190

was discovering his lower torso. A male psychologist, deaf in one ear, sought to straighten a spine that had become deformed through years of straining to listen to patients with his other ear. A 38-year-old mom-and-career superwoman was putting chronic fatigue and immune deficiency disorder behind her by discovering the mind-body-spirit connection in movement. A young woman, used to hiding from sexual harassment, was rediscovering her femininity by moving with pride in her own body.

What did we all have in common? We had each failed to perceive our own body as a whole entity rather than a bunch of parts. We had disassociated our bodies from what we did, how we felt, and how we acted. We had overlooked that *every* movement and action of our lifetimes is stored in the body's memory — a memory more powerful than that of the most powerful computer chip ever invented.

The Energy Connection

Learning to understand movement had a lot to do with pulling my body back from the brink. By attending to how I moved, I learned how fixed some of my thinking was, indeed, how rigid I had become. I was amazed to find that walking could be like landing on soft rubber springs if I stopped cutting myself off from my environment. Megan says we trap energy inward to protect our personal space, so we avoid connecting with the energy from the space around us.

Through various exercises, I've learned that conscious movement flows through the entire body; a hand movement is connected clear to my toes, and I can now feel movement ripple through my body. I was surprised to discover that I start every move by tensing my shoulders. I was living in my head; and my aching shoulders, as Megan puts it, were dragging my body along for the ride as if it were "hung on a hanger," where I could ignore it like baggage or dead weight.

My body is now a partner in my healing. Every time I work on an area of pain or stiffness in my body and focus on movement in that area, I am rewarded with a memory or a feeling that I've buried in that part of my body.

Breathing in Life

A few months after I began working with Megan, I took a spa vacation in Hawaii. Having in mind the goal of fitting into an impossibly slinky gold dress, I optimistically enrolled in the spa's "Cardioblast" workout. The bouncy instructor led me and seven far younger classmates outside for a quasi-boot camp drill. After running up and down 25 stairs five times, striding backwards up hill, and doing lunges down hill, and dropping to the ground to do push-ups, we began a 5-mile power walk up into the hills. I knew that I would probably die, as I certainly didn't have the stamina to continue, and my faulty sense of direction would never get me back to the hotel.

Suddenly, I straightened and looked up and out and was awed by what I saw and felt. The beauty that I was walking *through* entered my consciousness and energized me. With volcanic mountains to either side of me, the gorgeous ocean pulsing below, and the fragrance of grass and flowers swirling around me, tears of joy came to me as I acknowledged what I almost missed in my exercise frenzy.

And so I move — mindfully now. I exercise seven days a week, and I'm thankful to be able to do so. Now my sense of self is visualized from within and connected to others, not through needy approval, but with acceptance of my whole being. I vary my workout — some days aerobics, some days floor exercises and weights, sometimes a combination and some days a good brisk 2-mile walk.

Find Your Own Routine

Poor eating habits combined with sedentary lifestyles contribute to more than 300,000 deaths a year in America — more than sexually transmitted diseases, firearms, infectious diseases and toxic agents combined. We're dying early from issues firmly within our control. Kathy Smith, internationally known health and fitness expert, lost her father to a heart attack when he was only 42. Two years later her mom died in a plane crash. She was only 19. She shares that exercise helped to lift her out of the deep depression caused by her loss. She has devoted her life to getting people up and exercising. In more ways than one, exercise can save your life. All you have to do is get past the number one excuse for not exercising — *"I've got no time,"* — and find a routine that works for you.

This is one part of the workbook that is completely free form. You must find your own routine. There is no one right way to exercise. There is one rule, however. Whatever you are doing — vary the exercise. If our bodies get used to the same routines every day, the muscles don't get a good workout. Shape up your body by shaking up your exercise habits.

Recent government guidelines say that 30 minutes a day of any kind of physical exercise is enough to keep most people fit. This is enough to burn 1,000 to 1,200 additional calories a week which, studies say, accrues substantial cardiovascular improvement and protection from heart disease. Those 30 minutes don't even have to come all at once. The latest study to confirm the effectiveness of short, moderate bouts comes from Deakin University in Melbourne, Australia. It found that nine weekly 10-minute sessions offer the same cardiovascular benefits as three weekly 30-minute sessions. This allows you to turn your coffee break into an exercise break along with those breathing breaks from Chapter 25.

According to Porter Shimer's book, **Too Busy to Exercise** (Storey Communications, 1996), experts believe a daily exercise regimen should include three types of activity: a cardiovascular or aerobic component for improving heart and lung function and for burning calories; a strength-building component to increase muscle mass; and a flexibility component for relief of stiffness and stress. He goes on to give an easy way to fill those requirements:

Sample Daily Exercise Requirement

1) Five to 10-minute stretching routine before you get out of bed or while you're in the shower.

2) Five to 10 minutes of strength exercises.

3) A 10-20 minute brisk walk or aerobics routine.

To lose weight, additional exercise must be added, of course. This is a maintenance program to *keep* fit.

I love exercise videos and I have lots of them from "The Firm" Time Life series to Jane Fonda, Kathy Smith and *Basic Yoga* from the American Yoga Association. They allow me to work out when it's best for me. I used to exercise at 6:30AM before going to work. Recently, my body asked for a new routine. It was tired of the yoga/stretch, followed by meditation, ending up with aerobics schedule that I had been doing for several years. I was in the midst of writing this workbook, and that's what my body wanted to concentrate on in the early hours of the morning. I began getting up at 5:30AM, doing ten minutes of yoga and stretch exercises, 15 minutes of meditation, breakfast, then 3 to 4 hours of writing. I then broke up my day by doing aerobic exercise for half an hour around 10:30 or 11AM After that I showered and dressed. This is obviously an at-home office routine. Although, a lunch hour exercise routine could work for those in offices.

The point is to be creative. By getting a good block of writing done early in my day, I found my mind continued to create and write the rest of the day whether or not I was at my computer screen. By splitting up my exercise, I was making sure to get good breathing breaks, too. When I'm between books and traveling more, a different exercise routine will be born. The point is JUST DO IT — AND VARY WHAT YOU'RE DOING!!

Be Creative — Ideas for Travelers & Commuters

Here are a few other ideas: If you travel a lot, make sure to take the stairs whenever possible instead of escalators or elevators; Walk briskly to as many of your appointments as possible; Do floor exercises in your hotel room. I remember partial routines from my videotapes that I do on the road.

Even if you're in the car commuting a lot, there's an exercise routine for you. Cynthia Targosz had recorded a tape called "Drive to Fitness," to energize, tone and reduce stress. Again, be creative.

Exercising While Sedentary

* You can tense individual muscle groups, hold the tension, then relax.

* You can do isometric exercises, letting your muscle groups provide resistance by pushing or pulling against each other or an object — for example, hold your knees together like you're squeezing a grapefruit, then relax and do that with your elbows, squeezing them into each side, like you're trying to squeeze your mid-section out, so your elbows can meet — then relax. Squeeze your lower back into your seat back like you're trying to push the seat into the trunk. Tense your stomach and pull it into your back bone, taking a deep breath and holding it as you hold your stomach in, then exhale and let your stomach relax, pushing it out as full as it will go. Repeat this one five times slow, then five times fast, because you'll love the way it can help flatten troublesome tummies. Push your fanny into your car seat as hard as you can, then relax.

* Twist and stretch your shoulders. Twist and stretch your neck. What you are doing is checking in with various body parts, becoming mindful of them, waking them up and breathing energy into them.

While you may feel like you're going nowhere in traffic, you'll be getting all systems flowing in your body. If you do these exercises while driving, please remember to always keep your eyes on the road and stop exercising when you're moving in heavy traffic.

Young At 70

> "There is no drug in current or prospective use that holds as much promise for sustained health as a lifetime program of physical exercise."[1]

That statement appeared in the *Journal of the American Medical Association* in 1982 and remains the closest thing we have to fountain of youth wisdom. A new study from the NASA/Johnson Space Center and the Institute for Aerobics Research in Dallas indicates that the previously accepted age-related decline in aerobic capacity of 10% per decade after 25 IS NOT INEVITABLE; that much of the functional losses that set in between the ages of 30 and 70 are, in fact, attributable to lack of exercise. The study shows that a 70-year-old man who remains lean and does three hours a week of aerobic exercise (such as cycling, running, or vigorous walking) will lose only 7% of his aerobic capacity.[2]

Still Asking "Why *Should* I Exercise?"

Dr. Leslie Dornfeld, founder of Protective Medicine, Inc., finds that men historically have been more inclined to exercise because of their affinity for sports, while women have been more inclined to think of exercise primarily as a means to avoid obesity. "Perhaps neither sex fully appreciates how important exercise is to overall health," Dr. Dornfeld asserts. "It has clearly been shown that women who exercise regularly can increase the strength of their bones and obtain the same benefits as men as far as their heart, circulation and stroke are concerned. There is even evidence that shows that the risk of developing breast cancer might decrease with exercise. Male or female, if you ask me, 'Should I exercise?' I respond with a resounding, Yes, why take the *risk* of *not* exercising?"

Repeat after me, this simple mantra of benefits:

Aerobic activity improves heart and lung function;

Weight bearing exercise builds bone;

Both increase lean body mass.

And for those of us interested in weight loss: Adding exercise to a low-calorie diet not only burns more calories, but also helps prevent the loss of muscle and drop in metabolic rate that usually accompanies dieting.

---

[1] *Reprinted by permission from the University of California at Berkeley Wellness Letter,* © *Health Letter Associates, 1997. To order a one year subscription, call 800-829-9170.*

[2] *Ibid., Volume 2, Issue 8, May 1995, "Young at 70", pp. 2–3.*

The bottom line, according to the *University of California at Berkeley Wellness Letter*, November '96 issue, is *exercise creates stronger bones, better control of blood sugar, higher HDL ("good") cholesterol, more vigor, and a greater sense of well-being. And, it's an excellent way to maintain weight loss and prevent future weight gain.*[3]

And, don't forget, greater confidence, sexual aliveness, increased awareness and, in some cases, better memory can also be benefits of exercise.

"O.K.," you may say, "I'll buy all of that, but stretching is boring. Can't I skip that?"

No, and here are the reasons why: Stretching builds flexibility, the range of motion of a joint or group of joints. Here are the benefits as listed in the April, 1997 issue of the *"Harvard Women's Health Watch"*: *A more symmetrical body, better posture, improved balance, relief of muscle cramps, alleviation of low back pain. It can help you reach the top shelf, button the back of your blouse, and stay upright on icy streets. Moreover, stretching is one form of exercise that feels great, even at the beginning. For verification, just ask the nearest cat."*

Below are flexibility training exercises recommended by *Harvard Women's Health Watch* with the following advice: *"Because flexibility varies widely throughout the body, the exercises illustrated below are designed to work each of the major joints. Do as many repetitions as you like. If you feel any pain while doing them, stop."*[4]

Gastrocnemius and Achilles Tendon
Stand upright, slightly more than an arm's length from a wall. Bend one leg forward and keep the opposite leg straight. Lean against the wall, bracing your lower arms against it. Keep the heel of your rear foot down, sole flat on the floor, foot pointing forward. Hold the stretch for 10 seconds and relax. Switch legs and repeat.

Abductors
Sit upright on the floor with your buttocks against a wall, your legs flexed and your heels touching each other. Grasp your feet or ankles and pull them as close to you as possible. Lean forward from the hips without bending your back and attempt to lower your chest to the floor. Hold the stretch for 10 seconds and relax.

[3] *Ibid., Volume 13, Issue 2, November 1996, "The Real Effect of Exercise on Weight Control".*

[4] *Excerpted from the April, 1997 issue of the Harvard Women's Health Watch, © 1997, President and Fellows of Harvard College.*

Hip Flexors

Lie on the bed or floor, with your legs out-stretched. Flex one hip, and raise the knee toward your chest. Interlock your hands behind the raised knee. Bring your knee to your chest. Hold the stretch for 10 seconds and relax. Reverse legs and repeat.

Quadriceps

Stand upright with one hand against a surface for balance and support. Flex one knee and raise your heel to your buttocks. Slightly flex the supporting leg. Reach behind and grasp your raised foot with one hand. Pull your heel toward your buttocks. Hold the stretch for 10 seconds and relax. Reverse legs and repeat.

Lower Back

Sit upright in a chair with your legs separated slightly. Extend your upper torso, bend at the hip, and slowly lower your stomach between your thighs. Hold the stretch for 30 seconds and relax.

Buttocks and Hips

Sit upright on the floor, with your hands behind your hips and your legs extended. Bring your left foot over your right leg and slide your heel toward your buttocks. Reach over your left leg with your right arm. Press your right elbow into your knee and look over your left shoulder. Hold for 30 seconds. Relax. Reverse legs and repeat.

Lower Back

Lie flat on your back with your body extended. Flex your knees and slide your feet toward your buttocks. Grasp your thighs and pull your knees toward your chest, elevating your hips slightly. Hold the stretch for 30 seconds. Re-extend your legs slowly, one at a time.

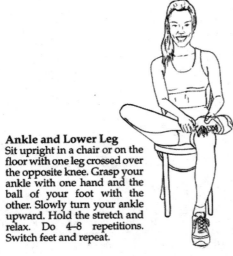

Triceps
Sit or stand upright with one arm behind your lower back, placed as far up your back as possible. Lift the other arm overhead, while holding a folded towel, and flex your elbow. Grasp the towel with your lower hand. Work your hands together. Hold the stretch for 10 seconds and relax. Reverse arm positions and repeat.

Ankle and Lower Leg
Sit upright in a chair or on the floor with one leg crossed over the opposite knee. Grasp your ankle with one hand and the ball of your foot with the other. Slowly turn your ankle upward. Hold the stretch and relax. Do 4–8 repetitions. Switch feet and repeat.

Deluxe Exercise Combo

We close this section with an invitation to experience a once a week deluxe combo of meditation, breathing, and exercise that can literally energize all the systems of your body. I call it the "Theme Regime." Treat yourself to this sensual experience at least one day a week. It will take 40 to 45 minutes.

1) Do five minutes of gentle stretches to wake up your body.

2) Sit on the floor Indian style or sit straight and relaxed in a chair with both feet flat on the ground. Close your eyes and select a color which will stay with you for the entire routine. (For example, let's use the color green)

3) Rotate your body from the waist up counter-clockwise as you take five deep breaths — each time breathing in the color green.

4) Now meditate for 15 minutes, visualizing the color green and all of its many embodiments and wonders. Meditate on the many shades of green. What does green smell like? What does green feel like? What does green sound like? How does green taste?

5) After completing your meditation, immediately get up and go for a 20-minute walk. Do not speak to anyone. Remain silent. Take that concentration on green into your walk and actually experience the sight, smell, feel, sound and taste of green.

You can do this with colors, objects, days, months, events — whatever comes into your mind. The result is a wake up call to your concentration, your senses and all of your systems while you receive the benefits of meditation and exercise.

The Too Young To Be Old People

Once upon a time there was a very young man and a very young woman who were married to each other and who had gotten very old — old beyond their years. They got up every day and did all the things they were supposed to do. They got dressed, they went to work, they made money, they ran the house and paid the bills. They ate three nutritious meals a day and kept up with all the mail, electronic and non. They read their newspapers, watched public television, contributed to charity, saved for retirement, and said they loved each other right before they went to sleep every night. They did everything right. They even had two children, a boy and a girl, and raised them very carefully to be just like them.

One day, the very young man and very young woman who had gotten very old noticed that something very strange was happening. Their children, not yet five, looked like very old little people. They got up every day, ate their meals, busied themselves with toys, games and learning. They never made a mess or a fuss. They never raised their voices or got out of line. They were all very busy, but something was missing in the lives of this very young family who had gotten very old. They were puzzled through and through. What were they to do?

A week later, the very young mother took her very young children to the grocery store. They rode silently in the car, watching the road and looking very old. When they got to the store, just outside the door was a grassy area full of kids doing something the two very young/old children had never heard before.

"What's that Mother?" the very old little girl asked.

"What's what?" Her mother replied.

"That pretty sound coming out of all of their mouths," replied the puzzled very old little boy.

The mother listened and got very sad. "It sounds like something I used to do a long time ago. I think it's laughter.

"Why are they laughing?" asked the little girl.

"What are they doing that makes them laugh? asked the little boy.

The mother looked very hard at what the children were doing and tried very hard to remember. She thought and she strained and she closed her eyes tight. Then she opened her eyes and nodded no as a tear rolled down her very serious, very old cheek. "I can't remember what it's called. I just don't know how. I think I used to do it, but I don't do it now. I'm so sorry."

Just at that moment several of the children ran up to the little boy and girl and said, "Do you want to play with us?"

"What is play?" They both asked together.

All the children giggled and one said very proud, "You two are very funny. You make us laugh out loud. Come on and play with us."

The little boy and girl wanted very much to learn to play and laugh. They asked their mother if they could go, but were so afraid she'd answer no.

The mother quickly nodded and took a big breath, "Oh, yes, you must go. It's what I had forgotten. What I didn't know. Then she did something the children had never seen her do before. She smiled.

The children were amazed. "Mom, you look so pretty with your face that way. Whatever has changed, you should do everyday!"

She took out her compact and looked at her face. It was young again with her smile back in place. "I'm smiling," she shouted with joy, "and I will teach you how. First, you must laugh and play — that's what to do now. I will watch, because I must remember how."

The children played and began to look as young as they were. Their very young mother watched and a beautiful sound came from her. The sound was one she had not made in years. She was humming a joyful song for the ears. She turned and skipped into the store. Her song made shopping enjoyed even more. She smiled at other shoppers who smiled back and stopped, whispering one to the other, they all seemed shocked!

They asked, "Whatever has she done? The old looking mother looks young?"

The woman heard them and smiled bigger than before. She'd learned to laugh and play! What a great trip to the store!

The above is a fairy tale for children and adults. Its purpose is to unite them in activities learned as children which often slip from adult consciousness without concerted effort. Often in our desperate search for survival, we forget a time when fantasy filled our lives, when our minds were teeming with creative pictures, when we discovered and honored the muse, when we believed that anything and everything was possible.

At times we actually run the risk of losing our imaginations to excessive television, mass-media advertising, struggle and stress. To find our imaginations again we merely have to look at children playing in a grassy field and remember the children we were. We must remember what it was like to live and speak from our hearts before the barriers and filters of society sprang up around them.

In the worst case of losing our emotional lives to stress, an increasing number of Americans are reversing home with work and work with home in terms of time, pleasure, accomplishment, and fulfillment being recognized. Often people are with a company longer than they are with their spouses. The corporate world has created a sense of family that is often more workable than home life. Arlie Russel Hothschild writes about the phenomenon in his book, **When Work Becomes Home and Home Becomes Work**. In the process, people begin to limit their lives and make emotional sacrifices in many areas of their lives. Their hearts and imaginations become less active as their minds take over with increasing regimentation and resignation.

A great compliment to someone aging in our society is to say, "Ah, but you are very *young at heart*." And, what does that mean? It means they have imagination, they love to play and sing and dance and live a vibrant life full of possibility and love. They are heart directed. They still have dreams and a belief that dreams can come true. The imagination speaks for the soul, and the keeper of imagination is the child within us all. That child never loses his or her desire to play, yet we adults often prohibit, shortcut or even refuse to allow it to happen. Passion then seeps from our wounds as we cry for what is lost — our emotional memory, psychic life and heart-directed and felt imagination. Soon it is hard to feel very strongly about anything because our hearts aren't involved. We become like the very old young people in the fairy tale. We get everything done, but without emotions and without fun. It's like we are sleep-walking thorough a numbed-out existence — going from event to event without processing how we feel about the event's impact on our lives.

Family Life Magazine recommends that every day adults should spend a few moments imagining life from a child's point of view. An extra benefit of this exercise for parents is that they often are motivated to modify the way they speak to their children. This is also interesting to do with your co-workers, bosses, and friends. It's a great reality check to see just how you are coming across to others.

One way to keep all of this from happening is to play. Through the simple act of playing, the keeper of our creativity, imagination and loving heart is kept alive — our youthful spirit, the innocent child within us all. Here are a few rules to help you get back into playing.

Rule 1: There is no right way or wrong way to play as long as it is enjoyable for all involved.

Rule 2: There can be no judgment or criticism involved in playing.

Rule 3: One must not be self-conscious when playing. Don't worry about how you look or sound. Just let what comes natural flow from your heart.

Rule 4: Everybody's a winner when playing. There are no losers.

Rule 5: *Do Not Worry About What Anybody Else Thinks. The Only Perception That Counts Is Your Own.*

Speaking of being a kid — list five physical things you liked to do as a kid. This was a tough one for me, because I was afraid of almost everything physical. My dad taught me to play catch by throwing the ball smack between my eyes. That's where it landed and I've never had the courage to catch. I loved to go out on boats, until my mom kept saying, "Don't you feel sick yet?" After enough questioning, I was pretty sure I felt seasick. In my adulthood, I've never been seasick, even through storms at sea.

I finally listed: Sing and dance, Go to the beach, Swing, Play hopscotch. Your turn:

Five Physical Things I Loved To Do As A Kid

1) _____

2) _____

3) _____

4) _____

5) _____

Now, when was the last time you did some of those things? Too childish, you say. Well, that may be exactly the point. When I don't dance enough, I feel seriously dance-deprived. Sometimes just dancing around the house makes me feel light-hearted. I know I don't sing enough, but every once in awhile I do belt out a good one when alone in the car. Fortunately, I live on the beach. That makes all ages of me extremely happy. I swing whenever I get the chance — at a resort, on the beach in Mexico, on a playground in Malibu, with my granddaughter in her back yard. And, I gave an indoor hopscotch mat to my granddaughter, maybe so I'd have an excuse to play with her. We spend a lot of time and money looking for youth, but play can't be sold as a magic elixir — it's FREE! All we have to do is PLAY!

Now, it's up to you. Take some time to play everyday. It will put youth in your life, a smile on your face and a song in your heart. Try it! Here are 52 suggestions — one for each week of the year.

52 Play Prompters

1) Play with your children or someone else's. Play just like they do. Try hop scotch, jump rope, hide n' seek, jacks, marbles — join in and play.

2) Try a board game or two. Remember Monopoly and the strategy that always worked for you? How about Clue? Life? Chinese Checkers? Choose your favorite — just make it fun and not too hard.

3) Color your hair or change your hairstyle.

4) Sing out loud while driving. Belt it out — let them hear you in the back row of your make-believe stadium.

5) Gossip with friends.

6) Flirt. Come on! A little harmless flirtation — you can do it with your own spouse or significant other. Just don't forget how to put a little sexy edge in your communication.

7) Mimic voices on TV or see how many voices you have inside of you.

8) Hug a tree.

9) Play in the mud. Build a sand castle. Make love outside. Get down on the ground and get involved with the earth.

10) Make a batch of cookies and eat the cookie dough. Take some cookies out with you and give them to people who are always in the position of waiting on you— the checker at the grocery store, the toll taker at the shopping center, the mechanic, your dry cleaner...

11) Go barefoot on wet grass.

12) Go to a toy store and buy something that appeals to you.

13) Buy a compilation of music from the time you were growing up — play it full blast and sing and dance your heart out.

14) Invite someone you love out on a date. Plan it all and be mysterious.

15) Plan an adventure — something you've never done before — could be hiking, fishing, snow shoeing — as long as you've never done it before. BE SPONTANEOUS. Do something completely unexpected!

16) Do something you really loved to do as a child — view one of your favorite movies from childhood, make a meal on French fries, catsup and a chocolate malt — you name it.

17) Buy yourself something you feel sexy wearing.

18) Go to a concert — the ballet.

19) Spend a day in a museum.

20) Play hooky from work and spend the day doing "stuff" you love to do — not one chore involved.

21) Smile when you're talking. Make an effort to smile at everyone you see.

22) On your morning walk alternate between walking and skipping. When you skip, try humming a little.

23) Play a game of make-believe with someone you love. When you're in a French restaurant, pretend you've just met in Paris...

24) Reward yourself visibly for doing fun things — give yourself a gold star on the calendar.

25) Put on some classical music and pretend you are the orchestra conductor.

26) Buy a giant tablet and some crayons and write notes to someone in huge letters.

27) Color.

28) Paint a picture.

29) Spend the day taking pictures of flowers.

30) Make a very special wish and pretend like it has already come true.

31) Dance in the moonlight.

32) Walk in the park and really take in nature. Notice how many colors there are — how many trees, flowers, birds, insects…

33) Redecorate — or just move things around.

34) Go to a professional sporting event… baseball, basketball, football, soccer, tennis — choose your favorite.

35) Go to a local high school sporting event.

36) Read for fun!

37) Take music lessons.

38) Learn another language.

39) Take up a hobby — start a collection…

40) Take a dance class.

41) Volunteer to help out your community theatre.

42) Go to a local carnival.

44) Go to the circus.

45) Spend a day at the zoo.

46) Throw a party.

47) Go shopping — any kind of shopping that you like to do.

48) Take a class — acting, writing, drawing, painting, decorating…

49) Pretend for a day that you are your favorite character in a movie or TV show.

50) Help needy children, become a Big Brother or Sister, take a senior citizen confined to the house or a retirement home for an outing.

51) Go for a bicycle ride.

52) Go to a playground — watch the kids — join in — swing…

LET YOURSELF GO — PLAY — LAUGH — ENJOY — HAVE FUN —BE SILLY — LET YOURSELF GO — PLAY — LAUGH — ENJOY — HAVE FUN — BE SILLY — LET YOURSELF GO — PLAY — LAUGH — ENJOY — HAVE FUN —BE SILLY — LET YOURSELF GO — PLAY — LAUGH — ENJOY — HAVE FUN —BE SILLY — LET YOURSELF GO — PLAY — LAUGH — ENJOY — HAVE FUN —BE SILLY — LET YOURSELF GO — PLAY — LAUGH — ENJOY — HAVE FUN —BE SILLY — LET YOURSELF GO — PLAY — LAUGH — ENJOY — HAVE FUN —BE SILLY — LET YOURSELF GO — PLAY — LAUGH — ENJOY — HAVE FUN —BE SILLY — LET YOURSELF GO — PLAY — LAUGH — ENJOY — HAVE FUN —BE SILLY — LET YOURSELF GO — PLAY — LAUGH — ENJOY — HAVE FUN BE SILLY — LET YOURSELF GO — PLAY — LAUGH — ENJOY — HAVE FUN —BE SILLY — LET YOURSELF GO — PLAY — LAUGH — ENJOY — HAVE FUN —BE SILLY — LET YOURSELF GO — PLAY — LAUGH — ENJOY — HAVE FUN —BE SILLY — LET YOURSELF GO — PLAY — LAUGH — ENJOY — HAVE FUN —BE SILLY — LET YOURSELF GO — PLAY — LAUGH — ENJOY — HAVE FUN —BE SILLY — LET YOURSELF GO — PLAY — LAUGH — ENJOY — HAVE FUN —BE SILLY — LET YOURSELF GO — PLAY — LAUGH — ENJOY — HAVE FUN — BE SILLY — LET YOURSELF GO — PLAY — LAUGH — ENJOY — HAVE FUN —BE SILLY LET YOURSELF GO — PLAY — LAUGH — ENJOY — HAVE FUN —BE SILLY — LET YOURSELF GO — PLAY — LAUGH — ENJOY

Movement	Connection	Awareness
_____	_____	_____
_____	_____	_____
_____	_____	_____

If The Spirit Is Willing

There once was a very astute and prosperous horse farmer in Minnesota who had the most fabulous stable of stallions in the whole area. All the other farmers looked up to him and his success. One day the farmer's most prized stallion took off and could not be found. When the other farmers in the area heard about it, they were desolate for the man, and immediately came over to console him. They all lamented, "We heard, about your stallion, and it's really terrible."

The farmer calmly replied, "Well, ya' never know."

A few days later, his prize stallion came prancing home, accompanied by another equally fine, if not better, stallion. The other farmers couldn't believe it. They quickly came over to see the new stallion that would make this farmer even richer than he had been before. They exclaimed, "Oh, you're so lucky, what good fortune you have!"

He said, "Well, ya' never know."

Three days later, the farmer's son was outside breaking in the new stallion. He was doing a good job, but the stallion's wildness overpowered the son, who fell and broke his leg from the ankle up to the hip. Doctors weren't sure they could mend the leg in a way that he could ever use it again. The farmers heard the news and came over to express their concern, "Oh, we heard about your son, what an awful thing this must be."

The farmer replied, "Well, ya' never know."

A week later, war broke out. Recruiting efforts took all of the farmers sons away — except the son with the broken leg. As the farmers worried about their sons going off to war, they looked on in astonishment at the farmer and his son with the broken leg only to hear him say, "Well, ya' never know."

This wonderful Sufi teaching story uses the simple phrase, "Well, ya' never know," to illustrate what it means to have faith and reliance in a power that is greater than the individual. That power resides within us all in the form of spirit. There are many names for that spirit; God, Buddha, Allah, Higher Power, Divine Light... It is this workbook's mission not to define or confine spirituality, but to demonstrate it's role in Health-Esteem.

We cannot fully plan our life story. We do not know the outcome, other than that eventually we will die. We do know to expect change, ups and downs, bumps along the road, stress, joy and all the emotions on life's scale. When we come to a crossroads, there is always a point where we must make a leap of faith: When we must look for what we are meant to learn, how we are expected to change, what we are guided to do. Our spirit is there to help us through all of those phases. We don't know everything. Sometimes a bad thing happens, but it brings a greater good. Sometimes a crisis occurs to guide us to a new path. Sometimes pain comes into our lives to make us wiser, stronger, more true to ourselves. Sometimes there is not an answer available for us to immediately discern. If we give up to the crisis before endeavoring to find the good, the message, the purpose, the healing, the direction in which change will lead us — then from my experience, I have only one thing to say, "You may miss the potential of your life by shutting yourself off to the possibilities."

If you just look back on a time in your life that you thought was disastrous and follow it through for three to five years by using the "Well, ya' never know" comment after every turn and change of events, you could have a surprise in store. Things may have turned out completely different from your worries, fears and dire prognostications. For instance:

I once owned a multi-million dollar advertising agency and thought I would die if it went out of business, and I lost its power to define who I was. I worked obsessively to the detriment of every other part of my life, especially my love life. Then one day I was diagnosed with MS, and my fear shifted from losing my business to losing my health... "Well ya' never know."

Time away from the business to discover holistic medicine revealed a woman who would help me decipher the meaning of my life. She also helped me to reach out to other women who became my healing partners. My health improved and so did my business. I decided that I was completely happy with my life as a single, health-directed, business person without a man in my life to complicate issues and possibly break my heart again. "Well, ya' never know."

Two years into my healing, I had learned to love myself, life, healing and the many possibilities around me. When I least expected it, I met a man unlike any I had known before, and we fell head over heels in love. He was my soul mate and we married four months after meeting. His philosophy was to wake up every morning with joy in his heart for what that day would bring. "Well, ya' never know."

In our first year together, my business began to falter. I worked round the clock in a desperate attempt to gain new clients and to save the jobs of the staff I had gathered around me. I all but ignored my husband, thinking that I was nothing without my business, and no one for my husband to love. My MS symptoms worsened. I was in a car accident precipitated by my faulty vision. "Well, ya' never know."

One year later my business was gone. I had time to write scripts and to co-produce a movie with my husband, which became a film festival favorite and allowed us to travel all over the world together. I concentrated on the healing knowledge around me and took it into every part of my life. One by one, my symptoms subsided. As my vision broadened outside of myself, I began to see what healing meant to my entire generation and the world in which we live. "Well, ya' never know."

With my new world perspective, my husband encouraged me to write a book about the process. I was shocked and frightened. I thought it would lead to complete isolation, that I would be shackled to my computer. I wanted to produce — not write! More arguments ensued. "Well, ya' never know."

Two years later my marriage was stable and happy, my book was practically finished, and the concept of Health-Esteem was born. Soon I was asked to do what I had prepared for and excelled in since high school — public speaking. In addition, two concepts for movies sprang from the stories in my book research. My life was different and better in all ways. From failure came recognition of a new way to do what I'd always wanted — teaching — and perhaps making movies, my life long dream. "Well, ya' never know."

The "Well Ya' Never Know" Experiment

Think of the biggest disappointment you have suffered in life. Explain that disappointment in Stage 1 below. Then chart out three major changes in your life that occurred in the three subsequent years. Can you find some ups and downs and twists and turns that are surprising to you now? Did the big disappointment have the long term effect that you expected? Were there some surprising results to your disappointments? Look for those. Please add as many events as you desire to make the twists and turns of this experiment complete.

Stage 1: (Big Disappointment)

_____

_____

_____

_____

_____   "Well, ya' never know."

Stage 2: (Six Months To One Year Later — change in events)

_____

_____

_____

_____

_____   "Well, ya' never know."

Stage 3: (One Year Later — change in events)

_____

_____

_____

_____

_____   "Well, ya' never know."

Stage 4: (One Year Later — change in events)

_____

_____

_____

_____

_____   "Well, ya' never know."

Tobes explains that the philosophy behind these kinds of teaching stories has to do with the need to have spiritual development in our lives. Twelve years after my MS diagnosis, I can look back at the stages in my life that I capsulized above and see how I fought, sometimes against myself. My philosophy was mind over matter. Instead of "Ya' never know," I'd say, "I'll die trying" or "I'll change that any way I can." Only when I started listening to my body, my heart and the world around me could true change move in and transform my life. Solutions were there, ready to reveal themselves when I took off my blinders. I needed balance in my life, but I didn't recognize that fact until my body forced me to see by almost blinding me.

It seems like such a conundrum, this maze that we must go through, to get to the heart of the matter, the truth in our lives — our spirit. Once we find it, however, living life from that center is so worthwhile. That is not to say that pain and hurt and fear and anxiety won't still happen. It is to say that we won't be lost in those feelings as long. Truth, will indeed, set us free.

Often we don't even see what's right in front of us — even when it's the truth. Much like the ancient story of a group of blind men who are asked to experience what an elephant is. They touch the elephant, and after examination are asked "What is an elephant?" One blind man responds — "It is like a tree trunk." Another says, "It's like a snake." They each describe only the part of the elephant personally perceived, mistaking it for the whole.

We're easily deceived by half truths, inappropriate perceptions, and negative or biased lessons that we've been programmed with throughout life. They serve as barriers to our own truth, until we walk away from the old programming that's no longer working in our lives.

An extremely successful magazine publishing executive I interviewed, Joslyn, put it this way, "We spend the first 18 years of our lives with our parents. We spend the next 18 years undoing what they did. At 36 we become adults. There are no more excuses. We cannot blame anyone else. At 36, we better start figuring it out." Joslyn's European heritage found her born to be a pragmatist. Her philosophy is to live life it to its fullest, and she takes full responsibility for that. "There's a freedom," she says "in knowing that whatever I do, it's me — my decision — not anybody else's."

36. Is it a magical year? It was at 36, one year after my diagnosis, that I began looking for answers and was directed inside myself. When I asked Nancy what her spiritual turning point was, she answered with this story from her life:

I've been in a progressive pattern since my early 30's, but the turning point was when I was 36. The guy I was going to marry was having an affair with his secretary, and I broke up with him. A month later, my cat died — which trust me — was much worse for me — to lose my 14-year old cat. I couldn't go home for three days after Dusty died. My mother was out of town, so I stayed at her place. When I mustered the courage to go home, I walked up the stairs to my apartment with dread. I just couldn't face not having Dusty be there to greet me. I walked in and threw myself on the floor where Dusty used to lie by the heater and I cried and cried — it was pathetic.

*A month later, I went to Orange County for a seminar. I ran into friends who invited me over for the weekend. There was a book on their coffee table — they didn't hand it to me — it was just there, **The Game of Life and How to Play It**, by Florence Scovell Shinn. I picked it up, began to read and was intrigued.*

It was New Year's Eve, my life had gone from utter structure to utter chaos, and since I wasn't feeling well, I decided to leave their house early. Even with a sinus headache, I stopped and bought the book I had started to read at their house. I took it home and passed out. I slept through New Year's Eve. I woke up the next day and felt a little better. I spent the next day reading the book. I thought, "Oh my God, can this really be?" It was all about affirmations — I wasn't religious, but I was presented with a lot of God language in Shinn's book. The book deals with the premise that everything you need in life is there for you once you learn how to get it. The author takes excerpts from the Bible and shows you how to interpret them to know that you will be provided for. Without much of a spiritual upbringing, I read the book wanting to believe it, but I needed evidence. "How could I believe it?" I wondered. If this were true there wouldn't be any bad stuff in the world. But every morning I'd get up at 5:30 and go into the living room while it was still dark outside. I'd wrap up in a comfy afghan, turn on a soft incandescent lamp and read parts of the book for half an hour or an hour. I said, "OK, I'll try it — I'll try to believe. OK, God, I'm going to give you the benefit of the doubt." I took a leap of faith. That was 1991.

Nancy's story shows that you can still have a little doubt when you make your leap of faith and start your spiritual exploration. The key is to be open, to listen, to become a student of life. Nancy did just that. She made a comforting ritual out of her exploration and study. Today her doubt is replaced with spirituality and knowing. Nancy explains:

I believe more strongly now that we'll always be provided for. Everyday when I'm driving around, I make a point of noticing how everything is connected to everything else. There really is a greater plan. Even today, I was late to work — I was rushing to the elevator and I panicked when I saw a guy ahead of me. I thought that he was going to get my elevator and I'd be even later if I had to wait for another one. Then, I caught myself and said, "Okay, don't worry about it." He did get the elevator and before I could push the call button, the door opened and three people got off the other elevator. I was reminded that there's more than one thing happening at a time in life. The guy got his elevator — another elevator was coming for me. I had to change my focus — I had to see the connections.

There may be dozens of turning points in a person's life, because each one of us is constantly evolving. The point is to recognize the turning points and to see where their evolution and resolution will take us. Take the leap of faith. You may ask, "What can happen?"

"Well, ya' never know."

It's Elemental

Continuing in the cycle of this workbook, we now need to go back and take a look at the Elements we discussed in Chapter 26. In this chapter we will use the Western interpretation of the elements which includes four elements; water, earth, fire and air. These represent the four qualities that make up creation: Light (fire), airiness, fluidity, and solidity.

The chart below looks at the elements through many different filters including astrology, psychology, ancient spirituality, physics, philosophy and mythology:

	WATER	**EARTH**	**FIRE**	**AIR**
Physics	Liquid	Solid	Plasma	Gaseous
Primary Needs	Water	Food	Warmth	Air
Greek Philosophy	Soul	Physical	Moral	Intellectual
Astrological	Feelings/ Emotions	Physical	Spirit	Mental/ Intuition
Emotions	Fear	Caring/ Concern	Joy	Grief/Sadness

There are many more ways to interpret the elements, but one thing becomes clear as we look at all they are documented to represent; the elements are vital forces that comprise everything we experience in life. We may be guided more by one element than another, but the rest come into play in varying degrees in our lives. The optimum situation is to balance them to our best advantage.

Tobes explains that "When the four elements snap into the proportion that is right for us as individuals, they create harmonious energy that allows a fifth element to become active in our lives, the Universal. We then can function as whole human beings with the awareness to explore our spiritual nature."

Universal Awareness Experiment

To help you get in touch with the physical, mental, emotional and spiritual aspect of yourself, Tobes suggests the following experiment:

1) Using the spirals that have been started for you below, create your own spheres by coloring the spirals in, using red for physical, orange for emotional, bright yellow for mental and green for spiritual. Use crayons or colored pencils. When drawing the spirals, take the time to use many circular lines for each one.

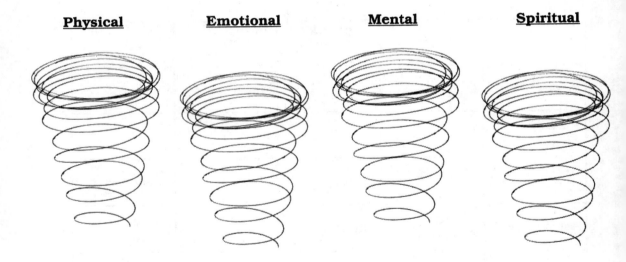

Physical   **Emotional**   **Mental**   **Spiritual**

2) Now, take all four colors and use the space provided below "Universal - the Creator," to mix all of the elements in one dynamic spiral. You may want to hold all the crayons at once to see what mixture evolves, or hold them individually to create the proportional blend that feels right to you. You are creating your own mixture and balance of the elements. This illustrates how the elements ebb and flow in all of our lives — one or two being dominant and the rest finding their appropriate balance.

Universal - the Creator

When the five levels of awareness are functioning in our lives, we become conscious of our world and what we can do for it and for all with whom we share the world. We are directed outward to seek answers to heal the whole not just the individual.

The Reaching Out Experiment

You may ask, "What do I need to move out into the world?" One way to find out is to do a graphic inventory. In the sample below, I began with the "Me" circle in the middle. I then drew lines out like an atomic cluster with a ball at the end of each line. Each ball represented an activity in my life — some balls were closer and some farther away, dependent on how much of my life they encompassed. I labeled each ball accordingly. You will see room for your own cluster below the example. Fill in the activities in your life and see what your world looks like.

At the time I made my cluster, work-related efforts, my husband, and my family of birth monopolized my life. Even community efforts were work related. When I looked at the components in my life, I could begin to see what was missing. I could see what my world looked like, and how I needed to grow it in order to continue my own development. I looked at the "Oh No to Outstanding" list from Chapter 8 and asked myself questions. As you fill in your cluster, I encourage you to do the same. Do I have my city in my life, my community, my friends? Or, am I just stuck with the things that are closest to me?

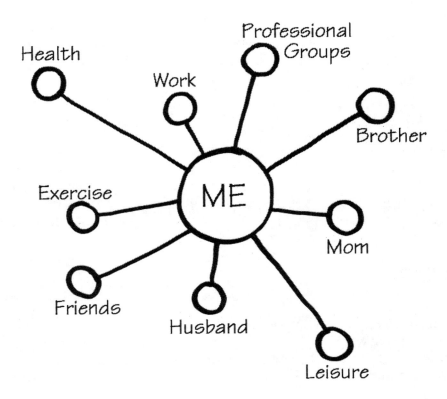

I was stuck, but not for long. Since I was now coming from an attitude that I wanted to create balance in my life, answers came to me as soon as I asked the questions. I will give two examples. I was missing children in my life as well as community involvement. My work creating public service announcements for Women In Film introduced me to Para Los Niños, a charity for homeless children. I found community involvement that satisfied my mothering instinct.

Example two was simply a matter of refocusing on a current activity and connecting it to missing elements in my life. I was a member of Women In Film for professional reasons. My atomic cluster indicated a lack of friends/ sisters in my life. When I became open to going deeper in my relationships, incredible women were already there for me to get to know.

Perhaps the most rewarding work of a lifetime is that involved with charity. Do not ever allow yourself to believe that the giving is one-way. The rewards come in the form of love, wisdom, human experience, inner peace, fulfillment and connection — all things that money cannot buy, but that our soul cannot flourish without.

I will end this exploration into our spiritual connection with an ancient teaching story that Tobes shared with me:

There once was a woman who was a very good spiritual teacher. She went to visit a man friend, also a good spiritual teacher, and listened to him teach. He stressed to his students, "You must work very hard and use all of your energy to knock on the door to your spiritual life. In order for that door to open, you must focus and devote your energy. If you keep knocking and knocking, someone will hear and know that you are serious about your spiritual journey. Then, they will answer."

The woman listened and was increasingly perplexed. She asked her friend, "Why do you keep telling them that you have to knock on the door and the door will be opened, when you know that the door is already open?"

Tobes explains: *The lesson from this story is that both are true. We don't know that the door is open until we knock, yet the door is always open. The first phase of healing or any kind of learning is to invest effort. We say, "I've got to find out." Then, when we do find out we say, "I already knew that." We all move very far away from what a child knows — the innate knowledge with which we were born. Education, conditioning, warnings, injunctions, and false perceptions all cloud this knowledge. It becomes a matter of relearning.*

We are reminded that the choice is not I've got to do this or that, but that I've got to do both — either/and, not either/or. Healing happens where we are not looking, in some deep, organic place, a place that becomes accessible when we function as a whole, balanced human being.

Movement	Connection	Awareness
_____	_____	_____
_____	_____	_____
_____	_____	_____

Love

Now that you have arrived at the last chapter of the workbook, you have the knowledge to get to the heart of the matter — love. You have discovered ways to free yourself from outside perception and definition by realizing that you are the author of your own thoughts. You have learned the importance of expressing those thoughts in your own voice. You have probably even begun to chip away at, or even demolish, some of the barriers that you defensively erected around your heart through the years. Now your heart is ready to find another, not to complete each other, but to enjoy the wholeness of each other.

Exposing the Half-a-Heart/Half-a-Self Theory

I remember a jagged heart necklace that I was given by the first love of my life. Each one of us wore half of a broken heart that when put together made a whole. I used to love that sentiment. Unfortunately, the concept fostered the belief that when we are alone, without our love, we are broken, incomplete, flawed. I believed that philosophy through several unsuccessful relationships in my life. My broken heart kept looking for its princely other half to make it whole. Each time my prince would leave, part of my heart was ripped away, and I felt as if my life force was draining out of me. Recuperation took longer each time, as I patched up my heart and vowed not to let any one else ever again tear open my sensitive wounds. I made up lists to live by: ways I would not be hurt again; behaviors I would perfect to attract the ideal soul mate; attributes my perfect soul mate must exhibit... The problem is my lists were based on molding myself and my future man to fill in all the broken places in each other in order to form a complete, mutually dependent entity. How many wedding ceremonies have you seen that symbolically depict that half-a-heart/half-a-self theory? How many times have two candles been blown out after lighting one candle symbolizing the marriage union?

I now look back with some amusement that I actually believed that civilization was set up to foster half human beings wandering around looking for their other half to complete themselves. Because I bought that perception, I functioned like half of a human being. The half that existed was made up of everyone else's perceptions of what I should be. Ironically, the answer to finding love *was* to find my other half. As we've seen throughout this workbook, however, that half was not on the outside. That half was discovering my heart, my voice, my thoughts and feelings about life independent from outside influence. I became whole when I discovered my health-esteem. I stopped looking for love outside and found it inside. Inherent in the phrase, "I am worth being healthy," is "I am worth love and loving — of myself and of others." It took a crisis to wake me up to that fact. To heal from MS, I had to fall in love with myself, which entailed falling in love with healing, which engendered falling in love with my soul mate. I had to throw out my old lists and make room for a whole person worthy of loving and being loved by others.

Trash The Old Lists Exercise

It's purging time. Just for old times' sake, write down your old wish lists for love — what you wanted in your perfect mate and who you wanted to be as a mate. I wanted a tall, dark, handsome, successful in business, intelligent, humorous, sensitive, athletic, totally devoted, great father, loving son kind of guy. I wanted to be a beautiful, blonde, successful in business, intelligent, humorous, sensitive, in shape, totally devoted, good mother, loving daughter kind of gal. In short, I wanted the male version of what I wanted to be, except I wanted him to be even better at all of it — a little stronger, a little richer, a bit more successful... I wanted perfection plus.

It's your turn. This exercise is for everyone, regardless of your current relationship status. Go back to your ideal wish list. The one that makes you start asking questions like: "Why can't he or she be more like...? If only he or she would... If I could just change one or two things about him or her..."

Personal Top Ten Mating Lists

What I Want In a Mate	What I Want To Be As a Mate
1) _____	_____
2) _____	_____
3) _____	_____
4) _____	_____
5) _____	_____

6) _____   _____

7) _____   _____

8) _____   _____

9) _____   _____

10) _____   _____

Now take the Expectations List on the right, "What You Want to be as a Mate" and see how it compares to your "Wish Wellness Chart" in Chapter 13. Does your mate self compare to your balanced life self? Are there things you could be doing that would make you a more satisfied person if they were self-motivated rather than driven by the need to please a potential mate? For instance, "healthy" wasn't in my wish list, yet it's a dominant force in my life now. I wanted to be fit, but I wasn't exercising. I wanted humor, sensitivity and devotion, yet all three were lavished only on my work, while my friends, community and world around me were ignored. I was waiting to pair with someone in order to round me out. But why wait? I could do it myself I had to let go of all false expectations before I could love. My first step was to "X" out my Top Ten Mating Lists. I encourage you to do that now. You will replace them with LOVE lists like the four that follow. Fill in some blanks now, but remember, these lists are works in progress.

Things I Love About Myself   **People I Love In My Life**

_____   _____

_____   _____

_____   _____

_____   _____

_____   _____

_____   _____

_____   _____

**Things I Love About My
Significant Other**

**Activities, Charities,
Involvements I Love**

_____	_____
_____	_____
_____	_____
_____	_____
_____	_____
_____	_____

When I began to heal from my crisis, I started to learn how to love myself and to accept love into my life. I began to appreciate different levels and types of love and to experience a heart connection to the world in which I live. That connection was dramatized for me the first time I visited a charity for homeless children, Para Los Niños. A darling 5-year-old girl with a smudge on her tiny nose suddenly appeared and hugged my legs. I looked down and saw her little arms reaching up to me to be lifted. I did so, and she enthusiastically wrapped her arms around my neck, pressing as close to me as possible. I spontaneously hugged her back and felt her heart sharing love with mine. Like a sponge she soaked up the nurturing I had to give her. She also left behind an imprint of innocence. We shared an immediate connection beyond words and thought.

One 42-year-old male author that I interviewed has started two corporations, written three books, and devoted the majority of his time to counseling seriously ill and handicapped people after becoming 80% blind and numb over most of his body with MS. He believes in life not thought. He says, If you put importance in the illusions of your mind, it's not as good as putting importance in your life. Nothing you think is as important as your life.

That thought helped me express the bond I share with my husband Jack in a different way. We met two years into my healing process, fell head over heels in love and married four months later. Since then, I have always marveled how we could disagree, sometimes with loud anger and verbal force, then have the fights pass quickly into oblivion, as we return to our loving bond, which grows ever stronger. Our fights are over thoughts, but the connection we have is much deeper, thereby making the thought fights insignificant.

What is a soul mate, after all, if not someone we connect with at a living level, not a thought level? When Jack and I met, we each had an uncanny sense of the other, and we fit into each other whether dancing or intimately entwined. I suddenly knew words to songs I'd never sung and steps to dances I'd never danced. I was being swept off my feet by a man who didn't smoke, drank only one cocktail on occasional days, exercised every day, ate a completely healthy diet, hadn't tried to ravage me on the first date, hadn't asked me to live with him yet, and confidently controlled the direction of his life, without being even slightly intimidated by mine. He could even say the dreaded "C" word, so repugnant to men in and around my generation: Commitment.

Up until a year prior, he would have had nothing to do with the cigarette smoking, junk-food junkie, workaholic woman that I had been, the one who felt mercilessly abused by the vagaries of life. I had changed, taken control of my life, substituted healthy belief systems for sick ones. When I got too sick to pretend any longer that I was comfortable with the way my life was going, I stopped the charade and started looking for the real me. That was when a man who had lived a life full of the values I was looking for could come into my life.

For once we each fell in love without facades. I fell in love with his zest for life, his humor, his wisdom, his voice, his ability to dream. And, sure enough, this man fell in love with my humor, my spirit, my heart, my mind and my very feminine self. Each of us held the antidotes for the other's lifetime wounds. We also held the grow lights for each other's unfulfilled promise. While decades apart in age, our experiences and value decisions in life mirrored one another's. We were whole human beings ready to connect at the deepest level of living. And, that is what we do everyday.

I am living proof that when you have Health-Esteem and take good care of yourself, you are more likely to attract people, things, events and times into your life that are good for you. That is what I wish for all of my workbook readers — a life full of Health-Esteem and love.

Movement	Connection	Awareness
_____	_____	_____
_____	_____	_____
_____	_____	_____

Health-Esteem Crisis Recovery Sheet

Crisis Name _____

Fill in the crisis name you chose in Chapter 5, and refer to your answers from the Crisis Break Down List and the Crisis Progress Sheet, midway through the workbook, before filling in the sentences below. Many things have probably changed since you began this workbook, perhaps even the crisis you're working to solve. Most importantly, your answers are likely to be dramatically different as you put the power of Health-Esteem to work in your life. You know now that you are worth being healthy, and that the thoughts and emotions that have troubled you in the past are within your power to change. That wisdom leads to a lot more positives in sentences like the ones below, and a lot more answers than questions when facing difficult times in your life.

I have faced my fear, I understand it, and _____

_____

I know where my anger originated and I can let go of it now and move on because

_____

I don't have to hate thoughts anymore because they belonged to: _____

_____

I can do so much more now than in the past because _____

_____

Because this happened, I have changed _____

_____

I am different in the way I _____

_____

I have the power to _____

_____

It's my choice to _____

_____

I can do what I need to _____

_____

My thoughts and feelings belong to _____

_____

Workbook Glossary / Index

This glossary covers many of the terms used in this workbook as well as an overview of selected alternative health processes and concepts of particular importance to the author.

Acupuncture: Developed by the Chinese thousands of years ago, the theory is that certain points on the skin affect and control certain organs in the body and by the use of needles these organs, i.e., the liver, heart, intestines, gall bladder, etc. can be affected and if diseased, healed. Acupuncture works with the dual flows of energy called yin and yang contained within the overall conception of energy known as the Chi or life force. These are expressed in everything in the universe; day and night, hot and cold, life and death. Yang stimulates and contracts and is the positive principle, Yin sedates and expands and is the negative principle. Health is dependent on the equilibrium of yin and yang — within the body and within the entire universe. *p. 2.*

Acupressure: (See Shiatsu)

Ayurvedic Medicine: A system of medicine from India that uses a holistic approach to healing based on maintaining balance in the body, mind and spirit. Their philosophy maintains that freedom from sickness depends upon individuals contacting their own awareness, bringing it into balance, then extending that balance to the body.

Balance: A stable mental or psychological state; emotional and physical stability. *chap. 12.*

Body Therapy: A general term that applies to a wide variety of physical therapies, emphasizing skillful touch, which affect posture, function, and behavior. *chap. 4, 25, 28.*

Chinese Medicine: It balances the chi flow in the body with acupuncture and Chinese herbal remedies to cure disease. Some practitioners use Qi Gong, a powerful technique of direct manipulation of chi to facilitate healing. *p. 182, 186, chap. 30.*

Chiropractic: The word chiropractic is an adaptation from the Greek meaning 'manual medicine' or 'manual practice'. Chiropractors look to the spine for the cause of disease as it contains and protects the spinal cord through which vital forces flow that are mediated to all parts of the body through the spinal nerves. Treatment consists of spinal manipulation, soft tissue muscle work, strengthening exercises, and nutritional advice. *p. 102, 149, 150.*

Crisis: A crucial or decisive point or situation; a turning point. An unstable condition involving an impending abrupt or decisive change. An emotionally stressful event or a traumatic change in a person's life. *chap. 5, 6, 9.*

Disease: A pathological condition resulting from various causes, such as infection, genetic defect, or environmental stress, and characterized by an identifiable group of signs or symptoms. Lack of ease; trouble. *chap. 8.*

Esteem: To regard with respect. *chap. 2.*

Health: A condition of optimal well being. *chap. 2.*

Healing: Restore to spiritual wholeness; evolution into consciousness. One of the earliest therapeutic discoveries of man, there is evidence that healing has existed for thousands of years. Most healers agree that in order for healing to take place there must be harmony and balance between the five natural elements contained in all life forms; mind, body, emotional, spiritual and soul. *chap. 2, 7.*

Hellerwork: An integrating process combining structural body work, movement education and dialogue in an exploration of how your body reflects your mind. The aim is to free the patient of set patterns, both mentally and physically, and to enhance to ability to adapt more easily to life's changes.

Herbalist: This describes the general practice of using naturally occurring herbs, rather than pharmaceuticals, to treat disease. Chinese, Ayurvedic, and Naturopaths commonly use herbs in their treatments.

Holistic Practitioner: A general term for any practitioner that considers the body as a whole and approaches treatment of dysfunction with that in mind. Holistic practitioners are often associated with just Alternative Medicine, but many western Medical Doctors use holistic principles.

Homeopathy: Based on "like cures like," it uses natural remedies that stimulates the bodies own healing processes. Homeopaths view the person as a whole a prescribe a remedy to cure what physical, emotional, and life problems that underlie the physical symptoms. *p. 149, 150.*

Immune system: The integrated body system of organs, tissues, cells, and cell products such as antibodies that differentiates self from non self and neutralizes potentially pathogenic organisms or substances. *chap. 12.*

Jungian: Carl Gustav Jung was a Swiss psychiatrist/psychologist who developed analytical psychology emphasizing the roles of conscious and unconscious processes and mythological archetypes as they influence human behavior. *chap. 10, 22.*

Manifestation: An indication of the existence, reality, or presence of something. *chap. 22.*

Mantra: A sacred verbal formula repeated in prayer, meditation, or incantation, with the intent of attaining mystical or spiritual potential. *chap. 2, 20.*

Massage Therapy: A general term for a discipline that utilizes many body work techniques (e.g. neuromuscular therapy, sports massage, visceral manipulation, etc...)

Meditate: To engage in contemplation, especially of a spiritual or devotional nature. Meditation can take many different forms according to an individual's needs. *chap. 20.*

Motivation: an incentive for movement to action. *chap. 11.*

Movement Therapy: A method to teach the body more efficient ways to move, creating correct posture and effective use of the body. It facilities new patterns of balanced movement. *chap. 28.*

Naturopathic Medicine: Viewing the person as a whole, naturopathy uses natural remedies (homeopathy), manipulative techniques, and Oriental Medical Practices to stimulate the bodies natural ability to heal.

Neuro-emotional complex: A mind body pattern in which a subluxation of the spine (nerve pressure) is present in linkage with a negative emotion. Not all emotions are linked with a subluxation.

Neuromuscular Therapy: Specific treatment massage designed to reduce facilitation of traumatized neuropathways, reduce hyperconstriction in the tissues, and restore proper bio-mechanical function.

Nourish: To provide with food or other substances necessary for life and growth; to keep alive; maintain, develop or promote. *chap. 26.*

Nurture: To nourish, to help grow or develop, to cultivate. *chap. 26, p. 176.*

Osteopathy: A comprehensive system of diagnosis and therapy based on the interrelationship of anatomy and physiology for the study, prevention, and treatment of disease. Utilizes hard manipulative techniques (adjustment of the spine), soft tissue massage, and CranioSacral Therapy.

Perception: Recognition and interpretation of sensory stimuli based chiefly on memory and the resultant insight, intuition, or knowledge gained. *chap. 13.*

Physiology: All the functions of a living organism or any of its parts. *chap. 25, 26, p. 187.*

Recuperate: To restore to health or strength, to regain, to recover.

Reflexology: Whenever an organ is out of order, the corresponding reflex in the feet will be very tender upon pressure. Special foot massage techniques are used to releases tension, encourage the full blood supply to areas in distress, and stimulate energy flow within the whole body.

Remission: Abatement or subsiding of the symptoms of a disease. *p. 6, 18.*

Shiatsu: In Japanese, Shiatsu means finger pressure. Shiatsu massage involves firm pressure to various points and areas on the skin known as meridian paths, most of theses points are the same as those used in acupuncture. Referred to as acupressure massage, both arts are based on the same philosophy of medicine — to aim at promoting better health by stimulating the flow of Chi or Ki energy.

Sufi: A school of mysticism that originated out of Middle Eastern philosophy. *chap. 30, p. 207.*

Susceptible: Easily influenced or affected; especially sensitive; highly impressionable. *chap. 16.*

Tai Chi: A non-contact martial art and weight-bearing exercise that combines slow, graceful movements to increase mobility of the joints, muscles and tendons. *chap. 4.*

Yin and Yang: According to Taoist belief, the activating force of all phenomena is the movement of energy between two poles known as the yin and yang. The varying combinations of these two tendencies, yin (the feminine principle) and yang (the male principle) gives all things their distinctive character. (see Acupuncture) *p. 183, chap. 30.*

Yoga: A system of meditation, breathing and postures deeply embedded in Indian culture. The yoga philosophy is to heal the spirit with the body. *chap. 24.*

Wellness: The condition of good physical and mental health, especially when maintained by proper diet, exercise, and habits. *chap. 2, 17.*

Perhaps you think you feel about the same every day, or swing between eight to ten very big emotions. It's more likely, however, that you experience a gamut of emotions just like the rest of us.

There are over 100 feelings listed below. When charting your feelings and exploring your emotional family tree, refer to this list to discover and explore the many sides of you. Think of these feelings as paints—you may want to use a broad brush stroke with some and eliminate others from the canvas of your life. The key is to identify and own your feelings, good and bad, and to notice the shadings, variety, intensity and longevity represented in the overall mix.

Feelings Chart[1]

accepted	affectionate	afraid	angry
annoyed	anxious	ashamed	bashful
bewildered	bitter	bored	brave
calm	compassionate	concerned	confident
confused	defeated	defensive	desperate
detached	disappointed	disgusted	disturbed
eager	edgy	elated	embarrassed
enthusiastic	envious	ecstatic	excited
fearful	foolish	free	frustrated
furious	glum	good	guilty
happy	hateful	helpless	high
hopeful	hostile	humiliated	hurt
inadequate	inhibited	insecure	intense
intimidated	irritable	jazzed	jealous
joyful	lonely	loving	lustful
mean	miserable	needed	neglected
nervous	nostalgic	numb	pained
passionate	peaceful	pessimistic	playful
pleased	pressured	protective	puzzled
rejected	relieved	remorseful	resentful
restless	sad	scared	secure
sensual	sentimental	sexy	shaky
shy	silly	strong	subdued
tender	tense	terrified	tight
tired	trapped	ugly	uneasy
unlovable	uptight	vulnerable	warm
weak	wonderful	worried	

[1]© *The Family Guide To Domestic Violence by Jim Gordon, Ph.D. and Michael Selsman c/o Los Angeles Counseling Center, Beverly Hills, CA 90212.*

Health-Esteem Reading List

Suggestions from Judith Parker Harris

These are just a few of the books that inspired me and my healing team.

Deepak Chopra, M.D.
  • *Quantum Healing*
  • *Perfect Health*
  • *Ageless Body, Timeless Mind*
  • *Unconditional Life*
  Magical Mind/Magical Body
  (cassette tapes and workbook)

Martin E.P. Seligman, Ph.D.
  Learned Optimism

Lee M. Silverman
  Consider the Change...
  The Choice is Yours

Florence Scovell Shinn
  The Wisdom of Florence Scovell Shinn

Melody Beattie
  Codependent No More

Shakti Gawain
  • *Creative Visualization*
  • *Living in the Light*

Dan Millman
  Way of the Peaceful Warrior

Barbara Hoberman Levine
  Your Body Believes Every Word You say

Dr. Howard S. Friedman
  The Self-Healing Personality

Joan Borysenko, Ph.D
  Minding the Body, Mending the Mind

Susan Jeffers, Ph.D.
  Feel The Fear And Do It Anyway

Robert Gerzon
  Finding Serenity in the Age of Anxiety

M. Scott Peck
  The Road Less Traveled

Carolyn Myss
  Anatomy of the Spirit

Jason Elias/ Katherine Ketcham
  FEMININE HEALING: A Woman's Guide to a Healthy Body, Mind and Spirit
  Originally published as
  In The House of the Moon

Daniel Goleman
  Emotional Intelligence

John K. Pollard, III
  The Self Parenting Program

Jacqueline Small
  Awakening In Time

Jeanne Elizabeth Blum
  Woman Heal Thyself

Mark Gerzon
  Coming Into Our Own

Andrew Weil, M.D.
  Spontaneous Healing

Judith Viorst
  Necessary Losses

Music List

Music is highly individual, and that is part of it's healing magic. Music that was there at the high and low points of our lives, when replayed, can take us immediately back to those memories. Barbra Streisand had the right songs for me to sing out being in love, falling out of love and finding independence. Whatever artists have been there for you — keep them in your lives. Listen to them — sing along. When you want to go back in search of something, music will definitely take you there. Keep an ear open to new music, as well. It keeps you attuned to the pulse of life.

Elizabeth finds a song for every feeling and shares this advice: "What moves one is simultaneously individual and collective. Singing or humming along with your favorite musician is a sure and simple way of inviting the muse to be a part of your healing circle. Lying down and allowing the musical vibrations to wend their way through the fiber of your being will certainly break through to the darkest corner of your psyche where fear, doubt and worry weigh heavy. Listening and honoring the words and tunes, old or new, can provide information and guidance unique to you. It's never too late to reawaken that part of the brain that wants to sing and dance."

Visit a music store that allows you to sample recordings and find one that gets the feelings moving that you want to explore. Here are a few suggestions that we have found particularly healing.

Shepherd Moons —Enya

Thursday Afternoon —Brian Eno

Miracles —Rob Whitesides Woo

Chants of India —Ravi Shankar

Inside the Taj Mahal —Paul Horn

Music For Healing
—Stephen Rhodes

LIBANA —Libana

Vangelis Themes —Vangelis

Structures From Silence
—Steve Roach

Earth Tribe Rhythms

Silent Joy —Anugama

Sky of Mind —Ray Lynch

Garden of Dreams —Ali Akbar Khan

Temple in the Forest —David Naegele

Fill Your Being Full —Rachel Bagby

Mozart's Concerto in C
—the London Symphony Orchestra

Ocean Dreams —Dean Evenson

Music to Listen To —Raphael

Enchanted Canyons
—Native Flutes

Heath-Esteem For Children
The next book by Judith Parker Harris

"I'm going to make sure that my feelings have a place to go all the time, to make me feel better, so when I get old, I won't be mean or sad." These words were said to me by 5-year-old, Danielle, who listened to my Health-Esteem tape being played by her mom and dad. At that moment I knew that I had to write a Health-Esteem book for children.

Coming soon, **Health-Esteem for Children** is a primer for feeling life mind, body and soul. It's designed to make learning feelings as natural as learning numbers and the alphabet. Through imaginative stories, interesting games, thought and talk provoking examples and fun exercises that families can do together, children will learn:

- How many feelings there are and how to feel them.
- Why hiding bad stuff can turn into shame and sickness.
- Ways to listen to the wisdom in their own bodies.
- How to connect to others and the world around them.
- What it means to be true to one's self.
- How respect, honesty, truthfulness and love build strong bodies and minds.
- How to embrace change as a natural part of life.
- The responsibility of health.
- Exercises for the mind, body and soul.

Children have an endless supply of "Why?" questions. Now they can lead their families in an exploration of the "Who, What, Where, When, Why of Wellness." Together, families will: Chart their emotional family trees; Meditate; Find fun ways to fit exercise into busy schedules; Learn to be completely authentic with each other; Play together; Wake up each morning with joy in their hearts for the opportunity the day may hold.

Like this workbook, Health-Esteem for Children is written with a healing team of contributors including teachers, wellness experts, moms, dads and, of course, kids. You can be a contributor, too.

If you have a Health-Esteem for children story, game or exercise you'd like to share in this book, please send it to:

Sayrite Publications
P.O. Box 3755
Beverly Hills, Ca 90212
or contact our web site www.healthesteem.com

Form Your Own Health-Esteem Group

As you get to know yourself better and embrace ownership of your thoughts and feelings, it's natural to want to know others beyond a surface level. In fact, it's difficult to stay separated from one another when we realize the tremendous energy that comes from connecting to those with whom we share this lifetime, this world, this space. I'm always surprised and delighted to discover who holds the next gift of awareness for me. When we're on the path of wellness and full of questions, answers come naturally in the events of each day. If, however, we stay locked behind our barriers of self-protection and refuse to connect with the world around us, our own particular answers may come and go unnoticed, unacknowledged, and unable to get in to enrich our lives. We often keep pounding on the wrong doors when we refuse to go through the doors that are open to us. A tragedy of isolation and useless effort unfolds.

I lived that tragedy of working without connection or awareness. Then multiple sclerosis threatened my life with indefinite periods of numbness and blindness. I was jarred into realizing that I had to see and feel the answers within myself in order to discover a world of possibilities outside of myself. I chose the winged heart as the symbol of Health-Esteem, because when I broke through the barriers of other people's perceptions and found my own truth, my heart began to fly. The things I wanted most out of life presented themselves to me, and I was able not only to recognize them, but to embrace them. Those things included my soul mate, new professional opportunities, a life path, spirituality, community and world connections, awareness and appreciation. I encourage you to give your heart wings by flying with others.

A friend and professional colleague who has read this workbook offered valuable input to me recently when she said, "I just wish I had your team right now. I need it, but I don't have time to find it!" Deborah, a devoted wife, mother of twin daughters, and an entertainment executive launching a new company, is battling to stay healthy in an anxiety-filled time. As we talked, however, she realized her life is already on the path. Her new company is devoted to creating quality children's programming. Her new lifestyle allows her to work from her home and be with her children more. Her new awareness has connected her to my healing team and to suggestions of those around her, as she communicates with them in a deeper, more meaningful fashion. Her determination to expand the Health-Esteem concepts to work for families finds her working with me on the upcoming Health-Esteem for Children book.

And so it happens. As you set your course with determination, integrity and healing energy, the people and projects you seek come to you. You worked in Chapter 4 to form your Health-Esteem Healing Team. Give that effort a boost by starting your own group, *The Winged Heart Network*. Simply invite friends you wish to know better and grow with to work together in the mutual development of Health-Esteem.

Winged Heart Network
How to Work With Your Group

There are many ways to use this workbook in your Winged Heart Network. You can discuss a chapter at a time and/or a question at a time from the Health-Esteem or Susceptibility Equation questionnaires. When you first come together, I suggest using the Health-Esteem questionnaire as a point of departure. Then decide as a group what topic to work on in the coming week. Meet in a mutually convenient location, such as a restaurant, or rotate meeting in each other's homes. Decide on a day of the week and time and stick to it. Limit the meetings to an agreed upon length of time and honor that so that the commitment does not become too great for anyone. Stick to the suggested format so that small talk does not limit the effectiveness of your purpose.

1) Start The Group With A Meditation: Hold hands or at least close your eyes. Repeat together: *"I am worth being healthy and I respect the health of others."* Select one person in the group each time to read the rest of the meditation. *"I am thankful for the people in this room, the life I am living, the opportunities around me, and the energy we share to heal. My heart is open to the uniqueness of each individual and aware that no one is more or less worthy or important than another. I am not here to judge or to criticize, but to share my stories, thoughts and emotions, which are uniquely my own, and to appreciate the stories, thoughts and emotions of those around me. I am receptive to the energy and information around me as I build my health-esteem."*

2) Share And Give Feedback: In one of the most effective groups I've worked in, created by Jael Greenleaf, she sets up a timed format in which one person shares for five minutes and then everyone in the group comments for one or two minutes each. The comments must be supportive and not judgmental. As we go around the circle in this manner, there can be no cross-talk (meaning no interruptions or conversations between others in the group). This has caused each of us to become wonderful listeners and to develop complete trust in the process. Over the course of seven years, the changes in this group have been dramatic. Each has changed professional direction, most have been helped trough a relationship or two, some have been helped through family deaths and illnesses, several through financial crises and all have grown spiritually. Our hearts have expanded to love and be able to accept love more easily. With gratitude to Jael Greenleaf, I suggest this same type of format for your group. You are free to set your own time limits based upon the size of your group.

Each individual is given five to ten minutes to talk about what the selected topic means to him or her and what feelings are aroused. When finished, each group member will have two minutes to comment supportively. Go around your circle in this way: share, then give feedback; share, then give feedback.

3) Group Q & A: After each person has shared and received feedback, take fifteen minutes for questions that arose during the first cycle of sharing, and answer these questions as a group.

4) Movement, Connection, Awareness: Take two minutes per person to talk about what movement, connection or awareness each individual received during the evening's discussion. Continue to go around the circle as in the previous steps. Each person should end this section of discussion by setting a goal for the coming week.

5) Next Topic: Together the group must decide whether this topic has been covered sufficiently and if so, what topic or chapter to work on in the coming week. This will determine which chapter has to be read in preparation for the next meeting.

6) Ending Meditation: Select one person in the group to read the closing meditation, or you may want to read it together as a group. *"Thank you for the connection this network creates, as we join in sharing our stories, thoughts and emotions. We are receiving insight, energy and power to give our hearts wings."*

Consider spending one minute to five minutes in group meditation — a powerful way to reinforce the thoughts of the evening and add personal and individual spirituality to the process.

Writing Groups

If you are on a chapter with writing exercises, you can decide whether to do them in group, or do them at home and bring them back to discuss in group. If you have done them at home, they will become the subject for your sharing segment. If you do them in group, set aside one half hour at the beginning to do the writing, then proceed with the above format, perhaps shortening the feedback segments.

Rules For The Winged Heart Network

1) This type of group work is extremely creative and personal. In advertising, when we were trying to come up with a new concept we called it brainstorming. Our rule was — no idea is a bad idea — just keep throwing them out there and see what works. That rule applies to groups. No one's thoughts or emotions are bad. They just are. The group must feel like a safe place for every individual to be open and truthful. Your role as a listener, is to do just that. Listen without judgment or criticism, and comment supportively. Start with a positive — "I understand how you must feel," or "I admire you for sharing that," or "Look what you've accomplished to come through that..." Then offer suggestions from your personal experience. Remember that each person's story is like pollen that when spread helps awareness in someone else to bloom. A personal story is a new color to bring to the canvas of life, a new note, a new instrument, a new way of playing a familiar song. <u>All stories must be respected.</u>

2) The Winged Heart Network is a place to work out feelings not to act them out. It is not a place for the shadowside emotions to be displayed. It is a place for them to be talked about. Perhaps someone's story makes you feel anger, or jealousy or resentment. It's healing to be honest about that. It's damaging to act it out. Simply say, "I find myself feeling jealous of all you've accomplished. You must be very proud. I wonder if I'll ever be able to do anything like that." All of that is good, because it gets a feeling out in the open to talk about and work on. Remember, talk about your feelings, then let them go, rather them keeping them inside where they can make you sick.

3) Create an atmosphere of trust. When working on Health-Esteem, you are pulling out disappointments and dreams and examining them in the light of friends. It can be frightening, but when those thoughts and dreams are validated it's empowering. You are each putting the wind of possibility beneath each other's wings. Listen carefully and shut off your own mind chatter so you can aid each other's flight.

4) Make this a place where failures are accepted as supportively as accomplishments. Find the strength in the experience. Move away from the negative and avoid dwelling on weakness. This is not a place for whining, but a place for growing. Show your belief in each other.

Above all, enjoy the process of increasing the energy of one by the power of the group.

Order Form
The Best Of Judith Parker Harris

Conquer Crisis With Health-Esteem™ Products

90 Minute Audiotape   only $15.95
Illustrated Workbook   only $19.95
1 Audiotape & 1 Workbook   combo $29.95 (save $5)
Copper cloisonne enameled pins   only $5.00
Watches and T-Shirts Available

Winged Heart Network

Five or more Audiotape & Workbook   combos $26.95 each
Five workbooks   only $17.95/each (save $2 each)
Six or more Workbooks   only $15.95/each (save $4 each)

Fax orders: 310-858-3774
Telephone orders: 310-858-1272
Toll free: 888-422-1272
Have credit card ready.
Online: www.healthesteem.com

NAME: _____ ADDRESS: _____

CITY: _____ STATE: _____ ZIP: _____

THIS BOOK PURCHASED FROM (STORE, CITY): _____

OTHER (CATALOG, LECTURE, WORKSHOP) SPECIFY: _____

OCCUPATION: _____ AGE: _____

Qty.	Item	Price	Discount	Net	Total

Sales tax:	Please add 8.25% for orders shipped to California addresses.	Total Price	
Shipping:	$4.00 for the first book and $2.00 for each additional book.	sales tax	
	$3.00 for the first audiotape and $2.00 for each additional one.	shipping	
	$1.00 for each heart pin.	**TOTAL**	

Mail order: Health-Esteem Intl. P.O. Box 3755 Beverly Hills, CA 90212

Payment: ❑ Check enclosed (payable to: Health-Esteem Intl.)

Credit Card: ❑ VISA, ❑ MasterCard

Card number: _____ Exp. date_____

Name on card: _____

Call *toll free* and order now!